BALLOONS AT
WAR

GASBAGS, FLYING BOMBS
& COLD WAR SECRETS

BALLOONS AT
WAR

GASBAGS, FLYING BOMBS
& COLD WAR SECRETS

John Christopher

TEMPUS

First published 2004

Tempus Publishing Ltd
The Mill, Brimscombe Port
Stroud, Gloucestershire GL5 2QG
www.tempus-publishing.com

British Library Cataloguing in Publication Data.
A catalogue record for this book is available from the British Library.

ISBN 0 7524 2995 7

Typesetting and origination by Tempus Publishing.
Printed and bound in Great Britain.

CONTENTS

	Acknowledgements	7
	Preface	8
1	Borne by the Wind	10
2	Bonaparte's Balloon Corps	17
3	Lowe Flying	29
4	Under Siege	40
5	Defending the Empire	51
6	Calling the Shots	65
7	Silver Sentinels	81
8	Doing a Man's Job	100
9	Most Secret War	116
10	All at Sea	130
11	Boo-Boo and the Doodlebugs	141
12	The Fu-Go Balloon Bomb	157
13	Cold War Encounters	166
14	Spy in the Sky	177
15	Mightier than the Sword	186
16	Rebirth	193
17	Farewell Boo-Boo and Bulgy	200
18	A Better Mousetrap	204
	Bibliography	218
	Index	221

DEDICATION

This book is dedicated to those unsung heroes of war – the many men and women who served with the balloons.

ACKNOWLEDGEMENTS

I would like to thank the many people who shared their memories and knowledge so generously. Several barrage balloon operators contacted me following an appearance on BBC Radio 4's *Making History* programme, including the remarkable ballooning couple Dorothy and Joseph Melford, who both worked with balloons during the Second World War. Dorothy began by repairing balloons and she was one of the first WAAFs to volunteer to operate them, while Joseph spent several years with the balloons at sea. They married after meeting during retraining for other duties.

Others who assisted include: Tony Gilruth, Anthony Smith of the Airship Heritage Trust, John Baker of the British Balloon Museum & Library, Tom Hamilton of *Balloon Life* magazine, Bob Baker, Larry Nelson, Jane Sloane, Rory Legge, Marcus Edwards, Goodyear Dunlop, David Williams, Rex Haggett, John Muxlow of Smelly Old Books for locating copies of American journals, Sally March, and, of course, the people at Tempus Publishing. Particular credit must be paid to Maureen and Chris Lynch of Valhalla Aerostation, an invaluable source of 'lighter-than-air' books, who also provided crucial information, images and support. Thanks to Herman Van Dyk for generously allowing me to use his illustrations and articles, to Barbara Moreton for French translations, to Mike Rentell for Russian, and to my wife Ute Christopher for the German.

And of course very special thanks are due to Ute. She didn't know barrage balloons existed before she met me and now, after the last few months, probably knows more than she ever wanted to. In addition to expertly scanning the images in this book, she spent many long hours proofreading and provided invaluable advice along the way.

Acknowledgements for individual photographs are included in the captions. Any errors or omissions in this book are entirely my own.

John Christopher

PREFACE

'I used to serve with balloons, but that was fifty years ago. I don't suppose anybody wants to know about that any more.'

Robert Butcher had come over to see me after I landed my balloon in one of his friend's fields near Yeovilton, in Somerset. Eying the heap of fabric, he explained that he had been with the barrage balloons during the Second World War. Not interested? I was very interested, and Robert was one of the many people I talked to in collecting material for *Balloons at War* – a book I have been intending to write ever since the RAF got rid of the last of its balloons in 1995.

There are several reasons for producing this book. Although excellent accounts have been published on the wartime career of its big cousin, the airship, the balloon itself had remained conspicuously neglected. That's not to say that some good books have not been written concerning specific periods of the balloon's illustrious military history – in particular, the Siege of Paris, the US Civil War and the observation balloons of the First World War – but none of these attempted to tell the whole story, to convey the bigger picture. What of the barrage balloons of the Second World War, for example, an application of balloons at war which has been virtually ignored over the years? But there remained many grey areas, especially in the twilight world of clandestine operations. Every now and then, when their guard was down, some of the old men of ballooning would hint at matters still secret, releasing little titbits spoken in hushed tones. And while a wink might be as good as a nod, it didn't give me enough hard facts to get my teeth into.

Then one day I happened upon a small second-hand bookshop tucked away in the back streets of my local town. As I entered its dark interior my highly tuned book-seeking radar went to work and I immediately spotted several cramped shelves right at the back of the shop. The collective heading of 'Women's Studies' was perhaps an unpromising hunting ground, but sandwiched between the well-thumbed paperbacks I struck gold. The book had seen better days, its once bright gold-blocked lettering faded to dull ochre on the broken spine, but I couldn't fail to be drawn by the title, *The Secret War 1939–1945*, because I had been researching the V1 and V2 'Vergeltungswaffe' or 'retribution weapons'. This was worth closer examination, and as the book fell open in my hands it did so at a chapter entitled 'The Wire Barrage'. Here, in black and white, was the story of the Free Balloon Barrage project – something which previously I had only come across in the briefest of references.

Armed with this piece of the jigsaw the big picture began to take shape, and I set to work sifting through the material, trying to get to the heart of the matter and hopefully laying to rest some of the oft repeated myths. In addition, many secrets of the Second World War and the subsequent Cold War were finally coming out of the shadows. It was absolutely fascinating stuff, with numerous surprises emerging along the way, but there was still one nagging concern. Some of the applications for balloons described in this book are still useful to the military, and the question then arises of whether publishing information about them would hinder their use or worse still, provide food for thought for the terrorists that have come to feature so prominently in our modern lives. As it turned out, my concerns proved to be unfounded for clear evidence was discovered in Afghanistan revealing that Al Qaeda had already been contemplating using balloons to spread anthrax spores. There was nothing I could teach them. And now as I sit writing this preface at the beginning of 2003, Hercules aircraft from RAF Lyneham drone overhead in preparation for a war against Saddam Hussein. If this conflict does go ahead then you can be sure that the humble balloon will be playing its part, sometimes in ways that we can only guess at.

This then is the remarkable story of the gasbags, flying bombs and the secret world of balloons at war... so far.

John Christopher
2003

1
BORNE BY THE WIND

The balloon was once described as 'a most unlikely candidate for war' and yet, as with so many technological innovations, it has not been immune to the interest of the military. From its conception it has been exploited as an aerial platform from which to spy upon the enemy, to scatter leaflets or drop bombs upon their heads, or to deliver human cargoes deep into hostile territory. It was not without good reason that the expression 'the balloon's gone up!' came to indicate the outbreak of hostilities, and the fortunes of that most peaceful form of aerial carriage, always at the mercy of the wind, have forever been linked to those of war.

Even before a single balloon had left the ground Joseph Montgolfier had envisaged his progeny as a means of launching a surprise attack upon the English forces holding Gibraltar. 'By making the balloon's bag big enough', he reasoned, 'it will be possible to introduce an entire army, which, borne by the wind, will enter right over the heads of the English.' Montgolfier's discovery of the principles of aerostation has often been portrayed as one of the great 'Eureka!' moments, with him watching in amazement as Madame Montgolfier's chemise flew upwards as it dried in front of the fire, and yet the invention of the balloon has in reality a somewhat more mundane origin. In the latter half of the eighteenth century great strides had been made in the scientific understanding of the physical world, including the properties of gases. It was an Englishman, Henry Cavandish, who in 1766 had identified the gas he christened 'phlogiston', also referred to as 'inflammable air', and which only later became known as hydrogen. Although potentially highly explosive if mixed with air, hydrogen possesses molecules that are less dense than the gaseous cocktail that makes up our atmosphere. As well as being the lightest substance on the planet, it happens to be one of the most common, being a constituent part of water. Joseph Montgolfier found his inspiration in the form of Joseph Priestley's treatise, 'Experiments and Observations on Different Kinds of Air', which had been translated into French in 1776.

Yet it is around this point that a degree of confusion regarding this 'inflammable air' seems to have set in for Montgolfier. He had begun his experiments by filling small paper and cotton globes with hydrogen – which seeped out through the pores of the paper and fabric like water through a sieve – before he turned his efforts instead to capturing a different source of lifting gas. Observing that smoke and cinders would rise above a fire he concluded that the process of combustion must in itself be generating quantities of this mysterious 'inflammable air'. Not quite appreciating that it is the hot air that is lighter than ordinary air, rather than the smoke, he set about generating the smelliest and most obnoxious bonfires he could muster, burning damp straw, wool, old shoes and even rancid meat, to generate as much smoke as possible. As luck would have it, this billowing sooty smoke also blocked the pores of the fabric and now, filled with hot air, his spheres took to the skies – which just goes to prove what a little healthy ignorance can achieve.

Joseph was joined in his experiments by his younger brother Etienne and on 5 June 1783 they organised a public demonstration in the square at Annonay, a small town in southern France and home of the Montgolfiers' paper mills. The atmosphere that day was one of carnival, but as the paper and cotton balloon was unloaded from a simple wooden cart the mood changed to one of hushed reverence. Measuring 25ft high, the yellow and red balloon was hoisted upright between two wooden poles above one of Joseph's special bonfires and in that moment, as the inanimate heap of fabric stirred into a living breathing creature, a powerful magic cast its spell. The townspeople watched with awe as the balloon swelled and once released soared silently upwards to a height estimated at around 6,000ft. It then drifted for ten minutes in the gentle breeze before coming back down to earth one and a half miles away.

The Montgolfier brothers were not alone in their ambitions to be upwardly mobile. In Paris news of these provincial successes was greeted with disdain and outright disbelief, and in order to restore the prestige of the Parisian Academy of Science a young physicist called Professor Jacques Alexandre César Charles took up the challenge. Charles possessed a much clearer understanding of the

Joseph and Etienne Montgolfier, the two brothers who devised and built the first manned balloon which flew on 21 November 1783.

composition and properties of hydrogen gas and with the aid of the two brothers Jean and Noël Robert, who had perfected a technique for coating fine silk with a solution of rubber to make it impervious to gas, he constructed the world's first hydrogen balloon. The race was now on to get a man airborne.

In September 1783 the Montgolfier brothers brought Paris to a standstill when they sent a cockerel, a duck and a sheep up into the uncharted province of the upper air, or 'aerial ocean', as some regarded it. There were some fears at this time concerning the dangers that might be involved – entirely illogical given that many people in mountainous areas lived at higher altitudes. But the animals survived, albeit with one broken wing inflicted by a swift kick from the sheep, and this flight propelled the Montgolfiers into the lead. Soon they were ready to send a human 'aeronaut' aloft. When King Louis XVI got wind of this he insisted that the risks were too great and that a volunteer should be sought among the prison inmates. Fortunately, the king was persuaded otherwise by a twenty-six-year-old daredevil and Academy member named Jean-François Pilâtre de Rozier, who had recruited the support of fellow aristocrat François Laurent, the Marquis d'Arlandes, and together they volunteered for the task.

The first cautious steps were taken as a series of tethered ascents, with de Rozier ascended at the Faubourg Saint Antoine in Paris on 15 October 1783. This experiment was repeated two days later and this time he was accompanied by André Giraud de Vilette, who was much taken by the new invention's potential for aerial reconnaissance. Writing to the editors of the *Journal de Paris*, he commented, 'I was convinced that this apparatus, costing but little, could be made useful to an army for discovering the positions of its enemy, his movements, his advances, and his dispositions, and that information could be conveyed to the troops operating the machine. I believe that it is equally possible, with proper precautions, to make similar use of this apparatus at sea.'

By 21 November 1783, the Montgolfiers' balloon was ready for free flight. With a volume of 79,000 cu ft – roughly the equivalent of a modern sporting hot air balloon – the paper and cotton envelope, magnificently decorated in blue and gold, was inflated over another obnoxious pyre. Then the two daring young men climbed aboard their flying machine and at 1.54 p.m. the restraining ropes were cut and the balloon rose up from the Chateau La Muette in the Bois de Boulogne. These two pioneers were the first air travellers, the first to experience that liberating moment of buoyant flight when the earth simply drops away to reveal a rapid change in perspective. So began the history of manned flight, but if the aeronauts did not tend to their tasks their moment of glory was going to be a very brief one. De Rozier and the Marquis were equipped with pitchforks to feed faggots of straw on to the fire, as well as buckets of water and sponges on long sticks to prevent any embers setting their fragile craft ablaze.

When not feeding the flames or dabbing away at the small burn holes smouldering in the envelope, the Marquis took time to marvel at the view. 'Astonished, I cast a glance towards the river. I perceived the confluence of the Oise. And naming the principal bends of the river by the places nearest them, I cried, "Paay, Saint-Germain. Saint-Denis, Sevres!"' After dodging the Parisian rooftops for an all too brief twenty-five-minute flight, the aeronauts were brought down to earth with an undignified bump at the Butte-aux-Cailles, some 900 yards from their starting point. It had been a modest first outing, with the balloon climbing to an estimated height of between 2,000 and 3,000ft, and it had been a risky one too, with the ever-present danger of fire engulfing their fragile craft. But it wasn't to be long before a more robust balloon flew over Paris.

Robbed of their place in history as the first aeronauts, Professor Charles and Noël Robert launched in their gas balloon from the Tuileries Gardens only eleven days later. Such was the ingenuity of Charles's balloon design that it has served as a virtual blueprint for gas balloons ever since. The spherical envelope was fitted with an open tube at its base to serve as a simple safety valve to release any excess pressure, thus preventing the balloon from popping as the gas expanded with the reduction in the ambient air pressure at height. It was covered by a net held in place by a ring around the envelope's equator and from this suspension lines ran down to the boat-shaped gondola in which the two men rode. In order to control the balloon, sand ballast was thrown overboard to make it climb and to come back down gas was vented via a wooden valve fitted at the apex of the envelope. Because hydrogen has about three times more lift than hot air, the balloon was much smaller than the Montgolfiers' and altogether a more robust craft with none of the inherent dangers of an on-board fire. The only

Only eleven days after the Montgolfiers' balloon had flown, the more robust gas-filled balloon of Professor Charles took to the skies and this type came to dominate the ballooning scene for almost 200 years.

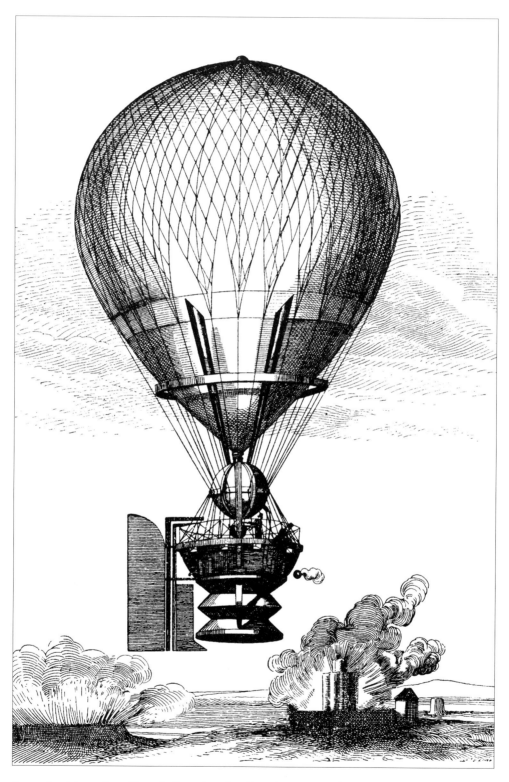

An early vision of a military balloon bombarding the enemy's fortifications.

drawback with this type of balloon was the difficulty in generating sufficient quantities of hydrogen, a long and tedious process involving the reaction of dilute sulphuric acid passed over iron filings. As this mixture bubbled away the hydrogen fumes were piped into sealed casks to cool before being fed into the balloon. An expensive process and one that might take many hours.

It is said that a crowd of 40,000 people witnessed this ascent as the balloon rose quickly to 1,800ft. 'Nothing will ever equal that moment of joyous excitement that filled my whole being when I felt myself flying away from the earth', Charles recounted afterwards. They made a perfect landing two hours later having travelled twenty-seven miles to the small town of Nesle. By this time the sun was setting but Charles was so exhilarated by the experience he couldn't resist the temptation to set off again, and after promising that he would return within thirty minutes he ascended beneath the now flaccid balloon on his own. Without his companion's weight the balloon shot upwards to a height of 10,000ft, causing Charles to suffer an acute earache, as well as rewarding him with a spectacular view of a second sunset. It had been a truly magnificent tour de force, demonstrating for the world to see the superiority of the gas balloon over its hot air rival.

Among the many spectators in Paris that day was the American diplomat Benjamin Franklin. When confronted by a bystander with the question, 'But of what use are these balloons?' he replied, 'And of what use is a new-born baby?' However, what Franklin failed to mention to that questioner was that he was not only in Paris to nurture diplomatic relationships and strengthen the alliance between France and America, he was also there as a spy, primarily to keep a watchful eye on their common adversary the English. Franklin was a key member of the American Committee of Secret Correspondence and he had some particular uses for the balloon in mind. He quickly penned a letter back to his masters – the nearest thing to a secret radio message in the late eighteenth century – which summed up the future of the military balloon in a nutshell. 'It may be sufficient for certain purposes, such as elevating an engineer to take a view of an enemy's army, works etcetera, conveying intelligence into, or from, or out of a besieged town, giving signals to distant places, or the like.' He also predicted the airborne invasions of the twentieth century when he wrote, 'Five thousand balloons, capable of raising two men each, could not cost more than five ships of the line, and where is there a prince who could afford to cover his country with troops for its defence as that ten thousand men descending from the clouds might not in places do an infinite amount of damage.'

As 'balloon mania' spread throughout both Europe and America, the notion of employing balloons as instruments of war soon came to be publicly acknowledged. In England, in early 1874, a pamphlet was published by an unknown author who proposed the adoption of balloons for reconnaissance on land and at sea, as well as for long-distance signalling:

On the first report of a country being invaded, an Air Balloon would save the expense of messengers, posts, etcetera, from the coasts to the main army. A general, likewise in

the day of battle, would derive singular advantage by going up in one of these machines;
he would have a bird's eye view of not only everything that he was doing in his own,
but in the enemy's army....

Such schemes were viewed with dismay in some quarters and the Englishman
Horace Walpole voiced his concern:

> In truth, I hope that these new mechanic meteors will prove only playthings for the
> learned and idle, and not be converted into new engines of destruction to the human
> race, as is often the case of refinements or discoveries in science. The wicked wit of man
> always studies to apply the results of talents to enslaving, destroying, or cheating his
> fellow creatures.

But it was too late, the genie was already out of the bottle and remarkably it was
to be only eleven years from the time of the Montgolfiers' initial demonstrations
until the formation of the world's first 'air force'.

2

BONAPARTE'S
BALLOON CORPS

In the years immediately following the outbreak of the French Revolution in 1789, France found itself almost constantly at war with many of its foreign neighbours. Accordingly, a Commission for the Study of Science in the Interests of the State was established so that the greatest minds of the Paris Academy could consider means of aiding the armies of France. Desperate times called for desperate measures and, as we have seen, several prominent figures had already advocated the use of balloons. It was therefore recommended to the Committee of Public Safety – the revolutionary government at that time – that balloons should be provided so that 'observers, placed like sentinels, hidden in the clouds, would observe the movements of the enemy'. In June 1793 the government accepted the proposal on one condition: that on no account could sulphuric acid be spared for the generation of hydrogen gas as every ounce of sulphur was needed for the production of gunpowder. The leading chemist Lavoisier was consulted to find an alternative and he proposed the production of hydrogen by passing steam over red-hot iron. Consequently, in October of that year, the government passed a decree ordering the construction of a balloon for the Army of the North, and allocated the considerable sum of 50,000 livres for its construction and the support equipment. Two scientists, Jean Marie Joseph Coutelle and Nicolas Jacques Conté, were put in charge of the work and over the next decade these two were to become the principle movers behind the introduction of military ballooning.

Coutelle, born in 1748, had by the age of twenty become first the pupil and then the friend of Professor Charles, creator of the gas balloon. Coutelle's younger companion Conté, born in 1755, had been a precocious child. At nine years old he had constructed a violin to concert standard, and at fourteen he demonstrated his artistic talent by completing the painting of a chapel at Séez after the original artist fell ill. Prior to the Revolution Conté had been an accomplished portrait painter and afterwards, deprived of his wealthy clients, he turned instead to the study of physics and mechanical invention – producing among other things machines for making medals and for whitening fabrics. In Paris he also created the Central Depot of Machines, the forerunner of the Conservatory of Arts and Crafts.

Above left: Jean Marie Joseph Coutelle.

Above right: Nicolas Jacques Conté with his distinctive eye patch, the result of an accident during his gas experiments.

The practicalities of producing hydrogen for the balloons were solved fairly swiftly, although poor Conté lost an eye when one experiment went wrong. (His portrait reveals a striking figure with a black band wrapped around his head to cover the damaged eye.) The biggest problem was that it took a large brick-built furnace to produce the heat required to generate sufficient quantities of gas. Such a generator would take time and resources to build and despite the ever-changing landscape of warfare this was clearly not going to be a mobile affair. Accordingly the balloons were best suited to siege situations, where they might be expected to stay in one location for some time. Conté also took great care to ensure that their envelopes were as gas-tight as possible by devising a coating for the silk fabric which, if his claims are to be believed, remains unequalled to this day. Sadly, this recipe has not survived.

While Conté set to his work on the practical side, Coutelle reported to the headquarters of General Jean-Baptiste Jourdain, the commander of the Army of the North which was holding the town of Maubeuge against the Austrian forces, with the intention of making preparations for balloon operations. Unfortunately, he was greeted with scepticism and suspicion by Jourdain and his staff. One officer, a zealot of the 'Terror', proposed that he be shot as a spy, while another reported back to the Committee of Public Safety that, 'A battalion is needed more at the front than a balloon.' Undeterred, Coutelle persevered until he had the ear of Jourdain and it was agreed that further experiments should be conducted in the secrecy and relative safety of Paris before any balloons were exposed to the dangers of the battlefield. He rejoined Conté in the capital where the Chateau at Chalais-Meudon was put at their disposal and it was here that the first military observation balloon took shape.

In appearance *L'Entreprenant*, or *Enterprise*, was much like previous gas balloons, but it had been constructed to be especially strong to withstand the buffeting of the wind and the strain of prolonged tethering. A spherical balloon tends to bob up and down with every gust, resulting in a ride that is said to be an alarming experience for the uninitiated. To prevent it spinning this balloon was held captive by two tether lines attached at its equator, although some contemporary engravings also show other lines leading from the basket. To maintain an approximate state of equilibrium – the point at which the balloon's lift more or less equals its load – Coutelle had devised a clever system whereby the balloon was ballasted at equilibrium at ground level, and as it climbed ballast was released to compensate for the increasing weight of the ropes. In theory, this put less strain on the balloon and helped to reduce the workload of the ground crew who raised or lowered it by means of a simple windlass. Many engravings depict this operation being carried out by the men themselves and on one exceptional occasion it is said that sixty-four men struggled to keep hold of their aerial charge. In none of the accounts have I found any indication that the pulling strength of horses was applied to the task and this may be because they were too valuable to be spared from the battlefield.

The first military balloon, *L'Entreprenant*, at the Battle of Fleurus on 26 June 1794.

It was decided that the balloon would be manned by two officers, one to observe the enemy and direct the guns of the artillery, and the other to manage the balloon and to send messages to the troops on the ground. This was achieved in two ways: by waving signal flags, or by sliding hand–written messages down the tether ropes in small weighted bags fitted with metal rings. In addition, a method was later devised to haul messages up from the ground in situations where the commanders sought information on specific aspects of the enemy's movements. Some sources have also suggested that the balloons were used to drop propaganda leaflets over the enemy's lines.

Early in 1974 Coutelle put on a demonstration of *L'Entreprenant* at Chalais-Meudon for appraisal by the members of the Scientific Commission. Tentatively the balloon was raised to the full extent of the tether line up to 1,770ft, where Coutelle and a companion, Adjutant General Radet, found that through a telescope they were easily able to distinguish the winding river Seine a full eighteen miles away. Clearly the performance had been a complete triumph and the Commission was so impressed that a few days later, on 2 April 1794, the Compagnie d'Aérostiers, or 'Aerostatic Corps' was formed. Now it was time to send the balloons to war.

Commanded by a newly commissioned Captain Coutelle, the corps was a well–organised unit consisting of seven officers and twenty men, including a drummer boy. Most of the men were selected because of particular knowledge in chemistry or skills in carpentry or masonry, the latter for the construction of the large on–site furnaces. Resplendent in distinctive uniforms of blue with black collars and cuffs piped in red, each man was also armed with a sabre and two pistols. The Aérostiers were immediately dispatched to join General Jourdain's forces at Maubeuge while the equipment was made ready. Dressed as they were it was only to be expected that their arrival was greeted with widespread derision. They had yet to prove themselves in battle and at Coutelle's orders they were sent into the thick of the fighting where, by all accounts, they acquitted themselves well enough to silence their critics and to earn the respect of their brothers–in–arms. And when *L'Entreprenant* arrived on the scene it was time to show just what they could do for the Republic's armies.

From the perspective of our modern world, in which a round–the–clock stream of media imagery informs us of every aspect of human activity from all corners of the globe, often as it is happening, it is hard to convey the utter shock and dismay with which the Austrian troops greeted this apparition on 2 June 1794. Few, if any, of the simple foot soldiers could have had any inkling of the remarkable developments in aeronautics over the previous ten years and the sight of this monstrous globe rising as if by magic or supernatural means above the hills was beyond all comprehension. In his memoirs of his time with the Aérostiers, Selle de Beachamp described the reaction of some of the Austrian prisoners who saw the balloon close to hand for the first time. 'They looked dumbfounded, on our enormous machine borne aloft with no visible means of support (for the ropes merged with their surroundings); some were prepared to throw themselves

Above and below: The envelope of a military balloon is varnished and sealed at Chalais–Meudon. Conté devised a windbreak skirt to protect the balloon from the worst of the elements.

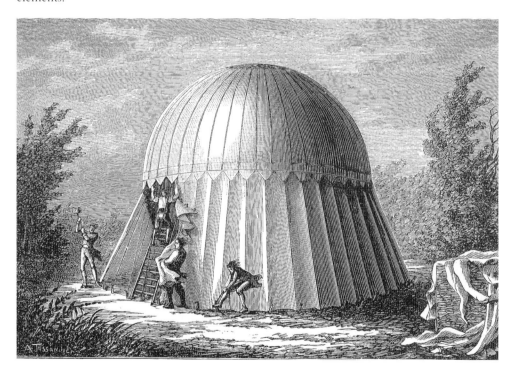

on their knees while others, waving their fists at it, declared in their own languages: "Spies, spies, you'll be hanged if you're caught".' Indeed, for many of their compatriots the sight of two French officers suspended in a basket slung beneath the balloon served to confirm their worst fears that the French Republic was indeed in league with the Devil himself. The Austrian and Dutch officers, however, had more practical concerns as every movement of their forces was now laid bare, like pieces on a chess board before the aerial interlopers, and they regarded this new development as an unsporting breach of the rules of gentlemanly conduct in warfare.

There was no question that the French now held the 'high ground', but on subsequent ascents Coutelle found himself the centre of some unwelcome attention. To create anti-aircraft guns the Austrian artillerymen had dug ditches in which to lower the rear ends of their cannon and thus elevate the barrels. They waited for their moment and when the balloon appeared on its fifth ascent the concealed gunners opened fire, sending one cannonball whistling over the top of the balloon and another grazing its basket. With typical sangfroid Coutelle responded with a rousing yell of 'Vive la République!' – much to the delight of the French troops, who hadn't noticed that all the while he was frantically signalling for more rope to be let out so that the balloon might climb beyond the range of the cannon. Such bravado soon earned the Aérostiers a reputation akin to the fighter aces of later wars and with it came the attention of the ladies. It has been suggested that on more than one occasion a young woman was taken for an unauthorised flight of fancy.

Towards the end of June the balloon was relocated to assist the French forces at Charleroi, about twenty miles away from Maubeuge. Because rebuilding the gas generating furnaces would have been such a major undertaking, the balloon was transported fully inflated. The band of sweating Aérostiers had to pull it along on ropes – with Conté riding in the basket, naturalment – as it was borne aloft like an arch of honour, just high enough to allow mounted cavalrymen to pass underneath. After fifteen hours of this hard slog under the unremitting summer sun, the exhausted and hungry balloonists arrived at Charleroi to the rousing cheers of their countrymen. Already the value of the balloon in raising the morale of the troops was evident, as was the reverse effect on their adversaries. The very next day *L'Entreprenant* was airborne and on 26 June the bitter Battle of Fleurus was fought, during which the balloon remained over the battlefield for more than nine hours. At times Coutelle was accompanied by General Antoine Morlot, who noted the Austrians' positions and identified their weaknesses from the air. His dispatches un-doubtedly contributed to Jourdain's shrewd deployment of his troops and the resounding French victory, but Coutelle remained characteristically modest on the matter:

I will not claim, as do those who praise or blame with exaggeration everything that is new, that the balloon won the Battle of Fleurus. On this memorable day, every corps did its full duty. What I can say is, that well served by my glass, despite the oscillation and movement caused by the wind, I was able to distinguish clearly the corps of infantry and cavalry, the parks of artillery, their movements, and in general, the massed troops.

After the triumph of Fleurus, the Aérostiers took to the road again and like children with a balloon on a string they followed Jourdain's advance into Belgium. However, *L'Entreprenant* was to fare no better than a toy balloon when it encountered a sharp object and as it was paraded through the streets of Brussels its silken fabric became snagged on one of the buildings. With a sigh of escaping hydrogen it sagged to the ground in a sorry heap. With punctured pride the Aérostiers repaired their balloon and by then a second one had emerged from Chalais-Meudon. Unlike its predecessor, the *Martial* was cylindrical in shape which meant that it was even less stable in the wind and too unsteady for useful observation duties. In addition to the second balloon, the Committee of Public Safety had ordered that a 2nd company of balloonists should be formed and a training school was to be established at Chalais-Meudon – another first in military aeronautics – headed by Nicolas Conté. Sixty balloonists were to be trained for the Republic's balloon service and it was clear that the authorities still held great store in their flying squad.

It took almost another twelve months before the 2nd Company was ready for action and along with two new balloons, the *Hercule* and *Intrepide*, it joined the

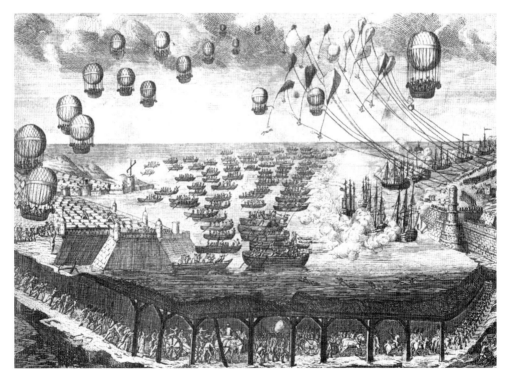

1803 portrayal of French invasion forces invading England via an aerial armada of cross-channel balloons, plus boats and even a tunnel!

Army of the Rhine where it served during the sieges of Mayence and at Mannheim. The following year, 1796, it moved on to Molsheim, near Strasbourg, and took part in the campaigns at Rastadt, Stuttgart and Donauwerth. The 1st Company, meanwhile, continued to serve with Jourdain's army until the Battle of Würzburg, when Jourdain was defeated by the Austrians and the balloon and its balloonists captured. Although hardly the fault of the Aérostiers, this proved to be a significant turning point in their fortunes. The remaining company, the 2nd, was transferred to the army of the Sambre-et-Meuse under General Hoche, who had nothing good to say about balloons and declined to put them into service at all. In August 1796 he even wrote to the

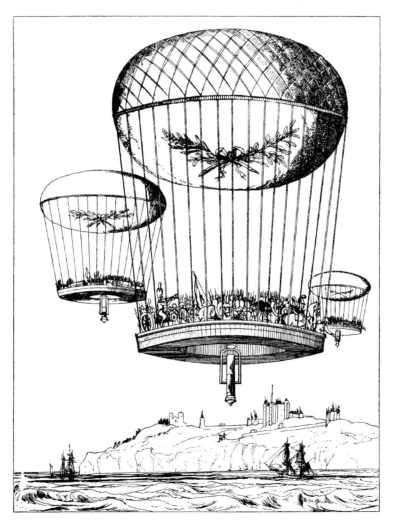

Another fanciful variation on the airborne invasion theme, with each balloon carrying a thousand French troops along with twenty-five horses and two cannon.

Minister of War asking for them to be removed as they were 'entirely useless'. It was as if the authorities had forgotten the lessons of the earlier campaigns, in which the observation balloon had proved very valuable, and they had become so detached from the realities of warfare that some quite outlandish schemes were commanding their attention.

That the French detested the English at this time goes without saying, and although England was tantalisingly close to hand it was defended by the waters of the Channel and the indomitable might of the British Navy. Several stratagems had been proposed to overcome these obstacles and, as previously anticipated by Benjamin Franklin, the notion of using balloons to deliver an army deep into enemy territory came into some prominence. On 3 December 1797, French periodical *L'Etoile de Bruxelles* announced, with apparent seriousness, that a 'numerous army was preparing to cross the sea and force the Cabinet in London to see reason… a mobile camp is being constructed, with a vast Montgolfiére to lift it and an army, and transport them across to England to effect the conquest'. Several contemporary engravings depict how this aerial armada might have looked had it gone into battle. One portrays a three-pronged attack with a flotilla of gas balloons bearing French troops over the channel, a fleet of small ships engaging the British Navy and deep below them a secret army marching merrily under the Channel by means of a subterranean tunnel – now there's a notion! Most curiously, perhaps, the English are shown defending their airspace by means of man-carrying kites which appear to be flying in exactly the opposite direction to the balloons.

Another variation on this airborne invasion involved huge balloons, each crammed with a thousand French troops along with twenty-five horses, two cannon and the associated trappings of warfare, including forage and food supplies for ten days. (It would be an interesting exercise to calculate just how vast such a balloon would need to be!) Whether such schemes were ever given any serious consideration by the French government remains uncertain, although it is probably doubtful, and the whole exercise may have been no more than sabre rattling to intimidate and unsettle the English. This it achieved to great effect, and in England many popular broadsheets of the time added fuel to the fire of national fears by keeping notions of an impending invasion in the forefront of the public's imagination. Often their message was delivered in the form of ballads to be recited or sung in the taverns, most likely with tongue firmly in cheek:

Should war again break out
As is not a doubt
With some that it may happen soon;
the French will invade us
Their troops will parade us
Brought over in an Air Balloon.
Their ships will appear,
Not in water but air,
And come in a twinkling down,
From Calais to Dover,
How quickly they'll be over,
Blown up in an Air Balloon.

Of course, the invasion force never materialised and as Bonaparte himself reluctantly concluded, 'We should give up any real attempt to invade England.' Even so, in the cause of baiting the enemy the rumours of invasion continued to be encouraged within France for some time!

Despite the tribulations of the 2nd Company under General Hoche, it was not entirely doom and gloom for the Aérostiers in 1797. In April of that year, the personnel of the 1st Company were liberated from captivity at Leoben and they were sent back to Chalais-Meudon for reorganisation. Better still, Napoleon Bonaparte was preparing plans for an expedition to conquer new territories and at Conté's personal suggestion the 1st Company was listed among the units to accompany him on this glorious campaign. The balloonists were going to North Africa, to Egypt! Though by the time they had reached the shores of Egypt Bonaparte seemed to have lost all enthusiasm for their deployment and, if most accounts are to be believed, the balloons and support equipment were never even unloaded from the ships. Yet this glib appraisal of events paints only half the picture in explaining the apparent sea-change in Bonaparte's attitude. Clearly something else, some external factor, had come to bear. And that something was Horatio Nelson and the British Navy!

The fact was that at least some of the ballooning equipment, including the materials for the gas generator, were destroyed at Aboukir during the Battle of the Nile in 1798, and the rest was then smashed during the Cairo revolt later that year. This left Conté, bereft of his beloved balloon, to turn his more than capable hands to assisting Bonaparte's armies in other ways, constructing cornmills, machines for printing, for making coins and producing steel, precision tools, surgical instruments and even trumpets for the cavalry. In between he found time to devise a system of signalling, using small captive balloons supporting pulleys on which the signals might be hoisted to be visible from afar. All this activity prompted Bonaparte to declare of Conté, 'the chief of these aeronauts, was a universal man, with the taste, the knowledge and the genius of arts, good to everyone, and capable of creating the art of France in the very midst of the deserts of Araby'. Conté was even promoted, and when Bonaparte decided to impress the locals with a display of French scientific mastery it is inconceivable that his services weren't called upon in the construction of three large Montgolfière balloons. The first was launched in Cairo on 22 September 1798. Sadly, there are very few known details; simply that the unmanned balloon went very high and disappeared before an immense crowd of onlookers who, faintly surprised, remained totally calm. The same reaction greeted the following ascent, and the next, and the displays were discontinued.

Then on 18 January 1799, two weeks after the last of these ascents in Cairo, the French government disbanded the two companies of the Corps d'Aérostiers without stating any reason. It may simply have been to save money, we don't know, but the balloon school at Chalais-Meudon was closed down. The old chateau was demolished and the grand marble columns from its portico used in the construction of the Arc de Triomphe. On his return to France the irrepressible Conté continued his inventing and it is said that when the

Frenchmen Biot and Gaylussa made their high-altitude ascent in 1804, Conté prepared the flight using a balloon he had brought back from Egypt.

In spite of the early successes of the military balloons, it is sometimes suggested that Bonaparte's inflated self opinion of his own talents as a military tactician may account for his apparent lack of enthusiasm for their continued use. At the end of the day he was tied to convention and relied upon his fast-moving cavalry to provide the reconnaissance information he needed. Or maybe he agreed with the Austrians that the presence of the balloons was not a gentlemanly act. What is certain, however, is that disdain turned to downright hatred when fate, chance, call it what you will, dealt this highly superstitious leader a most unwelcome omen.

On 16 December 1804 the Corsican corporal was crowned as Emperor and suitably lavish festivities were organised to mark the occasion. These included lots of fireworks plus the release from the gates of Notre Dame of a large hydrogen balloon which was elaborately decorated and bore aloft a huge gilded crown – a marvel that was to steal the show as it drifted away into the inky sky. So far, so good. But the following morning, by one of the most extraordinary strokes of mischance imaginable, the balloon was spotted by the inhabitants of Rome as it drifted overhead. It casually skimmed the dome of St Peter's before dipping down to ground level and finally disappearing off into the waters of Lake Bracciano. That is, except for the gilded crown which, according to popular legend, was

Napoleon's disdain for ballooning turned to hatred when one wayward balloon almost spoilt the celebrations for his coronation as Emperor.

found draped upon the tomb of none other than Nero! The odds against such a thing happening must be millions to one, and for a highly superstitious Bonaparte it was the final straw as far as balloons were concerned.

Napoleon almost encountered the balloon again in 1812. In an attempt to defend Moscow the Russians devised a 'dirigible' or 'steerable' balloon to drop bombs on the French forces – even on Bonaparte himself if they could manage it – but the concept was ahead of any suitable means of propulsion and this fish-shaped aerostat never left the ground. The Russians did, however, launch a small unmanned fire balloon as the signal for the burning of Moscow. Meanwhile, the pleas of some French officers to their Emperor to revive the Compagnie d'Aérostiers fell on predictably deaf ears.

By 1830, with Bonaparte out of the picture, the French government was inclined to give the balloonists another chance. To assist the army in Algeria the professional aeronaut Jean Margat set sail aboard the *Vittoria*, but unfortunately his carboys of sulphuric acid were broken en route in the rough seas, causing considerable damage to the ship. Little is known about Margat's subsequent experiments when he got to Algeria, although it is thought that at least one ascension took place.

In the first half of the nineteenth century several other countries, including the Danes and the Austrians, experimented with propaganda and bomb-carrying balloons. But for the next concerted surge of activity with observation balloons we must look to the other side of the Atlantic and the start of America's bloodiest conflict – the Civil War.

3
LOWE FLYING

The story of aeronautics in America's Civil War should have told of the military balloon's coming of age with the advent of telegraphic communication, aerial photography and efficient mobile gas generators. Instead it is one of petty rivalries and jealousy, inflated egos and deflated balloons, all tangled up in a web of bureaucratic red tape and confusion. Two names in particular came to dominate this war within a war – John La Mountain and Thaddeus Sobieski Constantine Lowe – and their rivalries can be traced back to the last years of peace.

John La Mountain, born in 1830, had spent much of his adult life as a merchant seaman before working with the veteran aeronaut John Wise, who was a firm believer in the future of ballooning as a viable mode of international transport. He had once stated, 'Our children will travel to any part of the globe without the inconvenience of smoke, sparks and seasickness, and at a rate of 100 miles per hour.' Wise had his eyes set on conquering the Atlantic, having identified a fairly consistent airflow at higher altitudes which roughly corresponded to the trade winds familiar to sailors. 'A current from west to east in the atmosphere is constantly in motion within the height of 12,000ft above the ocean. Nearly all my trips are strong proof of this.' It was a dangerous and difficult challenge, sure enough, but not an impossible one given the right balloon and a modicum of good luck with the weather. Wise raised sufficient funding to construct the *Atlantic* – a reasonably large gas balloon with a volume of 50,000 cu ft – and at dusk on 2 July 1859 he was joined by La Mountain together with two companions as they launched from the city of St Louis, Missouri, supposedly on a test-flight to Boston as a stepping stone to the transatlantic attempt. Alas, by the following afternoon the balloon was to be found 809 miles away, lodged halfway up a tree near Lake Ontario. All had started well, but by dawn they encountered fierce 90mph winds which slammed the balloon through a forest, ripping it to tatters. La Mountain rebuilt the *Atlantic*'s envelope, but he fared little better on his own shake-down flight; having launched from New York he ended up stranded for four days in the bleak Canadian wilderness.

Next off the starting blocks was the twenty-nine-year-old New Englander, Thaddeus Lowe, who launched from Cincinnati on 19 April 1861 and was carried by the wind on a long looping course that took him eastwards across Virginia before bending south-west over North and then South Carolina. After a journey of some 350 miles Lowe landed safely near the remote town of Unionville, but with war brewing he could hardly have picked a worse spot. Surrounded by a suspicious and threatening mob he was promptly arrested as a Yankee spy and faced the very real prospect of imprisonment or even execution. It was only by sheer good fortune that he was taken to the bigger town of Columbia where a local man recognised him and he was sent packing. Incredibly, the Atlantic Ocean would remain unconquered by the balloon for another 120 years, but Lowe was now more concerned by the obvious build up for war that he witnessed on his long train journey back north. 'I was fully convinced that my country was facing a severe struggle, and I would offer the breadth of my body and resources to its service.'

Military balloons had never been deployed by the Americans, although in 1840 it had been suggested that they could assist the troops in Florida to locate the hidden camps of the rebellious Seminole Indians. A few years later, during the Mexican War, John Wise gained some publicity for a proposal to bombard the fortress of San Juan de Ulúa at Veracruz from a balloon. But neither of these schemes aroused official support. Now with the USA on the brink of its bloodiest conflict, several professional aeronauts volunteered their services. With the support of the editor of the *Cincinnati Daily Commercial*, Thaddeus Lowe wrote to the US Treasury Secretary, Salmon Chase, in April of 1861 proposing to establish a balloon corps to serve the army. Just one month later John La

The famed Civil War aeronaut
Thaddeus Sobieski Constantine Lowe.
(Valhalla Aerostation)

'The war balloon at General McDowell's headquarters preparing for a reconnaissance', an engraving published in *Harper's Weekly* in October of 1861.

Mountain wrote to the Secretary of War, Simon Cameron, offering his services along the same lines. Already Lowe had demonstrated his political acumen by taking advantage of an influential supporter to gain the ear of the politicians and accordingly Secretary Chase arranged a meeting between Lowe and President Lincoln to take place in June. Once again Lowe was on the ball and he took with him his balloon *Enterprise* – another in a long series of aircraft so named, starting with the *L'Entreprenant* of the French Aérostiers right up to Captain Kirk's starship – and after outlining his vision of an air corps to the attentive President, Lowe offered to put on a practical demonstration.

On 17 June the *Enterprise* rose into the air 500ft above central Washington – a little short of the height of the Washington Monument when it was completed years later. On board were Lowe and two representatives of the American Telegraph Company, for Lowe had one more inspired card up his sleeve. With telegraph cables running down the tether rope and from there overground to the War Department and the White House, he transmitted the following message direct to President Lincoln:

> Sir. This point of observation commands an area nearly fifty miles in diameter. The city with its girdle of encampments, presents a superb scene. I take great pleasure in sending you this first dispatch ever telegraphed from an aerial station, and in acknowledging my indebtedness to your encouragement for the opportunity of demonstrating the availability of the science of aeronautics in the military service of this country.

With this brilliant tour-de-force Lowe had displayed the capabilities of the balloon and captured the ear of the President himself.

Although Lowe continued to make several successful tethered ascents around Washington, his problems were only just beginning. The civilian status of his organisation meant that, initially at least, he was forced to use his own equipment and even to pay his aides out of his own pocket. Added to which, he now had to bring some structure and order to the fellow aeronauts who were gathering under the Union banner. These included John Wise, James and Ezra Allen, and Samuel King – egotistical showmen to a man – not to mention La Mountain. Things started off badly for Lowe when Wise promised to build the government a balloon for $200 less than he had offered, but in July Wise's balloon was ripped by branches on its way to observe the Battle of Bull Run. Lowe seized the moment and hurriedly inflated the *Enterprise*, although by the time he got near to the fighting the Union soldiers were already in retreat.

These incidents highlighted the desperate need for a portable hydrogen generator. Lowe had designed one but without the funds to build it he remained tied to the municipal gas supply within Washington and so he continued to make ascents within the vicinity of the city. They were sometimes made as free-flights and on one of these he found himself drifting into danger over the Confederate lines. It was only by riding with the higher altitude winds that he made it back to friendly territory, to be greeted by gunfire from his own troops.

La Mountain – who publicly derided Lowe's ascents in Washington – had yet to hear from the Secretary of War, although he had received a letter from Major General Benjamin F. Butler who invited him to demonstrate a balloon at Fort Monroe, near the mouth of the James River in Virginia. Accordingly, on 13 August, La Mountain ascended in the old *Atlantic* in what turned out to be the first aerial observation in the USA of the enemy's forces. 'Having attained an altitude of 3,000ft, he found the encampment of Confederate forces to be about three miles beyond Newmarket Bridge, Virginia', reported the *New York Times*. 'There were no traces of rebels near Hampton. A considerable force is also encamped on the east side of James River, some eight miles above Newport. The two cannon mounted at Sewall's Point toward Old Point, he thinks, are only large field pieces. There are, perhaps, one thousand Confederates at Sewall's Point.' La Mountain also conducted a series of daring free-flights over the top of the enemy's positions. Using all his nautical expertise in judging the weather and wind conditions he calculated that on certain days he was able to drift over the enemy lines and then dump ballast to climb to a much higher level and fly with the contrary winds back to his own side. It was a calculated risk with the real likelihood of being regarded as a spy if captured by the Confederates, or conversely being shot at by his own people on the return trip.

If only the two aeronauts could have joined together the result would have been an 'air force' to be reckoned with, but it was not to be and the President appointed Lowe to form a Balloon Corps to serve under the Bureau of Topographical Engineers. Funding was also approved for the construction of

Lowe's first purpose-built military balloon which was ready by the end of the month. On 24 September 1861, Lowe ascended at Arlington and at 1,000ft he reported the presence of Confederate forces three miles away at Falls Church. Using the telegraphic equipment he was able to accurately guide the fire of the federal guns upon an opponent unseen from the ground positions. This had two immediate effects: it demoralised the enemy troops on the one hand, while convincing the Union commanders of the usefulness of the balloon on the other, and the following day Lowe was ordered to construct four additional balloons and 'such inflating apparatus as may be necessary for them'. At its height the Balloon Corp boasted six balloons, each brightly decorated with patriotic designs and bearing the names *Intrepid*, *Constitution*, *United States*, *Washington*, *Eagle* and *Excelsior*. They were controlled from the ground by crews using snatch blocks. At last Lowe had his field generators – twelve were constructed, working on the wet sulphuric acid and iron principle, and although bulky these could be drawn by teams of horses.

There is, however, one way in which La Mountain had stolen a march on Lowe. On 3 August 1861, he had taken to the water when an already inflated balloon was transferred to a windlass on the afterdeck of the armed tugboat *Fanny*. Even so, the honour of creating what is arguably the first 'aircraft carrier' went to Lowe. At a time when the opposing forces had become entrenched along the Potomac, Lowe identified the need for a vessel from which to ascend and he approached the Secretary of the Navy, who allocated an old coal barge, the *George Washington Parke Curtis*. The 122ft long barge was modified by the addition of plating over the hull to create a flat deck, and at the bow two hydrogen generators were installed. Lowe once joked that he thought the Confederate forces were afraid of his balloon-boat because it so much resembled the flat-topped ironclads of the time. On 11 November the balloon *Washington* alighted from the boat at Mattawomen Creek. Similar ship-borne excursions were later made by Lowe himself and also by John H. Steiner, who flew the *Eagle* from a simple flat-boat on the Mississippi, and by John B. Starkweather, who launched the *Washington* from the tug *May Flower*.

By the autumn of 1861 La Mountain had procured a second balloon, the *Saratoga*, to supplement the well-worn *Atlantic*, but in November it was torn out of the hands of the ground crew in stormy conditions. This left La Mountain ever more envious of Lowe with his fleet of balloons, a situation further exacerbated by his refusal to hand any of them over. The infighting continued into the new year, with either side vying for influential allies to press their cause, but by February 1862 even the army had had enough of the bickering and Major General George B. McClellan, commander of the Union Army of the Potomac, ordered that La Mountain be dismissed from the army's service.

Although the Confederates' attempts to establish their own air arm were severely hindered by a lack of resources, their balloon operations were more extensive than some historians might have us believe. By summer 1861 the Northern newspapers had reported five sightings of a Confederate balloon, but the names of the balloon or aeronaut have not been traced. And lest we conclude that these were phantoms – in much the same way that mysterious apparitions have been seen at other times of conflict, be they airships or flying saucers – in August 1861 a balloon was mentioned in a message from the Confederate General Johnston to General Beauregard at Manassas, 'It seems to me that the balloon may be useful… Let us send for it, we can surely use it advantageously.' In September the unnamed balloon was at Munson's Hill and during the winter was reported flying near Leesburg.

There is no doubt that the Confederate generals appreciated the value of observation balloons because the presence of the Union's aerial spies was causing them considerable inconvenience. Instructions were issued to the troops advising of the need to prevent the enemy from discovering their advanced outposts. 'No lights should be kept at night except where absolutely necessary, and then under such screens as may conceal the lights from observation. Further, tents, if used, are to be pitched under the cover of woods and sheltered in all cases as far as possible from accurate computation.' In other words, this was the first example of a 'blackout'. In addition, the Confederates put some effort into misleading the observers. Imitation cannon, known as 'Quaker guns', were constructed from tree trunks, and campfires were deliberately lit in an attempt to confuse the observers regarding the position and size of their forces.

In early 1862 Thaddeus Lowe reported seeing a strange new balloon that had 'neither shape nor buoyancy' hanging over the Confederates lines of General Johnston's forces at Yorktown. This hot air balloon, a throwback to the original Montgolfier aerostat of 1783, was an attempt to get airborne despite the absence of a mobile gas supply. A volunteer was selected, John Randolph Bryan, to act as an observer. He described the balloon as a 'large cotton bag' inflated with 'hot air, for a plentiful supply of pine knots and turpentine had been made to create a great heat under a flue, the end of which opened into the balloon'. Apparently

Entered according to Act of Congress, in the year 1862, by M. B. BRADY, in the Clerk's Office of the District Court of the District of Columbia.

This early stereoscopic card, featuring a photograph by Mathew Brady, shows Lowe's mobile gas generators in action at Fair Oaks, Virginia. (US Library of Congress)

The first aircraft carriers. 'War balloon on the James River', *Harper's Weekly*, September 1862.

observations had to be taken very quickly and this might suggest that the source of heat was not carried with the balloon, although some accounts suggest that the balloon did stay airborne for longer. Either way, it was a hazardous operation to say the least. Bryan also came under fire from the enemy's guns. 'Hardly had I got above the treetops and obtained a view of the enemy's line than I observed a great commotion among them, men running here and there and in a very few minutes they had run out a battery. I saw the officer in charge elevate the gun and give the signal to fire!'

As the Union forces advanced upon the Confederate positions, Bryan was ordered into the air to obtain information on their movements. His own troops had crowded around to get a closer view of the proceedings when one man got his foot entangled in a coil of rope, which, 'before he could step out again tightened around his leg and began pulling him up to the windlass, whereupon he screamed loudly'. One of his friends seized an axe and severed the rope, freeing the stricken man and in the process releasing the hot air balloon into the night sky. Bryan, finding himself unexpectedly airborne, appraised the situation all too aware that his cooling balloon could come down on either side of the lines. He was relieved to find himself being blown back to his own troops who, thinking he was a spy, took to the now customary practice of opening fire. 'In vain I cried out that I was a good Confederate… '

By the spring of 1862 the Southern forces had fallen back to the outskirts of the Confederate capital of Richmond. Unfortunately for General McClellan, commanding the Union army, his forces had become split on opposite sides of the river. But when the Confederates seized the opportunity to strike, Lowe's balloons played an active part in staving off a crushing at the Battle of Fair Oaks on 31 May and 1 June. On the first day, flying in the *Washington*, he was able to confirm that the attack was not a feint and his telegraphed warnings enabled the Northern commanders to send reinforcements. The following morning he ascended once more in *Washington*, but keen to ascend higher he quickly returned to the ground in order to switch to the larger *Intrepid*, which was six miles away. When he got to the balloon he discovered that it would take at least another hour before it was sufficiently inflated. The nearby *Constitution* also lacked sufficient lift. 'I saw the two armies coming nearer and nearer together. There was no time to be lost', Lowe recalled later. If only he could transfer the gas from one balloon to the other, but he had no equipment to connect the two. He searched around and latched upon a 10in cooking pot. The bottom was hastily cut off and with the pot serving as a short pipeline the *Intrepid* received its boost of flight-giving gas. Together with his telegraph operator, Lowe scrambled into the basket and the balloon rose high over the battlefield and soon the vital reports began to flow.

In June 1862 one of the most enduring legends of the Civil War – the Confederate 'silk dress' balloon – was born. 'While we were longing for the balloons that poverty denied us, a genius arose for the occasion and suggested that we send out and gather together all the silk dresses in the Confederacy and make a balloon. It was done, and we soon had a great patchwork ship which was ready for use in the Seven Days Campaign.' Or so wrote General James Longstreet in his memoirs. Obviously he didn't realise that not one of the Southern belles was deprived of a single dress, as a Captain Langdon Cheves had built the balloon at his own expense from pieces of new silk. As these were in a multitude of colours and patterns, this is probably where the story originated. The silk was then

Lowe ascends at Fair Oaks in the *Intrepid* balloon, decorated with the Stars and Stripes to deter 'friendly' fire from his own side. (US National Archives)

varnished with a rubber mixture produced from rubber train springs dissolved in naphtha to make it gas-tight. It was quite small – only 7,500 cu ft in volume – and because the Confederates lacked a portable generator it had to be taken to the Richmond Gas Works for inflation. 'It was the custom to inflate the balloon there. Tie it securely to an engine and run it down the York River Rail Road to any point at which we desired to send it', wrote Longstreet.

The 'silk dress' balloon made its first observation flight on 27 June with Major E.P. Alexander riding in the tiny basket; he was spotted by Lowe, who was not far away. Over the next few days it made several ascents as the Northern troops were forced back and McClellan fought to save his army. Lowe's Balloon Corps struggled to keep up with the rapidly moving front, and on one occasion was forced to abandon some of its gas generators to the enemy. Restricted by the extent of their railway transport system, which only came to within seven miles of the river, the Confederate aeronauts transferred their balloon, fully inflated, to the steam-tug *Teaser*, and it first flew from her decks on 1 July 1862. After several days operating in this manner the *Teaser* went aground on a mud bar and on 4 July the Union gunboat USS *Maratanza* blasted a hole in her boiler and both ship and balloon were captured.

A replacement silk balloon was hastily constructed, this time with funding from the Confederate War Department, probably of a similar size and design to the first 'silk dress' balloon. Completed by late August, it was flown several times over the next few months operating in much the same way as its predecessor, but this time obtaining gas from the works at Charleston where a 'charge account' had been opened. But the Confederates' forays into aerial warfare came to an abrupt end when the balloon was carried away in high winds and deposited into Union territory, where it was later cut up into small pieces as souvenirs.

Thaddeus Lowe was faring little better by this time. When McClellan was relieved of command of the Northern armies in 1863, Lowe lost his most valuable supporter. In his stead Captain Cyrus Comstock was assigned to oversee the organisation and it was clear from the outset that he did not have much interest in this bunch of temperamental and ill-disciplined aeronauts. He ordered cutbacks in both supplies and personnel, and in addition Lowe was accused of inadequate financial record keeping. This really must have rankled with Lowe at a time when he was wrestling to manage the corps while also trying to make ends meet personally. The final straw came when Comstock slashed his pay almost in half. Thaddeus Lowe, weary and disheartened, resigned from the Balloon Corps on 8 May 1863, barely two years after his triumphant demonstrations in Washington. The remaining Union balloonists struggled on until the summer under the direction of Ezra and James Allen. Then in August the corps was phased out altogether. That they had provided vital intelligence on many occasions is without doubt, but the opinions of the military commanders had become soured by the spectacle of the continuous bickering. For their part the Confederate commanders were equally delighted and bewildered by the demise of the Union's Balloon Corp. 'I have never understood why the enemy abandoned the use of military balloons in 1863, having used them extensively up to that time', wrote a Confederate artillery officer. 'Even if the observers never saw anything, they would have been worth all the cost for the annoyance and delays they caused us in trying to keep our movement out of their sight.'

One new reconnaissance tool which had come to the fore by this time was never put into practice by the Civil War balloonists. The first experiments in aerial photography had been conducted by a French army officer in 1849 using kites, and in 1858 the flamboyant French aeronaut Felix Tournachon, widely known as 'Nadar', declared the balloon to be an ideal and stable platform for his cameras. Now instead of relying upon sketches drawn in the basket,

This 1862 view of the attack on Fort Darling, in the James River, is a graphic demonstration of the advantages of observation from above.

The notion of an airborne army remained a constant theme from Napoleonic days onwards, and this 1862 cartoon portrays the 'Flying Artilliary' – a hint to General McClellan on how to advance on Richmond.

the day had come when commanders could see detailed images of the battlefield for themselves. Lowe certainly considered their use, but the bulky glass plate equipment was unsuited to his balloons. Photography did, however, provide a new way of recording history, one in which the idealised images of the engravers and artists is at odds with the much grittier photographic version of events. And it is thanks in particular to the work of war photographer Mathew Brady that we have such an evocative insight into the world of Lowe and his contemporaries.

A century after the war's end the balloonists on both sides were commemorated by a memorial erected by the City of Richmond at the site of the Battle of Seven Pines. 'Dedicated to the intrepid and patriotic men – the Civil War balloonists, Union and Confederate, known and unknown, who against ridicule and skepticism laid the foundation for the nation's future in the sky.'

Their legacy may also have led in another direction for aeronautics. A twenty-five-year-old cavalry officer named Ferdinand von Zeppelin was in the USA in 1863 as an observer for the Prussian army. On 18 May he ascended to 700ft in a tethered balloon at St Paul, Minnesota, flown by the German-born aeronaut John H. Steiner, and afterwards Zeppelin commented that the St Paul valley was 'exceptionally fitted for demonstrating the importance of the balloon in military reconnaissance'. How much this experience influenced Zeppelin's desire to build airships remains a matter of conjecture, though there can be little doubt that he was to observe more balloons on his travels, which later found him serving with some distinction in the Franco-Prussian War.

4

UNDER SIEGE

Despite the lessons of the American Civil War, the military authorities in Europe were unenthusiastic about ballooning and it remained for the most part the province of the showmen, sportsmen and scientists. One of these was the famous British aeronaut Henry Coxwell, who on 7 September 1854 ascended from the Surrey Zoological Gardens in order to demonstrate a method of signalling from the air. He also took with him a bag of carrier pigeons and these were duly dispatched with messages to the War Office, the Admiralty and the Foreign Office.

'Mr Henry Coxwell, ready like a true patriot, to serve his country when his country calls, and fly to her aid to Olympus high, when danger threatens, has turned his attention to the uses of which, in these piping times of war, ballooning may be applied', reported the *Morning Advertiser*. 'Indignant at the airy nothingness which the ascending experiment has hitherto revelled in, and resolved to entirely put aside all attempts to pander to the morbid appetite for objective performances, he has conceived the idea of "taking stock" of a threatened fortress, by balloon survey, and has invented a set of signals by which he can communicate.'

Later on, nocturnal performances using coloured flares took place at Leeds. However, despite the hyperbole of the newspapers, Coxwell's proposals fell upon deaf ears among his countrymen, although he did manage to arouse the interest of the Prussian army. In 1848 and 1849 he demonstrated the dropping of aerial torpedoes at Berlin and Elberfeld. The Prussians ordered two balloons and put Coxwell in charge of two balloon detachments, which made ascents at Cologne and during the siege of Strasbourg. The balloonists were then ordered to move their equipment to Paris, except that without mobile gas generators it was impossible to inflate them and the balloon detachments were disbanded on 10 October 1870.

The French authorities had not regained their appetite for military ballooning in the forty years since the Algerian campaign and it was not until the collapse of the Third Empire that the War Ministry was inclined to accept the offers of assistance from French aeronauts. Four private balloons were pressed into service

A French captive balloon ascends for observation of the enemy's movements in the early stages of the Siege of Paris.

at the Battle at Valenton on 17 September 1870, and during the siege at Metz small, unmanned hot air balloons made of paper or cotton were used to carry messages out of the city. Unfortunately, most of these fell into the enemy's hands, although ironically on 18 September the last telegram to reach Paris had contained news conveyed out of Metz by one of these balloons.

With Paris encircled by the Prussian forces by mid-September, its two million inhabitants settled down for a long siege. Contingency plans had been made and the city streets bustled with thousands of irregular volunteers as barricades were erected and in many places trees were cut down to provide a better outlook for the guns. Three balloons ascended on tether to observe the enemy's movements. An engraving in *The Illustrated London News* showed the *Le Neptune* ascending at Montmartre under the command of the celebrated aeronaut Nadar, with Camille Dartois and Jules Duruof as his lieutenants. Meanwhile, Eugene Goddard was in the *Ville de Florence* at the Boulevard d'Italie, and Wilfrid de Fonvielle flew in the *Céleste* at Vaugirard.

The biggest problem now facing the authorities was maintaining communications with the outside world, in particular with the temporary government set up at Tours and also the troops in the provinces. A few brave souls volunteered to run the gauntlet of the Prussian patrols by escaping on foot with vital messages, but this was clearly a very hit-and-miss affair. A secret telegraph cable had been laid along the river Seine, but this had been discovered by the Prussians and after attempts to tap into it had proved unrewarding they severed it – cutting the city off completely. If messages could not be conveyed by conventional means, then the unconventional had to be exploited and Paris was blessed with a loyal band of balloonists eager to play their part. But an inventory of the existing privately owned balloons was not at all encouraging. It consisted of the three already used for observational purposes plus three others, two of which were in a poor state of repair. However, the balloons were never intended to be the route for any large-scale escape from the city, and instead they served as the only avenue of communication still open to the Parisians, one that would later open up a two-way exchange. The balloonists immediately made contact with the director of the Post Office, M. Rampont, and working quickly, the first flight of the Balloon Post was soon ready to depart.

At 8.00 a.m. on 23 September the professional balloonist Jules Duruof took off from the Place St Pierre in Montmartre in *Le Neptune*. A large crowd had assembled to witness his moment of departure and they were astounded as the balloon shot heavenward like a home-sick angel, rising to 6,000ft. Duruof knew that the only way to get his leaky old balloon beyond the Prussian lines was to gain as much altitude as possible initially and to hope the winds would carry him far enough out as it gradually descended. Duruof travelled alone, although he was accompanied by 227lb of mail – much more than the weight of an average man. These weren't just official dispatches, as they included thousands of letters written by the public – produced on thin paper and without envelopes to save on weight. Another aeronaut later summed up the significance of these airmails when he wrote, 'I carried with me 400 kilos of mail; that is to say, 100,000 letters, 100,000 tokens of remembrance sent from Paris by 100,000 anxious families!'

To infuriate the Prussian infantry down below, Duruof dropped visiting cards on their lines as their canon fired and their shells exploded near enough to shake the balloon. After a little over three hours in the air he descended in the grounds of a chateau at Evreux, about fifty miles west of Paris, where he was taken to the nearest railway station and that same evening he presented himself and his dispatches at Tours. But of course there was, as yet, no way of getting news about his successful flight back to the besieged city.

Two days later a second balloon made its departure from Paris. This was the bigger *Ville de Florence* and this time in addition to the pilot, Gabriel Mangin, there was a passenger (probably an official courier) and more mail, and three pigeons in a small cage. For some time the pigeon fanciers had tried to impress upon the authorities the value of these birds for both inward and outward going messages, but now times were so desperate that even the most unimaginative official could appreciate the value of the birds returning to the city. It was a nerve-racking balloon flight and at first Mangin climbed to 14,000ft to gain more favourable winds, crossing the forest of St Germain before eventually creeping to the other side of the Seine after jettisoning some of the precious mail. Still dangerously close to the enemy, the balloonists were rescued by locals who bundled them up in peasant clothing and spirited them away. The lost mail was

Gaston Tissandier's balloon *Céleste* descends near Dreux.

recovered and, most importantly of all, the pigeons were released to fly back to their loft in Paris.

By this time the supply of balloons was dwindling rapidly and for the next excursion Louis Goddard linked together the two smallest balloons, the *Napoleon* and the *Hirondelle*. He launched this contraption from the Villette gasworks on 29 September, accompanied by another official courier, several bags of mail and this time six pigeons. Copies of a newspaper, which had been specially printed in Paris and contained news for the French peasants living in the occupied territories, were dropped en route, much to the wrath of the Germans. The two men landed dangerously close to the enemy and were rescued by French horsemen, and once again the pigeons returned to Paris.

The following day, 30 September, Gaston Tissandier lifted off in the little *Céleste*, the last of the airworthy balloons and well past her best. As he climbed to 3,000ft and drifted off towards Versailles, Tissandier was horrified by the scene that greeted him below. 'Not a soul on the roads, not a carriage, not a train. All the demolished bridges offer the appearance of abandoned ruins. Not a soldier, not a sentinel, nothing. You might think of yourself on the outskirts of an ancient city destroyed by time.' Despite throwing out ballast, Tissandier's aging balloon began to sink lower and lower and the Prussian cavalry began taking a keen interest in his progress. He eventually reached the little town of Dreux, which is about forty miles to the west of Paris, and encouraged by shouts from the peasants reassuring him that he was in a safe area, he thumped the *Céleste* into the ground.

On the same day another balloon, this time unmanned, had been launched from Paris to carry mail, but unfortunately it landed well within enemy lines and the experiment was not repeated. This test run may, in part at least, have been inspired by the unmanned balloons deployed during the siege at Metz, but it is more likely to have been seen as a solution to the exhausted supply of existing balloons. Fortunately, this situation had been foreseen and two makeshift balloon factories established at the redundant railway stations of Gare du Nord and the Gare d'Orléans were already in production. Women cut and stitched the gores of the balloons while bands of sailors prepared the intricate netting and constructed the simple baskets. The British journalist Henry Vizetelly was in Paris and he described the scene at the Gare d'Orléans.

> Under the vast iron and glass arched roof, on the long metal rafters sailors balanced themselves or sat astride engaged in suspending long strips of coloured calico reaching almost to the ground. Scores of women were occupied, either in spreading out and ironing long pieces of material or else in soaking the calico to get rid of its stiffness. Having been hung up to dry, the material was then cut out to various patterns, marked out to their full size upon the ground, and after a preliminary varnishing a hundred or more work-girls, seated at long tables and superintended by Madame Goddard, proceeded to sew the seams with a mechanical exactitude.

Because the balloons were only intended to fly once, they were constructed of calico – a coarse cotton cloth, which was cheap and readily available – coated

Balloon assembly line at the old Gare d'Orléans – note the sailors working on the rope rigging.

with linseed oil and litharge to make it gas-tight. For some obscure reason the ones built at the Gare d'Orléans were multi-coloured while the ones at the Gare du Nord were plain white. Each had a volume of approximately 70,000 cu ft and they were filled with coal gas supplied by the city's gas company.

The first of these balloons was destined to carry a very important passenger. The war was not going well for the French and while Metz still held out, Strasbourg and Toul had surrendered releasing yet more troops to reinforce the armies besieging the capital. The provisional government was tottering under the pressure and decreed that the elections for a Constituent Assembly, which had been called for 16 October, well before the outbreak of hostilities, were to go ahead as planned. In Paris the government realised that they must immediately send a new delegate to Tours to cancel this disastrous decision, and the only way such a person could do so was to go by balloon. It was decided that the youngest of the ministers, the charismatic Léon Gambetta, Minister of the Interior, should make the flight as soon as possible with the imposing mission of steering the delegates at Tours and raising and arming an army to deliver France from its enemies.

After waiting several days for the weather to improve, the *Armand Barbès* was inflated beside the *George Sand* at the Place Saint-Pierre on 7 October, ready for its special task. The two balloons were surrounded by a massive crowd, including Victor Hugo, as the figure of Gambetta, wrapped in a long greatcoat and fur hat, clambered into the basket of the *Armand Barbès* accompanied by his secretary Eugene Spuller, where they were briefed by the aeronaut J. Trichet. Aboard the

George Sand were pilot J. Revilliod, a French official and two Americans, who were going to buy arms on behalf of the French. At 11.00 a.m. they lifted off to the cheers of the crowd and cries of 'Vive la République!' However, the inexperienced Trichet found the over-laden balloon a handful from the start and once clear of Paris they crept over the enemy outposts at no more than 2,000ft. Shots came whistling past and after a rapid descent the balloon almost touched the ground before Trichet managed to gain some height by throwing out ballast. They came under fire once more near Criel, where a bullet grazed Gambetta's hand as he gripped the rim of the basket. The drama was far from over and still struggling to maintain height the balloon became entangled in the upper branches of an oak tree at Tricot, near to Montdidier. By nightfall one of the slate-grey pigeons was on its way back to its dovecote in Paris where news of the balloon's fate was eagerly awaited. It bore with it a brief message, 'Arrived after accident in forest at Epineuse. Balloon deflated, we were able to escape from Prussian rifle-fire and, thanks to the Mayor of Epineuse, come here, from whence we leave in one hour for Amiens… Léon Gambetta.'

As the world marvelled at this remarkable escape and Paris celebrated, the organised airlift continued at a steady pace. There were, regrettably, some exceptions to the rule and the day after Gambetta's departure a privately chartered balloon took off from the gasworks without the prior knowledge or approval of the authorities. On board were the pilot Racine and two merchants who had put up the money, but their flight was short-lived when the balloon landed near Stains in the no-man's land between the two opposing forces. The three men then spent several uncomfortable hours sheltering from enemy gunfire until French troops were able to rescue them under the cover of darkness. From then on it was not permitted to leave Paris by balloon without the permission of the government.

The flights continued whenever the weather conditions permitted and by the end of October a total of nineteen balloons had escaped the city, and in November a further thirteen followed. Naturally any news intended for Paris was eagerly awaited, and although not all of the pigeons were getting back to the city, a large number were and the messages they carried were duplicated between several birds in the hope that at least one copy would make it. However, there remained an obvious imbalance in the exchange of communications in and out as a handful of pigeons could carry only a fraction of the messages borne aloft by the balloons. One attempt to overcome this situation involved a photographic process in which up to 300 messages could be reduced to fit on to one sheet of paper. These could then be read with a powerful magnifying glass, although this often proved unsatisfactory as the texture of the paper made the messages difficult to discern. It was the Parisian photographer Dagron who devised what in effect was the first microfilm, using photographic film coated with finely grained collodion emulsion. This meant that each pigeon was now able to carry up to 5,000 letters in miniature, but before this system could be introduced Dagron and his equipment had to be got out of Paris. On the morning of 12 November he departed on board the balloon *Niepce*, which was flown by a sailor named Pagano.

Parisians post their letters for the 'Ballon monté' – the balloon post.

Microfilm messages were returned to Paris by pigeon and then projected and transcribed by a team of clerks.

As well as building balloons the Parisians needed many more aeronauts to fly them and these were picked from the ranks of the sailors who were sent off on their maiden flight with only the most rudimentary training. Consequently Dagron and his companion came down perilously close to the Prussian patrols and it took eight days for them to arrive safely at Bordeaux.

For the Parisians, Dagron's fate remained unknown until the microfilms began to arrive at the end of the month. Each precious film was swiftly taken to an office in the Rue de Grenalle where they were slotted inside a magic lantern and projected upon the wall. A team of clerks transcribed the individual messages, which were then delivered by normal means.

Infuriated by this constant flow of information in and out of the city passing over their heads, the Prussians introduced specially trained hawks to bring down the pigeons, and for the balloons Bismark ordered a new gun built by the famous Krupp armaments company. This first purpose-built anti-aircraft gun was capable of being tilted almost to a vertical position and it was mounted on a special lightweight gun-carriage for rapid repositioning. It is uncertain whether the gun was effective against the balloons – after all, it didn't shoot down a single one – but its reputation alone was enough to rattle the French and they decided that in future all departures would take place at night. This ruling was to lead to some extraordinary flights as the inexperienced pilots were liable to become lost in the darkness and tended to press on until daybreak. As a result several very long flights were made and tragically two of the balloons were lost at sea.

The first balloon to fly at night was *L'Archimède*, which launched at 1.00 a.m. on 21 November and by morning ended up at Castelré in Holland. Three days later *Ville d'Orléans* ascended a little before midnight, with the seaman Deschamps in command and one passenger on board, and the balloon flew for almost fifteen hours in which time it crossed the Baltic and eventually landed near Kongsberg in Norway – an extraordinary 800-mile voyage. The two men had carried with them a vital communique informing Gambetta of a plan to break through the siege, but by the time the weary aeronauts had reached Oslo and then travelled on to Tours, the breakout attempt was already underway and it subsequently failed.

The first to be lost at sea was the *Le Jacquard*, which took off on 28 November and was last sighted near Land's End as it headed out into the Atlantic. The second one was the penultimate balloon to leave Paris, the *Richard Wallace*, which on 27 January travelled south-west and was last spotted flying low over La Rochelle on its way to the Bay of Biscay. Both of these were being flown by seamen on their own, and it may be that they didn't realise where they were or they might simply have panicked. Spectators had shouted up to Lacaze, the pilot of the *Richard Wallace*, to come down, but inexplicably he threw out ballast instead.

Of course there was the ever-present danger of landing within enemy held territory and several balloons were lost in this way, the most celebrated case being that of the *Général Chanzy*. This launched on 20 December and flew almost due east – out of the frying pan and into the fire – ending up in Munich where its

Above: Krupp's 'anti-balloon cannon' forced the balloonists to stop their daylight flights.

Right: A dramatic illustration of a balloon launch at night, published in *The Illustrated London News* in December 1870. These later flights conducted under the cover of darkness created their own hazards for the inexperienced aeronauts.

hapless crew was immediately imprisoned. Some of the other balloons fared little better. On 18 January 1871 the pilot Vibert experienced the *Steenackers* travelling at 95mph and whisking him to a fast landing at Hynd, near the Zyder Zee, some 285 miles in three hours. On 28 January 1871 the last of the balloons, the *Général Cambronne*, left the city, and although several others were in production at the time they were not in fact needed as an armistice was declared. In all, sixty-six balloons had departed from Paris during the siege. Of these, fifty-eight made it to friendly territory, two had been lost and six fell into enemy hands. Between them they had carried 102 passengers, over 2,500,000 letters, more than 400 pigeons and five dogs. (It had been hoped that the dogs would travel back to the beleaguered city with microfilm messages, but they never made it through.) Gaston Tissandier, who was later joined by his brother Albert, had hoped to fly back to Paris, but in the end the right wind and weather conditions never materialised and one attempt from Rouen was aborted after they drifted into thick fog and wandered far off course. The government in Tours had also decided to place several balloons at the disposal of the armies in the provinces, including the *Ville de Langres* and the *Jean Bart*, and a balloon corps with two divisions was formed. However, the winter weather and problems with gas supplies hampered their efforts and with the declaration of peace this short-lived corps was disbanded.

5

DEFENDING THE EMPIRE

Following on from the period of intense military ballooning activity encompassing the American Civil War and Franco-Prussian War, there followed four decades in which the aeronauts were involved in a succession of lesser 'policing' actions in various far-flung corners of the world. But these were not fallow years as it was a time of reorganisation, modernisation and significant technological innovation.

Not surprisingly, among the European powers it was the French who got the ball rolling when in 1874 a Commission de Communications Aeriennes was formed to re-evaluate the balloon, and upon their advice a permanent military aeronautical establishment was founded in 1877. In charge was Lieutenant Charles Renard, who was later joined by his brother Paul, and together they set about organising a modern balloon unit at Chalais-Meudon, the site of the former home of Coutelle and Conté's Aérostiers.

Their first taste of action came in 1884 when General Courbet took a detachment with his expeditionary force to Tongking (now North Vietnam). It consisted of two officers, thirteen non-commissioned officers and twenty-three men. The balloon was small at only 9,200 cu ft – just big enough to lift one observer – and it was transported along with all ancillary gear including a winch and gas generator which worked on the principle of heating granulated zinc with bisulphate of potash, carried on specially constructed horse-drawn wagons. It is said that balloons were particularly useful in finding a way through the track-less marshes which the cavalry was unable to penetrate, and where reconnoitring parties were often prey to ambush in the dense bamboo forests. At the bombardment of Hong-Ha the French guns were directed from the balloon, and the retreat of the enemy was observed and consequently the order was given to advance. The French army continued to use balloons despite the relatively high cost of operation, and they were flown at Madagascar in 1895, at Taku in China in 1900, and used to scout for Muslin rebels during the 1907–1908 Moroccan campaign.

Where the French went their great rivals did not lag far behind, with a German Balloon Corps established in 1884, which within three years had eleven balloons at its disposal. Several other European nations followed suit and for the most part they were equipped with balloons and materials from the French constructors Yon, Goddard or Lachambre. The Russians started in 1884 with a balloon school near St Petersburg, Spain in 1884, Italy 1885, Holland and Belgium 1886, Denmark in 1889, Austria 1893, Bulgaria 1893, and Sweden and Switzerland in 1897. Further afield, the Chinese took to military ballooning in 1886, the Japanese in 1889, and finally, following a post-Civil War hiatus, the USA returned to it in 1893.

Invariably these embryonic air forces operated gas balloons, although experiments were conducted with the hot air variety as it was thought they might be more versatile on the battlefield in terms of rapid inflation, deflation and transportation. In 1886 the Russians inspected a 110,000 cu ft hot air balloon constructed by Goddard at Brussels, but the results of these tests proved unsatisfactory.

For most nations the balloons represented a high-profile accessory to their fighting forces, something to be displayed at the big set-piece manoeuvres or special occasions. While the German aeronauts were not to see any action until the First World War, those from most other countries played their part in a handful of minor campaigns. A typical example occurred in 1887 when the Italians took their French-built balloons on the Abyssinian campaign at Massawa and Saati, often transporting the heavy equipment including the new cylinders to carry gas – more on that later – over difficult and mountainous terrain by camel.

On the other side of the Atlantic it was almost thirty years after the Civil War before the US Army returned to ballooning, thanks to the efforts of Brig. General Adolphus V. Greely, who had been appointed Chief Signal Officer. In 1891 Greely sent an officer on a fact-finding mission to France, and upon his return set about organising a Balloon Service with the aid of the famous professional aeronaut William Ivy. They had just the one balloon, the *General Myer*, which lasted for several hundred ascents over the next three years before it was worn out and a replacement was constructed by Ivy and his wife.

When the Spanish-American War began in April 1898, Colonel Joseph E. Maxfield of the Signal Corps and Ivy were sent to Cuba to establish two balloon companies. They arrived on 28 June to discover that there was no gas generator and no acid or iron filings, leaving just about enough compressed hydrogen for one inflation of the lone balloon, the 14,000 cu ft *Santiago*. Worse still, when the balloon was unpacked it was discovered that the varnish had softened in the heat turning the envelope into one sticky heap. Undaunted, they nonetheless had the balloon in the air two days later and three flights were made. On 1 July the balloon was moved to El Paso Hill to observe the American attack at San Juan Hill, but it was positioned in a grove of trees just 2,000ft from the front line action. The 30 July 1898 edition of *Collier's Weekly* includes several photographs of the balloon being inflated from gas cylinders, the telephone equipment used to contact the ground, and the balloon in flight while attached to one of the trees. The Spanish forces could hardly believe their luck when the balloon's lines became entangled in the branches, trapping it just 300ft off the ground like a sitting duck and well within range. They riddled it with bullet and shellfire until it died a very public and humiliating death.

Not mentioned so far are the British who, despite a shaky start, embraced military ballooning with all the ardour of religious converts. They had no excuses, really – Henry Coxwell had been extolling the value of the balloon for some time – and thanks to the long tendrils of their massive empire they were to experience aerial reconnaissance in practice on a much wider scale than the other nations, in the process making some significant contributions to the art of ballooning.

During the American Civil War, Captain F. Beaumont of the Royal Engineers had been attached to Thaddeus Lowe's balloon corps and he was enthusiastic about what he saw. Back in England he repeatedly attempted to get balloons taken seriously and in 1863 together with a Captain G.E. Grover he arranged for Henry Coxwell to put on a demonstration at Aldershot. Disappointingly, for the next ten long years the authorities were moved to do precisely nothing, and in 1873 they turned down an offer from Coxwell to supply two silk balloons at a cost of £2,000 to join the Ashanti Expedition. It wasn't until 1878 that a sea change in policy was discernible and this is directly attributable to the efforts of Captain J.L.B. Templer, an enthusiastic amateur aeronaut who brought his own balloon *Crusader* to the Woolwich Arsenal. In 1879 the first British military aircraft

Early British experiment with balloon reconnaissance at the Royal Aldershot Review in the summer of 1863.

J.L.B. Templer, the enthusiastic
amateur aeronaut who became
the driving force behind the
British Army's ballooning
section.

ever constructed, the tiny *Pioneer*, was completed at the princely price of £71. The following year balloon training commenced at Aldershot and a balloon detachment took part in the army's manoeuvres there. Such was their success that subsequently a military ballooning school, balloon factory and depot were established at Chatham.

Originally the balloons were made of varnished cambric and inflated with coal gas, which was much cheaper than generating hydrogen, though not as efficient a lifting medium. Clearly this reliance on a fixed source of gas, albeit available in most towns, was a hindrance to mobility and experiments were conducted at Woolwich to produce a hydrogen generator along the lines of Coutelle's a hundred years earlier. This was not satisfactory and even the type of portable generator used by Lowe was considered too cumbersome and too slow. The suggestion that hydrogen could be compressed and stored in steel cylinders under pressure had originally been made in 1875 by a Lieutenant Watson and experimentation along these lines was resumed. The main difficulty was in perfecting a gas-tight valve, but by 1884 the cylinders were coming into use and were soon adopted by other countries. With improved gas pressure it was claimed that a small balloon could be inflated in fifteen minutes from cylinders, in comparison with several hours by the old method.

Using hydrogen meant, however, that a better envelope fabric was required to hold the gas. Templer turned to a highly specialised method of joining membranes from the lower intestine of an ox, known as 'gold-beaters' skin', which was being used to make small novelty balloons, often in the shape of floating figures. The skins were imported from the Continent in barrels and were handled almost exclusively by an Alsatian family in the East End of London, called the Weinlings. They guarded their ancient craft jealously, but Templer was able to persuade them to work for the British government building man-carrying balloons. The *Heron*, the first of the Weinlings's balloons, was completed in 1883, and while its volume of 10,000 cu ft is very small by most standards, its gold-beaters' skin envelope was light enough to lift one man to a reasonable height.

At the end of 1884, three balloons were sent with the British expeditionary force to Bechuanaland, in southern Africa. In the event there was no fighting and the balloonists were limited to giving a series of demonstration flights in the town of Mafeking. *The Graphic* reported that 'It was found that the buoyancy of the balloon was greatly affected by the fact that this place is about 5,000ft above sea-level.' It also commented that it was 'most satisfactory to see what a profound impression of England's greatness these practical and scientific exhibitions have made on the wondering native mind'. The following year a second detachment under the command of Templer was sent to the Sudan and at least one seven-hour tethered ascent was achieved with the balloon, at a height of 400ft, while attached to a wagon on the march between Suakin and Tofrik, but in general these operations were thwarted by the difficulties with gas supplies.

An example of a mobile hydrogen generator. These were later replaced by the widespread adoption of cylinders to transport compressed gas.

THE ILLUSTRATED LONDON NEWS

REGISTERED AT THE GENERAL POST-OFFICE FOR TRANSMISSION ABROAD

No. 2409.—VOL. LXXXVI.　　SATURDAY, JUNE 20, 1885.　　WITH SUPPLEMENT AND COLOURED PICTURE | SIXPENCE. By Post, 6½d.

1. The balloon taken out of the waggon at Mafeking.　2. Putting the net over the balloon.　3. The General about to enter the balloon car.　4. The balloon in mid air.
5. A catastrophe.　6. Expiring struggles.　7. Collapse and decease: funeral procession.　8. The native spectators.

BALLOONING IN BECHUANALAND.

FROM SKETCHES BY OUR SPECIAL ARTIST, MR. JULIUS M. PRICE, OF "METHUEN'S HORSE."

British army balloon being inflated at Mafeking in Bechuanaland, 1885.

It is a tribute to Templer's efforts that several other countries were to adopt the British gas cylinders and gold-beaters' skin for their balloons. One of Templer's innovations that didn't catch on to the same extent, however, was the introduction of steam traction engines to pull the wagons loaded with heavy ballooning equipment. In fact, he became such an advocate of these cumbersome all-terrain vehicles that the army appointed him as Director of Steam Road Transport in addition to his ballooning duties. For the Aldershot manoeuvres in 1889 a single engine was used to pull five wagons of gas cylinders, plus a further wagon with water for the steam engine itself. Progress was ponderously slow as they were preceded by the mandatory man on foot brandishing a red flag, and it took three days to reach Guildford. Even the pulling force of the traction engine couldn't get the combined load up the steep hill of Guildford High Street and amid the hustle and bustle of market day the engine was unhitched and positioned at the top of the hill to haul the wagons up by cable one at a time.

In the following year, 1890, the balloon section became a permanent part of the British army within the Royal Engineers, following an exemplary performance at the Aldershot manoeuvres. As *Sheldrakes Military Gazette* reported, 'The important part ballooning will play in future military operations is fully recognised by those who had the opportunity of witnessing the wonderful observations carried out.' For the bastions of the British Empire the observation balloon would be put to its greatest test soon enough against the Boers in South

Before the advent of the war photographer there were special war artists and this sketch shows a British balloon in the Sudan, on the march to Tamai in 1885.

Africa. The Boers outnumbered the British forces and, like a modern guerrilla army, used their extensive local knowledge to run rings around their adversary.

The Boer War began in 1899 and three balloon sections were sent to support the army. The first unit in action was the 2nd Balloon Section under the command of Major G.M. Heath, which arrived at Ladysmith on 27 October only to remain within the besieged town for the next four months. At first they continued to observe the enemy's movements, until the supply of hydrogen ran out. A small contingent of the 2nd Section which had remained outside of the town and with reserve equipment and gas saw action at Potgieter's Drift and Spion Kop.

The 1st Balloon Section joined Lord Methuen's advance on the Modder River and at the Battle of Magersfontein, observing the enemy and directing the artillery with great effect. In 1900 the balloonists provided vital information on the Boer's positions at Paardeborg, even though the 12,000 cu ft *Duchess of Connaught* was holed and leaking badly. The gas was transferred to the *Bristol*, which flew at the Battle of Poplar Grove, and in the advance from Bloemfontein it was kept inflated for twenty-two days on the 165-mile march. It then took part in the engagements at Vet River and Zand River. In June a balloon located at Pretoria assisted in the capture of the Boer forces, and although damaged by enemy fire in several places it was repaired with patches of gold-beaters' skin in the field.

The 3rd Balloon Section arrived at Cape Town in March of 1900, and was sent to Warrenton on the left flank of Lord Robert's advance on Pretoria. The observers were able to provide information on the position of the enemy guns and aided the directing of fire from the British 5in and 6in howitzers.

Transporting the balloon equipment was no easy task as Templer's traction engines had been lost on the way to Cape Town when HMS *Commonwealth* was wrecked. Instead they were moved, often fully inflated, on wagons drawn by teams of oxen or mules. These balloons were quite small, up to only 13,000 cu ft in volume, and their tiny baskets allowed just about enough room for one person sitting down, which explains why the habit of observers riding in the rigging became so commonplace.

The Boers had no balloons of their own, of course, and the effect on their morale was considerable as they relied upon their knowledge of the terrain to carry on a war of attrition. One Boer soldier in the Laager at Paardeberg wrote, '… it is all up, they will now be able to find out every hole and position we are in and will pour in a hell of shells'. He mused at the talk of his comrades. 'Do you call this fair play – that damnable big round thing, spying our positions. We would not be so mean to do a thing like this.' And, in truth, some of the British officers agreed with him.

In addition to the balloons in South Africa in 1900, the 4th Balloon Section was formed and sent to North China with the international force occupying Peking during the Boxer uprising. However, it arrived too late and ascents were made after the fighting was over. From there it transferred to India in 1901 to start an experimental balloon section in the Bengal Sappers at

Balloon Corps Transport, complete with wagons carrying hydrogen cylinders, with Lord Robert's army advancing on Johannesburg in 1901.

'A novel way of seeing the Happy Homes of England, now adopted by the Proprietor of Hudson's Soap. Hudson's War Balloons are travelling all over England – a facsimile of those now used by military authorities in South Africa.' From a contemporary advertisement.

Rawalpindi, but lacking adequate gas facilities, this was eventually disbanded in 1911.

In the aftermath of the South African action a special Committee on Military Ballooning considered the future for the British Army's balloons, and despite mixed opinions it concluded they still had a role to play in the twentieth century. Ironically this was 1903 – the same year in which the Wright *Flyer* made its first tentative forays across the sand dunes of Kittyhawk. Two years later the balloonists moved once again, this time to a site at Farnborough Common (now the Royal Aircraft Establishment, Farnborough). It was here that the army branched out into several new spheres of aeronautical activity, including airships, man-lifting kites and in 1908 the aeroplane. In 1912 Farnborough became the home of the new Royal Flying Corps (RFC) and on 13 May No.1 (Airship) Company Air Battalion, Royal Engineers, became the No.1 Squadron RFC.

The first decade of the twentieth century saw a distinct lack of interest in balloons among the military in most countries, with perhaps the exception of some activity in the Russo-Japanese War of 1904–1905. The East Siberian Balloon Corps had been formed by the Russian army, consisting of two companies initially operating spherical balloons, but as these were proving unsatisfactory several kite balloons were ordered from the Germans. A balloon

Rare image of a Japanese 'war balloon' operating at the rear of the besieging army at Port Arthur, 1905.

intended for the defence of Port Arthur, Manchuria, was on board a ship captured by the Japanese, but it is not clear if this was the balloon subsequently used by the Japanese army to spy on the port. It is said that, faced with the loss of their own balloon, one Czarist officer devised a replacement with an envelope constructed from bed linen coated with flax oil. The Japanese also used German balloon technology, including some elongated balloons, and a stereoscopic photograph issued at the time depicts a tail-less balloon belonging to the Third Division of the Japanese army said to be reconnoitring 'from a point about four miles north of Port Arthur'. Other photographs show the Russian balloonists operating spherical balloons and making use of cylindrical 'nurse' balloons to hold extra supplies of hydrogen.

In many ways these policing actions of the colonial powers were but a rehearsal for the 'big show' – a world war – in which a new shape was to fill the skies. It hadn't only been the military flying captive balloons and something of a vogue for these had flourished in the latter half of the nineteenth century. Since the birth of ballooning the professional aeronauts had sold places in their baskets, but only the wealthier members of society could afford a flight as it was such an expensive business. Alternatively, members of the public were sometimes taken up on short tethered rides and in 1867 the French balloonist Henri Gifford tapped into this market on a massive scale. His first captive ride balloon was big enough at 175,000 cu ft, but by the time of the 1878 Exposition in Paris he had created a colossal balloon with a gas volume of 882,000 cu ft – the biggest balloon the world had ever seen. Inflated with hydrogen it had a diameter of 118ft and could carry fifty passengers at a time up to a height of 1,600ft. Similar balloons soon became all the rage at expositions throughout Europe and although they contributed to the development of reliable steam winches to haul them up and down, they were without exception spherical. And while this shape is well suited to free flight, when tethered it tends to bob and rotate in anything but the lightest winds, and in strong winds it is a positive liability. What the military needed was a balloon that would actually become more stable in higher wind speeds, would turn into and actually ride the wind – in fact, something rather like a kite.

The idea of an elongated envelope was almost as old as ballooning itself, but simply changing the shape was not enough to make a captive balloon stable. Several aeronauts got it half right when they proposed using the position of the cable attachment to regulate the envelope's angle of attack and during the 1870s several French designs depicted elongated but tail-less observation balloons. At about this time a number of armies were taking an active interest in large man-lifting kites and it was perhaps no coincidence that in 1896 two German army officers, Major von Parseval and Captain von Sigsfield, took the kite as their inspiration to add two horizontal stabilisers and an air-filled tail, or rudder, to an elongated envelope to create the kite-balloon.

The kite-balloons were known as *drachen*, for 'kite' (although the same word coincidentally means 'dragon' in German), or more prosaically as 'sausages' by the British and *saucisse d'observation* by the French. The Germans enthusiastically

Henri Giffard's non-military *Le Captif* was hauled up and down on its cable by steam winch to provide pleasure flights for the public..

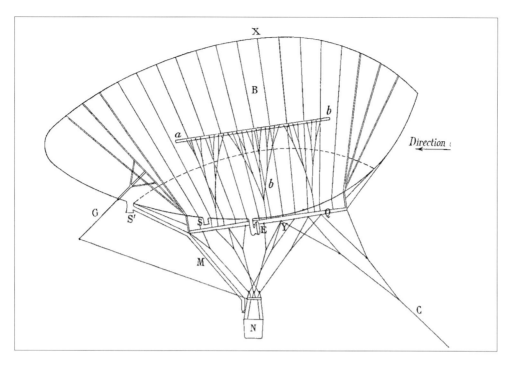

1870s design for a kiting balloon by Louis Godard anticipated the elongated shape but lacked the stabilising influence of tail fins.

This popular contemporary print, dated 1899, depicts troops of the German Imperial Army 'repelling a cavalry attack on a Balloon Detachment'.

adopted the new balloons, which represented the leading edge of aeronautical advancement at that time. A popular contemporary print, dated 1899, depicts 'Troops, repelling a cavalry attack on a Balloon Detachment', with a lengthy caption that reveals much about their self-image. 'To praise the German imperial army – bound by the Constitution of the German Empire (1871) to obey unconditionally the orders of the Kaiser – would be a work of superogation', it begins modestly. 'Such an array of men, with its simple but well-planned methods of recruiting, mobilisation, and efficiency on taking the field may well be Germany's pride, as well as the dread model for other nations…'

6
CALLING THE SHOTS

At the commencement of the First World War in 1914, it was the Germans with their superior equipment and expertise who took the lead with observation balloons on the Western Front. Eight Prussian and two Bavarian Feld-Luftschiffe-Abteilungen or 'observation balloon field units' were in existence, each with 280 officers and men, 194 horses and thirty-five carriages. The first balloons were 21,000 cu ft in volume and could rise to between 2,000 and 2,500ft, and later the bigger balloons of 35,000 cu ft permitted ascents up to 3,500ft. The disadvantage of the greater height was that it took longer to bring the balloon down and out of harm's way, a factor that was instrumental in the introduction of motor-driven winches. German balloons operated on the Eastern Front as well, especially in Serbia and Romania, and later in the Balkans and Russia. In the difficult terrain of the Dolomite mountains of Italy, both German and Italian balloons were also flown.

For the Allies, observation balloons were operated by the French, Belgians and British, initially at least, while on the Eastern Front the Russians had a considerable number. The French pressed several spherical balloons into service and these certainly had some advantage of being more easily repositioned, but the German *drachen* design dominated and was soon copied by the French. Lord Kitchener's British Expeditionary Force did not possess a single kite-balloon at first and examples of the French balloons were sent to England for copying. By the spring of 1915 the Royal Navy had a kite-balloon directing the heavy naval guns bombarding the Turks in the Dardenelles, but the British Army had to wait a little longer for the new kite-balloon sections to arrive at the Western Front. Part of the problem lay with the fragmented organisation of the British balloons, with the Admiralty and the Army's General Staff vying with each other and the newly formed Royal Flying Corps for control.

The role of the observers, scrutinising the zigzagging trenches running like an ugly scar from the North Sea down through Belgium and France, was divided between ranging for the artillery and general intelligence gathering. Equipped with telephone sets linked by cable to the ground and connected via the field telephone network, they could be in touch with individual gun batteries or even the Corps HQ if needed. American Craig Herbert later wrote of his experiences as an observer in *Eyes of the Army*. 'Hardly a train could move within five miles of the trenches, or a group of men come up for relief, or digging begun on a new series of emplacements or batteries, but a pair of eyes would take notice of it. Every movement, every activity would be registered until a schedule of usual enemy routine was built up and the average amount of motion known.' This degree of continuous surveillance led to the development of effective camouflage measures to disguise positions and troop movements, and arguably it was a significant factor in the stalemate of trench warfare. With the introduction of airborne photography from the balloons, officers on the ground could study the lay of the land for themselves. As the war progressed these cameras became ever more powerful with lenses starting at 300mm and culminating with 1,200mm – making them look like bulky canon as they poked over the sides of the baskets.

Riding in a tethered balloon above the combat zone took a certain and rare kind of nerve, though a healthy sense of humour didn't go amiss. The British balloonists referred to themselves as 'balloonatics' – a title that stuck – and many of them developed a great affection for their balloons. One of these was Goderic Hodges, who had volunteered to work with them in 1916. In his *Memoirs of a Balloonatic* he recalls, 'I took to ballooning like a duck to water… Once I was in the air all fears disappeared. I felt happy, exhilarated, even at the most hectic of moments.' And indeed, there could be something quite surreal about the experience, to be suspended above this vista of devastation but strangely aloof and detached from it. One observer wrote, 'For people with jaded nerves who are

A German *drachen* being manhandled into position at the Front.

Hauling down a French observation balloon – clearly based on the German design with its single air-filled lower fin.

perplexed with the ceaseless hurry, bustle and noise of modern life, I recommend a few hours up aloft in a kite-balloon as a tonic and respite from its cares and worries. There is a charming and attractive calm and quietness about the experience... Of course this is not recommended while there is a war on.'

In 1916, a distinctive new shape appeared above the trenches. Designed by and named after the French Captain Albert Caquot, this kite-balloon was more streamlined than the German *drachen* and it featured a tri-lobe air-filled tail arranged like a 'Y' – described by one commentator as looking not unlike a 'disordered bunch of bananas'. Maybe so, but early trials had shown that the balloon was capable of attaining 13,000ft and could fly in a 35mph wind with gusts up to 50mph; a far superior performance to the German balloons.

Down below, the troops at the front line cared little for such refinements as they regarded the balloonatics with disdain, dismissing them as having a soft option. After all, it was reasoned, they were positioned a little behind the lines and their crews lived in a degree of comfort. Yet this assumption couldn't have been further from the truth as the observers were sitting ducks for enemy aircraft, with only a flimsy wicker basket for protection and a bag of hydrogen bobbing just above their heads. This was particularly so during the earlier part of the war before improved winches could haul a threatened balloon down at 500ft per minute, and before observers were issued with parachutes. One study has suggested that the balloonists suffered the greatest level of nervous breakdowns among combatants because they felt so vulnerable and yet powerless to protect themselves. It was only after a series of appalling fatal falls in the early days of the war that the observers become almost exclusively the only airmen allowed a parachute – a policy based on the dubious assumption that aircraft pilots might not give their all if so equipped. The chutes, often referred to as 'guardian angels', were carried in upturned cones or 'acorns' attached to the side of the basket and they were automatically deployed by the weight of the observer when jumping. The Americans also conducted tests with a larger parachute rigged to bring the complete basket and occupants to the ground, but this was not popular with the observers.

Parachutes were never regarded as a guaranteed ride to safety as the falling observer faced the risk of either being engulfed by bits of the burning balloon as it fell, or of the parachute fouling the cable. This happened to Flight-Sergeant W.S. Lewis when his chute coiled around the cable and he heard the silk slashing into useless pieces. Then began the slow-motion unwinding, like a Maypole dance in reverse, from which Lewis fell like a stone, incredibly landing on his fellow observer's chute, also on its way down. 'Sorry! I couldn't help it', he shouted down to his companion who called back, 'It's all right, old man, but couldn't you have found some other bloody patch of field.' And grasping tight to the cords the two of them descended together for a heavy but survivable landing. Unfortunately, there were also many incidents when the parachutes failed to deploy, and in a perverse reversal of success a balloonist 'ace' was defined by the number of jumps made – in some cases more than one in a single day. And any suggestions that the airmen of the First World War fought with chivalry are largely spurious as an observer dangling beneath his parachute – in effect a white flag – was considered a legitimate target, certainly by the latter half of the war. One report from the Italian Front told of an attack by a British Sopwith Camel against an Austrian balloon confirming that 'the observer jumped out in a parachute, and Lieutenant Goode fired two bursts into his body at very close

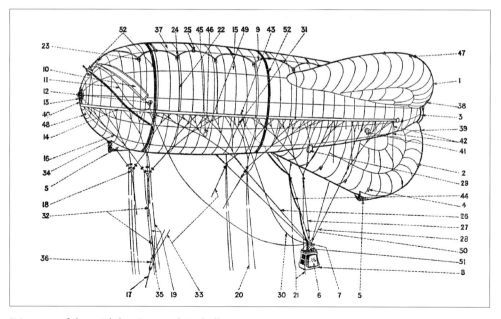

Diagram of the tri-lobe Caquot kite-balloon.

The War Illustrated, 8th June, 1918.

Regd. as a Newspaper & for Canadian Magazine Post.

The War Illustrated

Nº 199

VOL. 8 [Weekly Nos 183—208]   EDITED BY J. A. HAMMERTON   THREEPENCE

EYES OF THE ARTILLERY

Observer of a Royal Field Artillery Kite Balloon on
the Western Front with His Parachute Attachment

An observer of a Royal Field Artillery balloon demonstrates his parachute attachment,
which automatically deploys the chute when he leaps from the basket.

range'. There is also irrefutable evidence that both French and British army commanders gave orders to shoot at balloon observers.

It was the German balloonists who had been first to find themselves subjected to concerted attacks by a new breed of aviators colourfully described as 'balloon busters'. However, for the French and British pilots bagging a gasbag was a frustrating line of work as the damn things refused to pop as obligingly as they would have liked; their relatively low internal gas pressure meant they could take any number of bullet holes before it made an appreciable difference. Then, in one of those leaps of technology that combat often fosters, a French naval commander came up with the 'torpielle', a rocket with an 18in head, which could be launched from beneath the wing of an aeroplane. And although this air-to-air missile was somewhat erratic in performance, by the spring of 1916 the French rocketeers were experiencing some successes. But what they really needed was a bullet that could set the gas alight. Phosphorous-filled cartridges were tried, but they tended to perforate the envelopes rather than ignite the gas and they were also very prone to the effects of dampness. Only later would the answer come in the form of incendiary tracer bullets and even they could be frustratingly unreliable.

By 1916 the Germans had introduced anti-aircraft defences in the form of 3.7mm guns and dedicated fighter aircraft, and the task of the busters became increasingly hazardous. Sometimes the balloons bit back! Second Lieutenant Anton Wöstmann was an observer with the German 4th Army FLA 3, operating on the Eastern Front near the Belarussian city of Pinsk. On 11 August 1916 he was observing the Russian's positions from 4,000ft when he was advised of an approaching aeroplane. The aircraft came in slowly, but instead of taking advantage of a high-level dive it continued at the same height. This gave Wöstmann time to load his rifle with a twenty-round clip and as the aircraft opened fire he got into a kneeling position to fire back. 'My defence begins with well-aimed, slow single shots. After about the eighth shot the aeroplane begins to waver and darts down into a steep dive. I suspect this is a feint, not believing in having success after a few shots, but first I have to clear the gun chamber because, in jumping up so quickly when the opponent wavered, I caused the clip to jam. As I look out again, the aeroplane is far below me and trying to make it to the enemy lines.' It didn't make it home and despite the protestations of its embarrassed crew – reluctant to admit they had been brought down by a lowly balloon – Wöstmann received a telephone call from the Division general staff congratulating him on his 'kill'.

In some instances British balloons actually served as bait for attacking fighters, with a straw dummy taking the place of the observer and nearby a horde of defending aircraft poised at the ready. There is also a story from 1917 of the balloonists' revenge, one that borders on the apocryphal. In order to snare a persistent balloon attacker, an aging Caquot was booby-trapped with 500lb of explosives and a dummy placed in the basket. When the German Albatross aircraft duly approached the balloon it was consumed by an almighty explosion and, as the official report recorded, 'the machine folded like a book'.

Regardless of the antics of the balloon busters the balloonatics had other issues to contend with, as they were always at the mercy of the elements. In the summer they were scorched in their lofty perches, while in the winter months the cold could cut them to the bone. 'The icy wind blowing straight into our faces made us weep', recalled Goderic Hodges. 'Our tears froze on the lenses of our binoculars. We cleaned the lenses and started again. We wept again, cleaned again and so on.' Small hand-sized charcoal burners were issued to British observers, but they provided only a modicum of heat. Stormy conditions brought their own problems.

An ever present hazard was the breakaway, caused by either the weather or by enemy shellfire, and all observers were trained in the art of free-ballooning in case of such an eventuality. First Lieutenants Hinman and Tait – observers with the US 12th Balloon Company at Sommedieue, south-east of Verdun – were to experience one of those days when nothing goes right. Ascending in squally conditions, their balloon was engulfed by cloud at 1,600ft and, with useful observation out of the question, they were instructed to come down. However, the men on the winch brought the balloon down too quickly which, coupled with the effect of the wind funnelling through the valley, sent the balloon swinging in wild circles, barely missing the hills. 'The balloon swung out broadside to the wind, then suddenly shifted tail into wind. This caused a

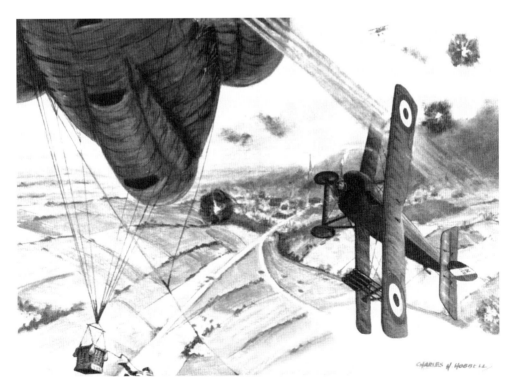

French 'torpielle' air-to-air rockets being launched against a German balloon in 1916. (NASA)

A German-designed observation balloon at an Italian training barracks.

nose dive from 400ft and the balloon hit the ground, the cable laying over the winch', reported Hinman. 'One man of the Basket Detail rushed at the basket, stepped on my parachute rope, pulled the parachute out of the container and took a tumble as the balloon rose.' The balloon broke loose and shot upwards like a cork out of a bottle, only impeded by Hinman's now deployed parachute. Suddenly he found himself being pulled by his harness, which had slipped from his waist and caught around his throat, strangling him with its pressure. Unable to free his partner, Tait vented hydrogen to halt the balloon's upward pull. He then cut Hinman from the parachute cords which allowed the unshackled balloon to take to the skies – and it was at this point that matters took a turn for the worse…

With their balloon drifting towards the trenches the two men found themselves in the thick hail of the shellfire they were meant to have been directing. They jettisoned all maps and equipment, including the telephone, and the balloon climbed high above the blanket of cloud, up to about 13,000ft, where it became as taut as a drum in the sunshine. Afraid of being spotted by enemy aircraft and minus a parachute, they initiated a descent by valving gas, and nearer to the deck Tait pulled the rip-line as hard as he could. The basket slammed into the ground, Tait lost his grip on the line and the balloon bounced up once more to about 50ft and then repeated this exercise four times until the men were tipped out. It was now Tait's turn to be caught by his parachute, and as the runaway balloon continued a succession of yo-yoing bounces, he was dragged on his belly until Hinman managed to scramble on to its deflated tail. Shortly afterwards the German soldiers arrived on the scene and took the bedraggled balloonists away for interrogation at Conflans, where they were bombarded by the British guns!

In another incident a twenty-one-year-old lieutenant of the RFC, Arthur V. Burbury, was alone in his balloon when enemy gunfire severed the cable releasing the balloon to drift towards German lines. Burbury destroyed his maps and papers, climbed up into the rigging and succeeded in ripping the envelope, to prevent it falling into enemy hands, and then parachuted within friendly territory. In recognition of his fast-thinking, Burbury was awarded the Military Cross by the King, and the French President presented him with the Croix de Guerre. Unusually, he was then transferred to aircraft and had his own share of balloon 'kills' until April 1917 when he was shot down behind enemy lines after going for a German balloon, and he spent the remainder of the war in captivity at Langensalza in Saxony. Other breakaways did fall into enemy hands, which gave the Germans the opportunity to copy the Caquot design with their own version known as the Ae-Ballon. (As Germany's rubber supplies were running short the envelopes were made instead from a combination of canvas and a synthetic substance called Zellon.) But perhaps the most extraordinary incident of all concerning breakaways occurred in the spring of 1918 when two British observers found themselves free-flying overnight and at dawn came down in Derbyshire.

Conditions for the ground crews were not necessarily that much better. When not in operation the balloons were 'bedded' down in a cleared area screened by trees or high ground as protection against the wind and hopefully out of sight of the enemy. Some attempts were made to camouflage the envelopes with bold stripes in much the same manner as the dazzle colour schemes on some warships. Nonetheless, the balloon beds were frequently visited by enemy shellfire and the effect on the hydrogen stored in small nurse balloons, or in cylinders, could be devastating. The risk of a breakaway was also ever present when ground handling or transporting a balloon, particularly if it was detached from the winch. One Flight Sergeant recalled such an incident. 'The men got worried and lost their heads. A few let go, and that made it more difficult for the rest to control the balloon. The panic spread and the balloon lifted off and took the fellows who hadn't panicked with it… two dropped off from 300 or 400ft and were killed.'

When America joined the war on 6 April 1917, it brought an influx of fresh blood to this aerial dance, although admittedly most branches of the US military were under-prepared and the Balloon Corps was no exception. A task force was sent to Europe to evaluate the usefulness of the balloons at the front, and when they reported back favourably the US War Department hurriedly established a training school at Fort Omaha in Nebraska – which still had its steel hangar, a hydrogen plant, and a handful of balloons including a leaky German *drachen* and an American-built kite-balloon. The Allies desperately needed more balloons and in September of 1917 the commander of the American Expeditionary Force (AEF), General John J. Pershing, cabled Washington, 'Kite

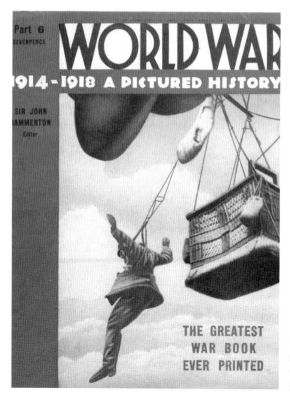

The leap from a balloon was often a leap of faith and a balloonist 'ace' was defined by the number of jumps made.

balloon situation French front very serious. Fifty companies urgently needed…' But it wasn't until 27 December that the first contingent of the 2nd Balloon Squadron, consisting of just four companies, arrived in France. In the event Pershing received thirty-six companies altogether, of which seventeen served at the front (and six arrived after hostilities had ceased).

All newly arrived balloon personnel were presented with a pocket-sized booklet published by the Department of Military Aeronautics, US Army, entitled *Balloon Terms – Their Definitions and French Equivalents*. This also contained useful 'hints for men going to France', including advice about travelling on the public transport, the art of tipping in hotels and cafes, buying tobacco and so on. 'Matches are always sold, never given away', it comments, before concluding with an important warning. 'Do not expect to find coffee, pies, etc., as "mother used to make them". When in France it may be well to do as the French do.' One of the first units to arrive was immediately sent to Marne to relieve a battle-weary French balloon company, and in July 1918 this balloon became the first of the AEF's shot down by the enemy. As aviation historian Maureen Lynch relates, 'The burning wreckage of the balloon had barely struck the ground before men went running up to claim souvenir pieces of it! There wasn't much left, one had to stomp out flames on remaining bits of fabric.' By the end of the war a further thirty-five AEF balloons were downed by enemy aircraft, twelve were destroyed by artillery fire on the ground

This modern DC comic is a tribute to the enduring appeal of the legend of the great 'balloon busters'.

and many more were scrapped due to damage from shellfire or lost because of the weather.

The last year of the war saw the art of balloon busting taken to new heights. By this time such attacks were considered highly dangerous thanks to the anti-aircraft defences, but that didn't deter the likes of German pilot Fritz Röth, who in a single, swooping strafing run burnt five British balloons in a little over ninety minutes. In his combat report Röth stated, 'On each balloon I opened fire at a very little distance and then righted my Albatross and flew close over the balloon and away. Almost all fell after 15–30 seconds, enveloped in flames. I attacked no balloon more than once.'

For many of the aviators their careers were a meteoric flash of brilliance that burnt out as suddenly as they had begun, but at least the Belgian Flying Corp pilot Willy Coppens lived to tell his tale. In the space of just three weeks in late April and early May 1918 Coppens had claimed five balloons, qualifying him as an 'ace', though in his memoirs *Days on the Wing* he recalls one encounter that didn't quite go according to plan. On the morning of 14 May he attacked a balloon over Houthulst at around 3,900ft, but although he had fired at point-blank range the balloon did not catch fire. Feeling annoyed, Coppens slowed down and approached the balloon horizontally, firing at the last moment. Then suddenly the balloon lurched upwards and Coppens found himself perched on the top of it. 'My wheels struck the gasbag, which gave under the shock...

My right wing also touched the envelope and for a second I pivoted on my nose, while the balloon sagged and sank under the weight.' Fortunately he had the presence of mind to switch off the engine and for a split second the aircraft sat there with its propeller idle. 'The next instant my machine began to slide across the spongy thing that gave way beneath me as we advanced, until it plunged over the side, nose-first, gathering speed as it fell.' As the airflow windmilled the propeller blades Coppens switched on the engine and pulled up in the nick of time. Looking back, he saw the wounded balloon sink to the ground where it burst into a ball of flame.

Without doubt the most famous of the busters was the American Frank Luke, an incorrigible freelancer who defied his superiors to become one of the most celebrated pilots of the war. The son of German immigrants, Luke attacked balloons with the vehemence of a man set on his own 'heaven-sent shortcut to glory and fame'. In a period of just seventeen days in September 1918 he brought down more balloons than any other 'buster' of the war – thirteen in one week alone. On one of those forays he had claimed two balloons in addition to shooting down two Fokker D-7s and a Halberstadt, and then, as was his custom, returned to base in an aircraft so shot about it had no right to be still flying. These exploits earned him the title the 'Arizona Balloon Buster' but such bravado had only one reward and on 28 September 1918 he made his last assault on German *drachen* during the Battle of Meuse-Argonne. As he was under arrest for going AWOL at the time, Luke stole a Spad 13 and dashed off to the front where he 'flamed' three balloons in quick succession. A swarm of Fokkers chased him down and he landed near the town of Murvaux, strafing enemy troops on the way. Surrounded and wounded Luke made his last stand, and in true Wild West style turned on his captors with pistol blazing. He died at the age of twenty-one, just a kid really, one of the highest scoring American pilots, second only to Eddie Rickenbacker, and one of only four to receive the Congressional Medal of Honour. Arrogant, courageous, Frank Luke was the stuff of legend.

In the final months of the war the Allied balloonists laboured to keep up with the advancing front while their German counterparts struggled to cope with a failing supply chain amid the turmoil of impending defeat. Sometimes mistakes were made in the heat of the moment and on the very last full day of combat friendly fire from two American Spads destroyed one of their own balloons. On their return to base the red-faced pilots were awarded mock Iron Crosses by their comrades.

It is estimated that by the war's end almost 500 observation balloons had been operated by Germany alone, with a similar number for the Allies. These ubiquitous balloons remain an enduring image of the 'Great War'. They had symbolised the start of hostilities, and on 11 November 1918 they signified its end. As the guns fell silent a British Army communique noted, 'All along the Front, the balloons are down.'

The balloons had also played their part in another war – the war of words. The first recorded instance of balloons being used to deliver propaganda occurred back in 1848 when the defenders of Milan had launched unmanned hot air balloons carrying leaflets to be released by time fuses. During the First World War the British army chiefs didn't take the distribution of propaganda seriously until the establishment of a propaganda branch within Military Intelligence in early 1916. But it was a fairly haphazard affair, with the German-language leaflets being dropped by aeroplanes while performing their ordinary duties. Even so, the German government did not take kindly to this development and a strongly worded protest was delivered via the Swiss intermediaries in which they were described as 'inflammatory writings, some in particular directed against His Majesty the German Emperor'. Claiming that such action was outside the scope of 'acts of war' they warned that any captured airmen found in possession of such material would be tried by Court Martial, with the implication that they could face the death sentence for treason. Matters came to a head when two RFC airmen were shot down in October 1917 and subsequently sentenced to ten years' imprisonment for dropping leaflets. A drawn-out exchange of protests and threats ensued, and against this background the British ceased their distribution by aeroplane. But that didn't stop them looking at alternative methods, and given the favourable westerly winds in France it was decided to use balloons for the purpose.

About 8 ft high and with a volume of 100 cu ft, the balloons were constructed of doped paper sections, inflated with hydrogen and could carry between 500 and 1,000 leaflets each. They were launched by small mobile teams usually consisting of one or two lorries to transport the balloons and the hydrogen cylinders. Once a launch location had been selected canvas screens were stretched across the windward side to provide additional shelter. The individual balloons were laid on a ground sheet, inflated, and the leaflets attached, then the slow-burning wick was ignited and they were released, all in a matter of just a few minutes. As the wick burnt through the leaflets were dropped, usually between ten and fifty miles behind enemy lines. The not so subtle message of the propaganda material was aimed at encouraging the German troops to abandon their long struggle, as this example shows:

In 1919 the training continued in the USA as shown in this picture of balloons lined up at a training camp. (US Library of Congress)

British troops releasing small propaganda balloons to drift over enemy lines.
(Valhalla Aerostation)

> For what are you fighting, Michel? They tell you that you are fighting for the
> Fatherland. Have you ever thought why you are fighting? You are fighting to glorify
> Hindenburg, to enrich Krupp. You are struggling for the Kaiser, the Junkers, and the
> militarists… They promise you victory and peace. You poor fools! It was promised to
> your comrades for more than three years. They have indeed found peace, deep in the
> grave, but victory did not come…

It continues in this vein and concludes, 'The whole power of the Western
world stands behind England and France and America! An army of ten
million is being prepared; soon it will come into battle. Have you thought of that,
Michel?'

The effect of these remonstrations on the morale of the German troops is
unquantifiable, but the appearance of the balloons heading eastward also served
to bolster the spirits of the Allied troops. As one recorded in his war diary for
18 July 1918, 'We noticed several propaganda balloons going over to Fritz today.'
In the latter months of the war the embargo on distribution by aeroplanes was
ended and it was estimated that 7 tons of leaflets were being dropped in a single
week, but with the enemy in full retreat one British official suggested that it
might be 'a great deal more efficacious to concentrate our efforts on killing him
than educating him'.

An example of a British propaganda leaflet delivered by balloon depicts the German soldiers being devoured by the figure of death. (Valhalla Aerostation)

Despite their earlier protests it is clear that the Germans also utilised balloons to deliver propaganda, and photographs reveal balloons of a very similar size and design to the British ones. These were also used to gauge wind speed at various levels, which was important for the operation of their big cousins, the observation balloons, as well as for aircraft. But there can be little doubt that they were also used as a means of testing the wind direction before the use of that most horrendous and deadly weapon, poison gas shells, which would claim the lives of 80,000 men.

Wind direction was also of paramount importance to clandestine operations. In *The Secrets of Rue St Roch*, author Janet Morgan reveals that balloons were deployed to carry both pigeons and agents behind enemy lines. Carrier pigeons are a marvellous method of sending messages, as witnessed in the Siege of Paris, but the problem facing the British Secret Service was how to get them where they were needed. Initially pilots of the RFC undertook the task, but landing an aircraft at night was dangerous and attracted attention. Volunteers were recruited to parachute down with the birds, but inevitably a high casualty rate brought these operations to an end. Perhaps balloons could be used?

Commander William Pollock, an experienced balloonist who was training observers to handle kite-balloons, was brought in to perfect the procedures. Small 8ft-diameter balloons of gold-beater's skin carried a clutch of pigeons, each in a small protective cage, to be released by timer beneath silk parachutes. In February 1917 the first pigeon balloon was launched and over the following months hundreds of birds were sent in this fashion. The results were surprisingly good, with a number of birds returning valuable intelligence information. However, the Germans soon countered, offering rewards for recovered birds and equipment or severe penalties, even death, for those who handled them. Together with a shortage of birds this resulted in the development of an ingenious balloon kit which included a simple hydrogen-making device and instructions for the finder, although only one of these 'surrogate pigeons' made it back to the British. Attention then turned to getting a human behind the lines. Riding silently under the cover of darkness an agent would bring the balloon down to earth, then hop out of the basket to leave all evidence of their arrival floating away. Flights commenced in the autumn of 1917, yet despite the balloons performing well the agents were frequently caught or they found it too difficult to carry out their work.

7
SILVER SENTINELS

The idea of a barrier or 'barrage' of deadly cables hoisted high into the sky was not exclusive to the Second World War. By all accounts the first application of balloons for this purpose can be credited to the Germans, who had begun experiments in the early years of the First World War, and by 1917 several balloon detachments were protecting key industrial locations. One British pilot, Second-Lieutenant L.G. Taylor, and his French observer, had a narrow escape when the wing of their FE2b was snagged by a cable while returning from a raid on Trèves. Forced to crash-land their aircraft, the two men were taken prisoner by German troops and thus they were unable to report back to their superiors on the incident until after the war.

The earliest known Allied barrage was raised at Venice by the Italians to thwart attacks from Austrian bombers, and approximately seventy balloons were flown from rafts floated around the city at heights up to around 10,000ft. In June 1917 an officer from the RFC went to Italy to evaluate this scheme, and as a result three months later Major-General E.B. Ashmore – commander of the London Air Defence Area – put forward a proposal for a balloon barrage to protect the capital. London had first been the subject of aerial bombardment back in 1915 when the Zeppelin airships had begun their raids. As it turned out the early hydrogen-filled Zeppelins proved too vulnerable once the British aircraft had been improved enough to attain the high altitudes at which they could be intercepted. For the airship commanders the answer was to fly at ever increasing heights and the second generation 'super-Zepps' were capable of reaching 20,000ft or more – a hazardous enough operation in itself. When their nocturnal raids declined in frequency there came a new breed of heavy aircraft, in particular the Gotha bomber. On balance, the effect of the German air raids was not great in strategic terms, but there were civilian casualties – by the end of the war in 1918 it was calculated that 1,413 fatalities and over 3,000 injuries had resulted from the combined attacks of the airships and bomber aircraft – and while the effect on morale might not have been as devastating as the Kaiser had anticipated, it was still a significant consideration. As more than half of these fatalities had occurred within London, Ashmore's scheme was aimed specifically at defending the capital from low-flying attacks by means of an 'apron', formed by a row of four or five balloons linked together by horizontal cables, from which would dangle a 1,000ft curtain of wire streamers.

In October 1917 the Commander-in-Chief Home Forces approved the plan and the establishment of five balloon squadrons with a total of 3,587 personnel. Initially the intention was to install twenty balloon aprons on a line to the east and south-east of London, running approximately through Tottenham, Ilford, Barking, Woolwich and Lewisham. By April 1918 seven of these aprons were in operation and an eighth was being readied. Their primary function was to keep enemy aircraft flying high in order to reduce the accuracy of their bombing. For the men who looked after the balloons, often in isolated locations, it was tedious work. Captain Goderic Hodges, originally a balloonatic, was transferred to No.1 Balloon Apron after being injured, but he found life at a remote camp near Barking on the banks of the Thames very dreary by comparison with the Western Front. 'After the daily excitement of life in the air in Belgium, this defence work was dull. It was the enemy that had the initiative. All that we could do was to inspect everything carefully every day, then wait.'

In practice the apron system proved to be inflexible and difficult to operate. The network of cables was heavy and had a tendency to sag, dragging the balloons into a bunch. Furthermore, when the apron was lowered the wires would drape themselves over whatever lay below, including electricity or overhead tram lines, and occasionally on the houses of the very people they were meant to protect. Opinion on their merit was divided. Major-General Ashmore, understandably proud of his progeny, commented at the end of the war, 'In my opinion, the balloon aprons are an essential part of the defence; to do away with them would have the worst possible effect. London would certainly be bombed from low heights at which considerable accuracy is attainable.' But others were more sceptical and one critic suggested that the balloons did not 'appear likely to form a very serious deterrent to a really determined enemy attack... They have little effect in altering or discouraging the enemy's intention. It would only be necessary, as a prelude to an attack, to send over a sufficiently large formation of fighters to shoot an avenue through the balloons to the centre of London.' Either way, the civilian population found their presence reassuring and the positive effect on public morale could not be denied.

When the 'war to end all wars' was over in November 1918, it brought an abrupt halt to the world the young men of Britain's newly formed Royal Air Force (RAF) had come to know, and a period of uncertainty began in which they were assigned other duties as they awaited demobilisation. A few of the airmen might have some prospect of working for the fledgling airline companies, whereas for the officers and men of the observation balloons the outlook was bleak. Some would later apply their specialist skills within the Imperial Airship Service – an ambitious programme launched by the government in 1924 to create an aerial link between Britain and its far flung colonies – but for most it meant exchanging their uniforms for civvies and finding a new job with both feet planted firmly on the ground. As for the balloons, turning these particular swords into plough shears would prove a more difficult task.

Three months after the cessation of hostilities a special Balloon Commanders' Conference was convened with one very important item on its agenda: 'Practical use to which balloons could be put during the Armistice and possibly during peace'. On the day of the meeting a cloud of despondency hung over the proceedings as several equally impractical proposals were put forward. These included using the balloons as 'air buoys' to be moored above clouds in order to provide passing aircraft with bearings and by 'means of signals on the balloons to show whether or not it is safe to descend through clouds' to an aerodrome below. Alternatively, it was suggested that they could serve as aerial lighthouses for night flying. But you can imagine the sort of reaction such schemes engendered in other aviators when contemplating the possibility of encountering 'friendly' steel hawsers hidden in the clouds! A handful of more realistic schemes were also submitted, one of which had the balloons located on certain stretches of coastline to assist the authorities in spotting smugglers. Nevertheless, at the end of the day the simple fact of the matter was that the peacetime RAF would be reduced to only a fraction of its wartime capacity. Its founder, Lord Trenchard, recognised that if the RAF was to remain intact and independent it could only do so by staying small in order not to become a burden on the government's purse. As it was, most defence experts were of the opinion

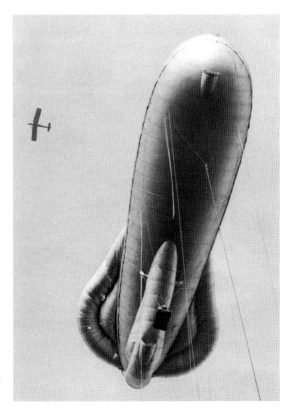

'Both can look out, but only one can sting.' This 1933 photograph taken at the RAF Balloon Section at Larkhill, near Salisbury, shows the old and the new methods of aerial observation and points the way to their future.

that there would be no war for at least another twenty years and public opinion had little appetite for further rearmament at this time. So just a few months after the Balloon Commanders' Conference, the government's Disposal Board began seeking tenders for 273 balloons 'of various types' and a surplus of waterproofed balloon fabric to be used in the manufacture of 'tarpaulins and wagon coverings'.

A handful of balloons was retained and some activity continued on a much reduced level at the RAF Balloon Section stationed at Larkhill, near Salisbury, for training and developmental purposes. Over the ensuing years the balloons were given an occasional airing. In 1924, for instance, one was flown to aid the police directing traffic going to the Derby horse races. Other former Western Front balloons made appearances at the annual RAF Air Pageants held at Hendon during the 1920s and early 1930s, but this was usually in the role of sacrificial lambs – soft targets in which the outmoded biplane fighters would sink their teeth – while others endured an even more humiliating second career as aerial billboards. Some appeared at public events, such as the one emblazoned with advertising for the *Daily Graphic* at the British Empire Exhibition at Wembley in 1924. Rides were offered to the public at half-a-crown to go up 500 or 600ft, and as one brave soul recalled, 'It was certainly a wonderful view we got of all the many brilliantly decorated pavilions representing the different countries that made up the British Empire.'

None of these activities deterred the school of silly ideas and for the most part the interwar years were epitomised by a series of highly 'imaginative' schemes. The *Popular Mechanics* journal in the USA published one outline for a balloon-borne mail service in which letters would be carried in a tethered balloon and whisked from town to town via an electrified rail. And according to *Mechanics and Handicraft*, the problem of supplying 'artificial rain' to large areas of farmland within the Trans-Volga district of the USSR had been solved using balloons. Apparently tractors – for which the Soviets were renowned – would pump water up from irrigation ditches for it to be sprinkled on the crops via a 600ft perforated pipe suspended from balloons. Believe that if you will.

There was, however, one proposal from a more reputable source. In *Flight* magazine on 3 May 1923 an article appeared arguing that the adoption of gliding as a recreational sport was being severely restricted by the requirement of a sufficiently high range of hills from which to launch. Accordingly a German inventor, Erich Oppermann, envisaged utilising kite-balloons to raise gliders up to 2,000ft before releasing them to return to the ground by their own means. Undeniably, this scheme did have some merit. Indeed, the British had already conducted practical tests a few years earlier; launching a BE2c fighter aircraft beneath a free balloon in order to overcome the aircraft's poor rate of climb when attempting to reach the high-flying Zeppelins. In theory, once his aircraft had been delivered to a sufficient height the pilot would release it from the balloon and engage the enemy – leaving the balloon to float away into the night sky. The initial trials looked promising, but in February 1916 everything went wrong when the rigging broke, sending the aircraft plummeting into the ground and killing its two-man crew. Despite the setbacks the technique was perfected two years later when a Sopwith Camel was launched from the underside of the British rigid airship No.23 and later from the R33. It is known that in the 1930s the Soviets successfully used manned spherical balloons to hoist gliders aloft. Regardless of the practicalities, the significance of this scheme from the German's point of view was that while they were prohibited from developing a new air force under the onerous terms of the Treaty of Versailles, they could accelerate the training of glider pilots for recreational purposes while at the same time expanding their balloon manufacturing base. Oppermann may have been acting in all innocence, but there is little doubt that the gliding schools which were so popular in Germany at the time would prove to be the breeding ground for a new Luftwaffe.

By the 1930s the political events in Germany and the all-too-obvious increase in the Luftwaffe's strength had come to the attention of the British Prime Minister, Stanley Baldwin, and in 1932 he addressed Parliament. 'I think it well for the man in the street to realise that there is no power on earth that can protect him from being bombed.' Although the context of this statement was to emphasise the need to develop an offensive bomber capability to prevent another war, it did nonetheless raise the question of how Britain could be defended. And

This magazine cover from November 1938 demonstrates that the balloons were maintaining a high profile in the public eye in the build up to war.

while the man on the street did not pay too much attention to the warnings of politicians, the release of Alexander Korda's film *Things to Come* – based on the prophesies of H.G. Wells – shocked audiences with its graphic depiction of a near-future war including scenes of air raids on 'Everytown'. As a film it is a somewhat ponderous procession of speeches set against an unremitting portrayal of the horrors of total war, and most critics condemned it as scare mongering. Nonetheless, it was time for Britain's wake-up call. Another war was coming and this time civilians were going to be in the firing line. In April 1937 fiction became ghastly fact when scores of Luftwaffe dive bombers rained deadly destruction upon the undefended town of Guernica, the cultural and spiritual home of the Spanish Basques. In lending his support to General Franco, Adolf Hitler was demonstrating to the entire world his brutal vision of how wars would be conducted in the future.

Fortunately for Britain some of the politicians had been paying heed and in 1936 the government had initiated an extensive and timely expansion programme of the RAF's offensive and defensive capabilities – both in quality and quantity. At last the Air Staff were being given the opportunity to make the service ready for a modern war and to leave behind its outmoded image of fabric-covered biplanes. In parallel the air defences would see the advance of new

Mr Hemm, the Works Manager of Dunlop's factory in Manchester, gives a party of VIPs, including the city's Lord Mayor and officers of the Territorial Army, an inside look at a barrage balloon in early 1939.

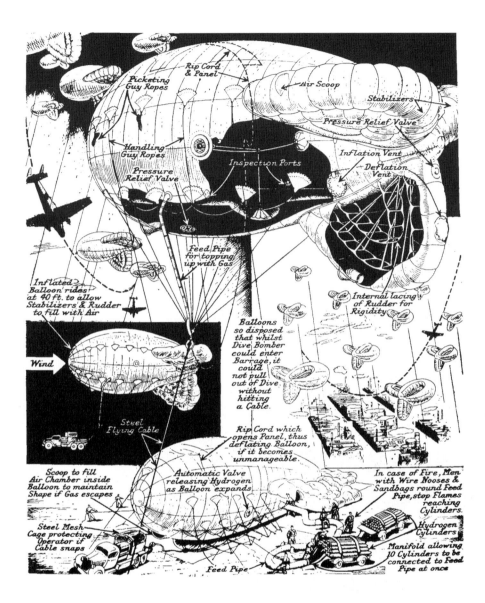

The not-so-secret secret weapon. In a bid to bolster public confidence, a surprising amount of information was published on Britain's air defences. It may also have been a deliberate ploy to deter the Luftwaffe's dive-bombers.

technologies – in particular the development of radar for early warning and fighter control – as well as a new lease of life for the more conventional measures, including anti-aircraft (AA) guns and, of course, a new generation of 'silver sentinels' to form a protective 'roof over Britain'.

With the decision to re-establish a balloon barrage for London, work was commenced under the direction of Colonel J.D. Macworth initially, and later continued by Air Commodore J.G. Hearson – formerly in the RFC, with experience in commanding two kite-balloon sections in the First World War. The main development effort on the technical side was undertaken at RAF Station Cardington, Bedfordshire – later to become the Balloon Development Establishment – where the former airship engineers and designers applied their skills to developing the LZ or 'Low Zone' balloon. In January 1937 the No.1 Balloon Training Unit was also established there and consequently it became the main centre for both the development and manufacture of the balloons, as well as the training of their crews.

Originally the new balloon barrage was envisaged as a thirty-mile-diameter ring encircling London. Learning from experience, it would consist of individual balloons and not a linked apron as is still sometimes suggested. They were to be spaced ten to a mile, approximately 200 yards apart, giving a total of 450 balloons. A preliminary survey was made of suitable locations, but almost before it had started the principle of 'perimeter siting' was abandoned in favour of 'field siting' – with the balloons randomly dotted throughout an area like a minefield – as it was recognised that modern aircraft could easily have flown over a protecting outer screen and then come in low to make an attack. The question of operational height had to be considered and while flying balloons at extreme heights might offer the greatest defence, it also

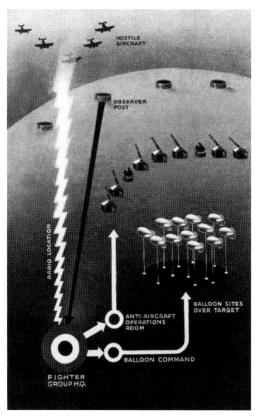

Official wartime diagram showing the position of the balloon barrage within the anti-aircraft defences.

'All blown up and nowhere to go.' The celebrated cartoonist Low couldn't resist depicting Adolf Hitler as a bloated 'super windbag' in 1939.

meant that longer and heavier cables required bigger balloons which could prove difficult to handle, especially in built-up areas with limited space. It was therefore decided to operate at medium heights, up to 10,000ft, sufficient to keep the bombers high in order to reduce their accuracy, and also to force them within a specific height zone in which the anti-aircraft guns and fighters could locate them – in hunting parlance, they were to 'position the pheasant'.

In appearance the balloons bore more than a passing resemblance to the Caquot-style observation balloons; hardly surprising, as they worked on the same principle. In fact they were squatter in profile and only about half the size with a capacity of 19,150 cu ft, a length of 68ft and a diameter of 27ft. Their shape was designed so that the forward component of the kite effect balanced the wind drag on the cable and envelope, keeping the balloons relatively stable and level whatever the wind speed. Because of this kiting, faster winds tended to push the balloons upwards rather than forcing them down as might be expected, although in gusty or turbulent conditions, especially when near the ground or on unsheltered sites, they could still be a handful. The fabric, a rubberised cotton, was coated with aluminium powder, not to make them more visible – as is sometimes suggested – but to reflect the heating influence of the sun on the gas and to reduce the effect of ultra-violet degradation on the fabric itself. Internally the main bulk was divided into two compartments by a membrane, with the larger upper part containing the hydrogen and the lower one – known by the French word 'ballonet' for a small balloon – filled with ordinary air via a small

mouth-shaped air scoop at the front of the envelope. This system dealt with the variations in gas volume caused by changes in temperature or the reduction in ambient atmospheric pressure with height. As the balloon climbed, the hydrogen would increase in volume forcing the membrane down and causing air to be vented from the ballonet. Another way of overcoming this problem devised by the French was to design balloons with elastic panels to allow for expansion, but the British preferred to stay with the tried and tested ballonet system. A gas valve was also fitted on the side of the envelope to release excess hydrogen if the ballonet became fully extended. The distinctive tri-lobe tail was inflated with air supplied by an air scoop on the lower fin.

The cutting edge of barrage balloon technology, so to speak, was of course the cable itself. To ensure that this was up to the job assistance was sought from the Royal Aircraft Establishment, Farnborough, in conducting tests to evaluate the damage caused to an aircraft. In addition, they looked into the possible countermeasures an enemy might devise to 'sweep' a safe line through the cables. The practical tests were flown by Flight Lieutenant A.E. Clouston, who began his hazardous task with a Miles Hawk which he dutifully flew into a length of ordinary fishing line suspended beneath a parachute dropped at a height of 5,000ft. The line was later replaced by light wire and the wooden Hawk by a much sturdier Fairey P4/34, and for the final tests the wire was suspended from a balloon over a remote part of Norfolk. Throughout the experiments it was found that the wires either wrapped themselves around the aircraft or bit deeply into its wings, leaving no doubt the balloon barrage offered a viable form of defence. When it was later discovered that some enemy aircraft still managed to limp on despite hitting cables, a device known as the Detachable Parachute Link (DPL) was introduced which featured small parachute canisters at each end of the

Opposite: Official Air Ministry photograph of a balloon amid obvious air-raid damage, possibly in Dover.

BALLOONS

or

Squaring the Circle!

By Bruce Sievier

We have received this amusing verse from the well-known broadcaster who is now Flying-Officer R. B. B. Sievier, M.C. (R.A.F.V.R.), of the Balloon Barrage

When I was but a baby boy
In coat and pantaloon,
My nurse would wheel me in the park
Behind a toy balloon.

When I arrived at walking stage
(An artful little mite!)
I used to buy a ball of string
And fly a baby kite.

But now I'm virile, big and strong,
I work from noon to noon
And all day long I sit beneath
A ruddy 'big' balloon!

The moral of this story is
Enough to drive one wild,
For those who try to wage a war
Just treat one as a child!

Right: Published in the *Radio Times*, a little wartime ditty on the plight of those who served with the balloons.

cable. When an aircraft made contact with a cable it activated cutter links, just below the balloon itself and above the winch, and two 8ft-diameter parachutes were deployed. These generated substantial additional drag – calculated at around 3 tons – enough to bring down any aircraft. Consideration was also given to equipping this device with an explosive charge which, in theory, would be dragged across the wing of the aircraft – see Chapter 9.

A large number of trained personnel was needed to operate the balloons, and as it was uneconomical to maintain a permanent strength of operators in peacetime, members of the Auxiliary Air Force (AAF) were organised into the first Balloon Squadrons – designated with squadron numbers in the 900 series – to man the balloons part-time or at weekends in association with a small nucleus of regular personnel based at four main depots in the London area. These depots were used both as storage and for training purposes initially, and later on as maintenance and supply depots for balloon squadrons in the field. To put the balloon crews through their paces regular public displays were carried out from 1937 onwards, and sometimes the older observation balloons were also dusted off and given an airing. A newspaper clipping, dated 11 August 1937, pictures one of these in action with the caption: 'War in East Anglia. An RAF balloon going up for observation work in co-operation with artillery manoeuvres, which began yesterday.' It takes more than one balloon to make a war, of course, but these displays became increasingly important in bolstering public confidence in the light of international tensions. By the time of the Munich Crisis in September 1938, some squadrons

Balloons pepper the skies over Cardington in Bedford, former home to the R100 and R101 airships – the hangars or 'sheds' can be seen on the right.

A beautifully preserved example of a balloon winch at the Imperial War Museum, Duxford. The winch mechanism is housed in front of the protective wire cage and the flatbed at the back carries a balloon still in its bag. (John Christopher)

were deployed to their intended wartime sites and they remained on a war footing for about ten days.

On 1 November 1938, Balloon Command was formed under the auspices of Fighter Command to administer and control the balloons, with Air Vice Marshall Owen Tudor-Boyd at the helm. By now the organisation was sufficiently developed to proceed with the establishment of the first provincial barrages for the cities of Bristol, Cardiff, Swansea, Portsmouth, Southampton, Plymouth, Liverpool, Manchester, Glasgow, Newcastle, Birmingham, Coventry, Sheffield and Hull. The provincial Balloon Groups were established shortly afterwards and additional barrages were earmarked for the Forth of Firth, Crewe, the Thames and Harwich. There is a marvellous short film made by the General Post Office (GPO) documentary film unit which depicts the training of the men of RAF Balloon Squadron 992 at Cardington. The film shows the new recruits being taught to splice ropes, make sailor's knots and prepare rigging attachment patches before they are let loose on the bobbing balloons that fill the vast interior of the airship hangars like porpoises at a tea dance. And, shock-horror, the narrator announces in clipped tones that the men 'even have to learn how to sew'. To which one of the new recruits chips in with a carefully rehearsed ad-lib, 'I hope my missus don't see this!' When the war started this squadron was swiftly deployed to defend the railway bridge at the Firth of Forth following an attack by a lone Heinkel.

The King and Queen did their bit to boost prewar morale and in April 1939 they dutifully toured No.2 Balloon Centre at Hook, Surrey, accompanied by the Prime Minister, Neville Chamberlain, to see the work of Balloon Command. A few months later Britain held what would prove to be its last prewar defence exercise involving the deployment of some 33,000 men, 1,300 aircraft, 110 AA guns, 700 searchlights and 100 barrage balloons. When Chamberlain made his fateful announcement to the nation on 3 September 1939, the balloons were flying in the clear autumnal skies over the capital. Balloon Command had already placed 444 of them into position in London, and an additional 180 elsewhere, on the previous Friday. (The balloon squadrons actually outnumbered the flying squadrons forty-four to twenty.) 'This country is now at war', Chamberlain had said. 'We are ready.'

On 31 August 1940 the Luftwaffe came to pay its respects to the balloons protecting Dover as a prelude to the Battle of Britain. At ten minutes to nine on a fine clear morning, the attack began with six Messerschmitt 109s disposing of the twenty-three balloons in just six minutes. Although this attack was more successful than any subsequently made, the cost to the Luftwaffe was two aircraft shot down by anti-aircraft fire and a third by rifle fire from one of the balloon crews. This 'first-hand' account of the incident was later published by the Ministry of Information:

> We were cleaning up the billet when the crackle of machine and cannon guns was heard. Everyone grabbed his rifle and dashed on the site. The sky was full of AA shell bursts while machine guns were going off everywhere. Several balloons were coming down in flames, ours included. The next balloon to us was being hauled down just as fast as the winch could pull it. It was about 800ft off the ground when one of the Me109s decided he would try and get it. He swept over our heads and got it all right. But as he turned and banked away to go out to sea again, he seemed to be standing still in the air for a few seconds. The range was about 700ft. The officer in charge yelled 'Fire!' Everyone pumped as many rounds as we could into it. The Me kept straight on with his dive out to sea, while a thin trail poured out from behind.

Worse still for the Germans was the fact that within forty minutes the first of the replacement balloons was already in position, by lunchtime there were eleven flying, and later that same afternoon their number had reached eighteen. At 7.30 p.m. the Messerschmitts came again, this time shooting down fifteen balloons. That night the balloon crews were kept busy and by the morning they had restored the balloon numbers to fifteen. The aircraft came once more, but by then the odds were starting to work against the Germans, who lost three aircraft at the cost of only two balloons. The game was not worth the candle – the defences had improved and the balloons were too easily replaced – and as a result, these attacks on Dover appear to be the only concerted effort at destroying barrage balloons in any number.

The first enemy contact with one of the cables is said to have occurred in June 1940 when a German aircraft struck the cable of a balloon defending Le Havre. The following month the crew of a Junkers Ju88 found themselves plopped onto the top of a balloon over Plymouth, which they had been trying to avoid when their aircraft stalled. Fortunately for them the gasbag was not punctured and the pilot regained control as the aircraft slid off the balloon and picked up speed as it fell earthward. The first aircraft actually brought down by a balloon barrage over the Home Front was a Heinkel He111 returning from a bombing raid on Merseyside on 13 September 1940. It struck a cable over Newport, Monmouthshire, and plummeted into a residential area killing the crew and also two young children on the ground.

Perversely it was the weather that accounted for far greater balloon losses than any action by the enemy. This problem had become apparent even before the war when, during the 1939 exercises, 53 per cent of the balloons were ripped from their moorings by gale force winds. Originally, the balloons were flown directly from the leading-off gear at the back of the winches, but a great improvement came with the introduction of a circular ground-bed and a central anchoring point, which enabled the balloons to be secured more effectively. Another problem was the tendency of the long metal cables to act as efficient lightning conductors. In September 1937, six balloons at Cardington were hit by lightning and came down in flames, and on another occasion as many as eighty balloons were destroyed over London in one afternoon.

Derek Fletcher was a schoolboy in Barrow-in-Furness during the war and he vividly remembers a lightning strike on one of the balloons protecting the Vickers shipyard. 'It was in the evening, getting darkish, when the lightning started. Us lads knew everything about everything and we could tell that the crew was pulling this balloon down on its winch. The lightning hit it and I saw it suddenly burst into flames and then it began to fall down with the middle still burning.' One night a stricken balloon landed on a local school and the following morning the children found their schoolyard littered with the remnants of silvery fabric. Later improvements in weather forecasting techniques and better lightning protection did help to reduce this rate of attrition by natural causes.

For the locals the arrival of a balloon team in their area was the cause of great excitement, and the first inflation would attract crowds of onlookers. It was not uncommon for the Air Raid Precaution Wardens to be called upon to keep people out of harm's way. Children in particular seemed to find the balloons fascinating and Robert Westall, the author of *The Machine Gunners* and *Children of the Blitz*, described how his gang would inspect the local defences at Derwentside on a daily basis, 'looking for improvements and making sure the crews knew their job. Best were the barrage balloons. We spent hours atDockwray Square, staring through the railings; the balloon was like a great silver elephant, whose sides crinkled with every breeze.' The term elephant was perhaps the best most people

Above, left and opposite: A definite camaraderie developed among the close-knit balloon teams, who lived, ate, and tended their balloons together day after day. Wherever possible general maintenance of the balloons was carried out on site, although occasionally things did not go quite according to plan.

could come up with to describe the balloons and it seemed to stick. Initially the sight of the balloons dotting the sky was a great novelty and few regarded them as harbingers of the terrible raids to come. Instead they became the natural butt of countless jokes, such as the apocryphal London woman who supposedly said that if the 'Nasties' thought they could scare her by sitting up in those balloons all day, they were very much mistaken! The notion that the balloons were manned was not that uncommon, but a tongue-in-cheek suggestion that they were filled with concrete received less credence. They were also a gift to the newspaper cartoonists, and the balloon crews joined in the fun by christening their wayward aerostats. The *Archblimp* bobbed above Lambeth Palace, *Mae West* appeared in the West End, and many others sported girl's names such as *Annie* or *Matilda*. But the curiosity value of the new arrivals soon faded as they became a familiar part of the wartime landscape, and after a while it was considered very old hat to point out that 'the balloon is going up'.

The balloons were sited in suitable open areas, often in public parks or squares – even the Oval cricket ground was selected – and for the crews their quality of life had much to do with the location. Accommodation was in tents at first, but after a while these were replaced with more comfortable huts. Those near enough to the balloon depots received some provisions delivered to the site daily – including hot or at least lukewarm meals in hay boxes – and sometimes the

The deprivations of war were tempered with a healthy sense of humour as shown in this 1940 Christmas card, and one bright spark has arrowed a figure and written 'Me?'

locals would take pity on their new neighbours and provide the occasional warming cup of tea, but for those in the more remote places it was very much a case of self sufficiency. Probably the worst billeting of all was at Scarpa Flow in the Orkneys, where the cold winds ripped the first balloons from their moorings and concrete bases had to be laid to secure the replacements. Balloons weren't only stationed on dry land, however, and one of the toughest jobs of all was 'manning' the ones that operated from barges to protect major river estuaries and ports from low-flying mine-laying aircraft (see Chapter 10).

Joseph Melford was typical of many who had joined the Auxiliary Air Force. 'I was just an ordinary bloke going to work, but I thought there was a war coming and I decided to join the AAF. My friend and I thought that by joining early we would at least get a uniform that actually fitted and so we joined up about eight months before the war started.' After training Joseph was posted to a balloon site situated on a sports ground near the Thames, where he found the food supplies were augmented by an unexpected source. 'In the beginning we met all sorts of people. A good friend of mine on the balloons called Dennis was a barrister and his father used to come down every Wednesday in a beautiful Bentley and bring food for us and even cigars. And we would sit there smoking cigars – I had never had a cigar before in my life!'

By January 1940 it was estimated that Balloon Command had grown to 40,000 personnel – that's more than the entire Royal Air Force of five years earlier. Clearly this was a considerable drain on manpower that was desperately needed elsewhere in the war effort. Yet the solution had been there all along. Members of the Women's Auxiliary Air Force (WAAF) were already carrying out a range of duties as drivers, on the AA guns, searchlights, aircraft recognition and even repairing the balloons, so why not tap into this resource of 'woman-power' and put it to work operating them?

8
DOING A MAN'S JOB

When, in 1936, the Ministry of Aircraft Production consulted with manufacturing companies and expressed the urgent need to produce larger quantities of balloons in a comparatively short period, two were contracted to meet the initial output – Dunlop, famous for tyres and rubber, and the RFD company which had made its nickname 'Rescue From Danger' by producing rubber dinghies and life jackets. New construction methods were introduced so that the initial work on cutting out the fabric panels could be done in conventional manufacturing facilities without the need for purpose-built hangars. Each balloon was made up of 600 individual panels cut from over 1,000 yards of 48in-wide fabric. Other components were also mass produced and it is estimated that the production time for each balloon was reduced from a hefty 3,500 hours to just 500 hours. (Methods of manufacturing meteorological balloons were also improved to cut the production time by up to 80 per cent.) The facilities for producing the rubber-proofed fabric for the barrage balloons were upgraded and expanded, and with the outbreak of hostilities work on all non-essential domestic rubber products, such as golf or tennis balls, ceased as the demands on war production intensified. Before the war the national output of barrage balloons had been at the rate of about two a week, but by its conclusion Dunlop alone had produced some 28,000 balloons.

Rigging and test inflating the completed balloons took place at either the rubber factories themselves, at certain RAF facilities around the country and, as demand increased, in any suitably high-roofed buildings that could be found. In Manchester, for instance, the old Victorian market hall was commandeered for the task and ironically this building now houses Manchester Museum's Air and Space Gallery. New facilities were also purpose built and in 1936 RFD erected a new inflation shed at Godalming, Surrey, at the cost of £14,000 – a landmark that became known locally as the 'balloon factory'.

As with all areas of war production, working hours were increased by introducing double shifts and it was said that the factory lights never went out, the machines never stopped. Just as in the First World War, the most obvious

Initially the women were viewed merely as valuable wartime workers, playing their part in assembling and repairing the balloons. This 1939 photograph shows balloons under construction at the Dunlop factory in Manchester.

change on the factory floor was a dramatic increase in the numbers of women workers as the men were called up for military service. In its post-war publication *VE VJ Contributions*, Dunlop described how the shift in the workforce had begun. 'It was in the proofing factory that female operatives were first employed on spreading machines and after a suitable period of training were found to produce a standard of proofing equal to that of male labour.' It was not long before the process of cutting the panels, overlapping and taping them, marking and fitting accessories, such as the fins, attachment points, valves, etc, became almost exclusively the responsibility of the women.

Many of these women were only teenagers at the start of the war, and although those employed by the rubber companies were civilians, others, especially on the repair side, were from the Women's Auxiliary Air Force (WAAF). Initially, the first influx of WAAFs at RAF operational stations came sooner than expected and many of these new recruits found that preparations had not been made for their arrival. One balloon repairer, Eileen Jacobs, recalls that her group turned up at Felixstowe to find a foot of snow and that there weren't even any greatcoats for them. 'We were issued instead with men's gumboots, dungarees and balaclavas. It was freezing working on the balloons in the seaplane hangars right on the sea front!'

Dorothy Melford was eighteen years old when she joined. 'I decided to volunteer for the WAAF as I didn't want to go into the Land Army, or the army.' She started off as a fabric worker repairing balloons at the RAF station at Fazakerley, north-east of Liverpool, where they often joked that the girls repaired the balloons that the men had torn. The balloons would arrive packed up in a bundle about 4ft high and they would then be inflated with powerful air pumps in order to make the repairs.

> We actually worked with two girls inside the balloon and another two outside. We took an electric light bulb on a long cable inside, and we would shine the light so that the girls on the outside could mark with a pen where repairs were needed. All the panels were numbered and then, when we had done one or two, we stood still and shouted 'Jump!' And as we jumped the girls on the outside turned the balloon round so we could get to the next panels. Very amateurish in a way, but it got the job done.

Another job carried out in a separate hangar was to re-dope the balloons because of the effects of weathering on the aluminium paint. 'They used to give us lots of milk to drink to counteract the doping fumes, but of course we were all high as kites.'

In January of 1941 Balloon Command was asked to consider a suggestion that operating the balloons could be carried out by the WAAF in an attempt to release the men for other duties. Clearly 'manning' the balloons twenty-four hours a day, seven days a week, and in all weathers was a physically arduous task and there was some concern that it might prove to be too demanding for the female crews. The only way to find out was to put the matter to a practical test and three months

WAAF personnel undertake training in the art of balloon handling. For many of the young women who joined the barrage balloons it was a welcome opportunity to learn new skills. (Imperial War Museum)

later twenty fabric workers, all volunteers, marched on to a balloon training site and under the guidance of eight male balloon operators, and closely watched by several RAF officers, they carried out a number of balloon operations. Although it poured with rain for the entire day the enthusiastic but inexperienced WAAFs proved their worth and a month later the first batch was sent to the balloon centre at Cardington, Bedfordshire, for ten weeks of intensive training. Another practical assessment followed at the end of the course and the women came through with flying colours.

'Training has proceeded to the extent that it has now been found possible to draft women to war sites in the balloon barrage', reported the Air Officer Commanding direct to the Secretary of State for Air. 'Sites which they will, in a few days' time, be in course of taking over from the airmen.' However, while the increase in the numbers of female workers building and repairing the balloons had been accepted without further justification, the introduction of female balloon operators was always dealt with in official publications in terms designed not to upset the fragile sensibilities of their male colleagues. 'The substitution of WAAF for airmen on balloon sites does not imply that the airmen, who have operated in all weathers and under aerial bombardment, have in any sense been doing a woman's job', announced the Orwellian-sounding Ministry of Information, which went on:

In the first place, it requires sixteen airwomen to replace ten airmen. Secondly, it must be borne in mind that RAF crews are incorporated in military defence schemes, whereas WAAF are not. Thus in a number of areas it is not practicable for WAAF to take over sites. Lastly, it is only the great progress in and simplification of balloon manipulation, for which the original officers and airmen of Balloon Command are responsible, that has made the substitution at all possible. Skill and intelligence will still be required, but the constant physical strain which was present in the past has been very much reduced.

Yes, progress had been made, principally with the introduction of a fixed bed with rings set in concrete to tie the balloon off rather than heaving heavy sandbags about the place, and the winches had also been improved. But the bottom line was that the women of the WAAF had demonstrated beyond doubt that they had the backbone to do the job, and to do it well. As even the

'Up to a Man's job – and equal to it,' proclaimed this Weetabix advertisement in June 1942. But don't tell the men, was the Air Ministry's initial response.

Trainee barrage balloon teams on parade in the vast airship hangar at Cardington.
(US Library of Congress)

Ministry admitted, 'This is undoubtedly one of the hardest jobs undertaken by
women in this war, but they have tackled it and succeeded at it.' And although
there may in some quarters have been a degree of scepticism concerning women
in uniform generally, the work of the balloon barrage teams was widely noticed,
especially when sites were situated in urban areas. Even the advertisers took up
the theme. 'On a Man's job – and equal to it', proclaimed the makers of Weetabix
in *Everybody's Weekly*. 'Of course she's tired at the end of the day, but not "played
out". Her power of endurance is amazing and, as she will tell you, this is because
she so regularly includes Weetabix in her meals.' Probably less palatable and
certainly less believable was an advertisement for Bile Beans, which features a
radiant WAAF still in pristine full uniform after a hard day on the balloon site.

    In September 1941 *The Aeroplane* also extolled the virtues of the WAAFs,
stating that 'experience has shown already that women take easily to this work
and that remarkably few accidents occur'. The article also gives an interesting
insight into the recruitment of the women:

Pay is good and recruits for this new branch of the Service open to women are wanted in large numbers. On completion of training pay rises from 1s 8d to 2s 8d a day. A girl need not possess any particular qualifications. She must be over seventeen and under forty-three years of age to be selected. If she is of athletic type so much the better. Those whose civilian work dealt with packing and fishing tackle have an advantage over those engaged in more sedentary occupations. But experience has shown an actress to be just as proficient as a fisher-lass when she is trained. Chances of promotion are good. All NCOs and Commissioned Officers have to serve in and are chosen from the ranks.

Actresses and fisher-lasses aside, at the front of the queue were the WAAF balloon repairers with Dorothy Melford among them. 'Of course we had a bit of head start because we knew all about the panels. We trained at Long Benton near Newcastle, a training station. We were the second intake there and we had to do all the rope splicing, topping up with gas, motor training for the winch, point attachment, storm-bedding, and so on.'

For many of the girls life in the WAAF was a liberating experience as this was their first time away from home. It was an opportunity to make new friends, of both sexes, and to discover something of the world. Ann Fox from mid-Wales was originally posted to Dyce in Aberdeen as a waitress in the officers' mess, but this really wasn't what she had joined up to do. She wanted to get more involved in the war effort, so she volunteered to become a balloon operator and was sent to Cardington for training. 'And my God, I realised that this is where the R101 went from – the airship I had heard about at school – from this hangar where we were now. I thought, well, I never thought I'd get to that.'

Dorothy Melford found that she was treated by the newer recruits like an old hand. 'By the time I became a balloon operator I had been in the WAAF about nine or ten months already. But the ones who had just joined up and been on the course had only just left home, and they could be very tearful until they got going.' Sometimes it wasn't just homesickness that upset the girls, as not all of them were happy with being posted to balloons. In her autobiography *We All Wore Blue*, Murial Gane Pushman recalls that she chose the WAAF because they had the best uniforms, but then came the order to report for balloon training at RAF Pucklechurch near Bristol. 'Most of my friends were being sent to well known fighter stations or Bomber Command... and here I was being exiled to this godforsaken spot of which no one had ever heard. To make matters worse it was Balloon Command, of all things.'

Once training was completed the women were sent out to the balloons and as Dorothy Melford recalls, 'The sites could be really rough and ready, nothing pretty about them.' It was all a matter of luck whether you were sent to some remote spot beside a steelworks or to a suburb of a large town or city. Dorothy experienced both, but in Manchester her team really landed on their feet when they found that their balloon was located right next to a social club.

We were able to have proper baths and so on. We even adopted a dog on the site. At Christmas a skeleton crew would look after the balloon and some would go over to the club, and then take turns. We were really mothered, I don't think any of us was over nineteen. We were very much left to our own devices, they had trust in us to behave. I was a corporal so I was in charge of the balloon site. There were about eight or nine WAAFs – there were supposed to be more – but you can imagine if one of the girls went sick, or we had leave, it was never more than about eight on site doing a twenty-four hour shift. You were on duty virtually all the time as we lived on the site.

Once a week a lorry would turn up with supplies and they gave us a menu to follow, but of course we used to switch it all around and make all sorts. Some of the girls liked cooking. Being women we made our Nissen hut look great. We had some carpets given to us to cover the rough floors and we even put some net curtains up at the window. It was very relaxed and we just called each other by our first names. It was like a family really.

Periodically a WAAF officer would pay a visit.

You might have been up in the middle of the night and felt like hell, but you still had to have the balloon looking spick-and-span, and get your gang all together and try to look smart. Polish the buttons quick, which were green with age. We had been among the first to be given tunics, for you couldn't work on a balloon site in a skirt, and sometimes we did look scruffy.

'Balloons speaking!'
The barrage balloons and their female crews attracted more than their fair share of humour as this 1940 cartoon illustrates.

One of war artist Dame Laura Knight's most famous paintings depicts a *Balloon Site at Coventry*. (Imperial War Museum)

Still, it was heavy work, and it could be dangerous too for the balloons were positioned where there was likely to be action. Just handling the balloons could be hazardous.

> It was when they were set to just 500ft, for example, that it would become dangerous if it was windy. The yawing effect sent the balloon thrashing backwards and forwards, sometimes coming down, and if you sent them up too quickly you might lose your balloon. Because we were a female team we had our legs pulled on one occasion because one of our balloons had come down in a brewery some distance away.

Dorothy admits with a sheepish grin that they sometimes broke the rules. 'When we had to send the balloon up quick we disconnected the lever and let the winch free-wheel, and the balloon would shoot up. But then you had to be very careful when you halted them or they would be gone!'

Probably the most frightening task was storm-bedding the balloon when it was brought right down to the ground and they had to get the air out of the tail fins and then roll them underneath.

I used to have to go up the ladder because I was the only one brave enough to do this. The balloon was moving about in the wind and it could be three o'clock in the morning when you got the call to "storm down". Then next day they had to be flying at point of attachment, ready to send up quickly. So of course when they had been storm-bedded, someone had to go under to prevent it getting tangled up. One day in the wind my foot got caught up and if the person on the winch hadn't stopped the balloon I would have lost my foot. That was close.

If the operators found their balloons hazardous, then the aircrews found them quite deadly for a cable could slice through the wing of an aircraft or smash its propeller to splinters. That the balloon barrage was more than just an inconvenience to the Luftwaffe is evident by the countermeasures that they developed and once again a woman came to the fore. The German aircraft designer Hans Jacobs had devised a protective 'fender' or frame, which extended from the nose of a bomber to its wing tips, thus protecting the engines and wings. In theory, if a wire struck the fender it would be dragged along the frame to a cutting device situated at the wing tip. But theory was all very well, the system still had to be put to the test. Recruited for this difficult task was none other than Hannah Reitsch, the diminutive but renowned female test pilot who undertook her duties with characteristic determination. As she later wrote in her autobiography, *The Sky My Kingdom*, 'Like few others, these experiments had laid hold of my imagination, for every test I flew brought us a step nearer to overcoming some of those perils which pilots and crews had daily to face in operations against the enemy.'

The initial tests were conducted at Rechlin, Germany, where a balloon was prepared starting with steel cables of 2.7mm in diameter. She would be flying in a Dornier 17 bomber, which had been specially equipped with duplicate flight controls built into the rear gun-turret and nearer to the escape hatch. This extra flight deck could only be used once in flight and was not suitable for takeoffs or landings. On low-level runs, however, there would be no question of being able to bail out. The accessibility of the escape hatch was very nearly put to the test on the first test flight. As Reitsch began her run the cable gleamed silver against the sky, but then as she closed in she lost sight of it and she was forced to gauge its position from memory and the aircraft juddered as it struck against the wing. In all future tests small strips of bunting were attached to the cable at 100ft intervals to make it easier to spot. Instruments recorded every detail of the impact and the stress inflicted and as the tests progressed the diameter of the cables was increased to correspond with what was expected to be encountered on the British balloons.

Having proven to be successful the cable-fender was ready for operational trials, although for the most part the Luftwaffe remained sceptical and many officers were concerned about the additional 600lb weight penalty. This inevitably meant a reduction in the bomb payload and there were fears about an aircraft's ability to fly with the fender should one of the engines be put out of action. In the summer of 1941 a Heinkel 111 was brought down in one piece while on a bombing raid to England and this gave the British experts their first chance to examine the German balloon fender at first hand. They considered it to be a somewhat cumbersome design and it appears that the Germans agreed as it was subsequently abandoned in favour of a protective strip of razor-sharp steel fitted to the leading edge of the wings. This strip, it was hoped, would cut right through a cable, but clearly it afforded absolutely no protection to the propellers or engines. Once again Hannah Reitsch was called upon to carry out the tests, which had been transferred to the balloon-testing station at Saarow in order to cope with the demand on balloons. Each time a cable was cut the balloon would tend to blow away, and as the British had discovered, a trailed cable could cause considerable damage, especially to the electricity power lines. Fighter aircraft would be scrambled to shoot down the silvery fugitives, and sometimes the pressure relief valves on the balloons had been preset so that they would rupture at a predetermined height and fall back to the ground. 'Neither of these methods was however, entirely effective', commented Reitsch.

On one of the last tests a thicker 5.6mm cable was to be used. This had been recovered from a British balloon which had drifted across the Channel, but because only a short length had been found the test was to be conducted at a much lower height than usual. Things did not start well, with the balloon slewing sideways in the breeze, pulling the cable at a steeply slanting angle. On impact with the aircraft the cable parted and the starboard airscrew was smashed into metal splinters which shot through the cabin leaving the engine racing at high speed. With only moments to spare, Reitsch switched off the damaged engine and engaged an electric motor, which would 'feather' the propellers into a neutral position. She struggled with the tail-heavy aircraft and managed to bring it down in one piece. It had been an extremely close escape from almost certain death, and in recognition of her bravery Hitler personally presented her with the Iron Cross, Second Class.

The British, too, had been working on protection against balloon cables – continuing their prewar experiments – for the Germans also had barrage balloons to protect important locations, as will be seen in Chapter 11. At the start of the war, Rex Haggett was a twelve-year-old country lad living in the village of Pawlett, situated to the north of Bridgwater near the west Somerset coast. This was a remote and sparsely populated spot far removed from the business of war – that is, until the day the lorries came trundling through the village. 'Being curious, we children followed them on our bikes and soon found that building work was going on, at the foot of Gaunts Hill and about 100 yards from the entrance gate to the Hams; a large area of meadow land without any hedges.' A barrage balloon hangar was constructed and tests of the cables and developing defensive measures soon commenced. The first deliberate collision with a balloon cable at Pawlett was carried out by Flight Lieutenant J.A. Kent on 26 September 1939. As the aircraft struck, the cable cut deeply into the wing and Kent limped back to Exeter with 500ft of it trailing behind.

Over the ensuing years Rex and the other village children would closely follow the experiments taking place over their heads.

When the barrage balloon site had been built on the edge of the Hams the main objective of the exercise had been the recovery of the paraphernalia which fell from the balloon after the plane had cut its cable. Where it fell was determined by the strength and the direction of the wind, and as children we learnt to gauge this quite accurately. Despite this, I never did achieve my burning ambition to catch one of the orange flags before it hit the ground.

The signal that tests were about to commence was the launch of the balloon itself. 'It was brought out of the hangar by several men holding on to the looped hanging ropes and was then attached by a coupling to the main cable. Also attached to the coupling was a very long length of piano wire with all the paraphernalia on it.' At the top of this subsidiary cable was a parachute packed into a detonator capsule, below this was a 6ft square orange flag, a loop of smaller black flags to indicate the target section of the wire, a second orange flag, and at the bottom an inverted parachute filled with ballast and a small drogue parachute to tip the ballast out when the cable was cut.

Initially these flags were made of silk, but when orange curtains started appearing in the village they were changed to cotton ones. At the bottom corner of each flag was a bag of lead shot sewn into it which acted as a weight to keep the flag taut. The second generation flags had large rubber stamps on them which offered a half-a-crown reward for returning them. However as we children were beating the men to it the third stage flags bore stamps which read 'Air Ministry Property, Return to Police', and the rewards stopped.

The main cable had a large black flag, about 18ft square, to indicate to the pilots not only that this was the main cable but also to show that this was the same level

An Air Ministry photograph of a downed Heinkel 111 night-bomber with its cable fender still intact. Registration numbers have been deleted by the censor.

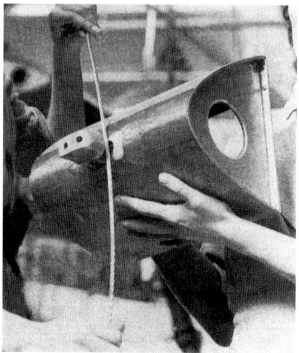

Above: The barrage balloon shed at Pawlett, West Somerset – the scene of the British experiments with balloons and cables – is one of only three surviving examples in the UK. (John Christopher)

Left: A British cable-cutter as fitted in the leading edge of an aircraft's wing. The cable would trigger a cartridge to fire a chisel against a small anvil set in the upper jaw of the gate.

as the target cable. As the main cable unwound, red and white windsocks were attached at intervals of approximately 200ft.

> By counting these we children could tell how high the balloon was. On a brilliant day it used to go up so high that it appeared as a silver dot in the sky. Other days when there was low cloud it went right through it and above and we could only guess what was going on. We would hear the aeroplanes come over, the crack of the detonator, and then suddenly the bits and pieces would come falling through the clouds.

The aircraft were coming up from Exeter and mostly they were Fairey Battle bombers fitted with cutters on the leading edge of the wings.

> They used to circle the balloon and when ready dive in, cut the subsidiary cable at the designated spot, and then fly home. First of all the detonator exploded and a largish parachute would open, supporting the top portion of the cut cable as it headed for the ground. The two orange flags would detach and also start streaking downwards, pulled down by their lead shot weights. The smaller black flags which were hit by the plane would float down at a more leisurely speed. The bottom half of the cable would also start falling. At this point the drogue parachute would pull at the inverted chute sideways and so tip the sand out of it. Then the two parachutes would right themselves and support the weight of the bottom half of the cut cable as it fell.

Further experiments were also conducted at Pawlett. On one very windy day the children were surprised to see the cable hoisted aloft by large box kites flying in tandem. Rex also recalls that very occasionally the flags were attached to the main cable. 'When this happened I knew we were in for a treat because, instead of the usual Fairey Battles, the much bigger Wellington bombers came over and cut the main cable of the balloon.' To prevent the balloon flying away it was fitted with a rip panel that was activated by a cord when the cable was cut, but it wasn't foolproof. 'One time they lost the balloon, presumably because the rip chord did not work. It just kept rising until eventually we lost sight of it.'

The British system to deal with cables had been designed by James Martin of the Martin-Baker Aircraft Company well before the war, and it utilised leading edge protection on the wings combined with a cutting device which was not dependent on the speed of the aircraft. A balloon cable would slide into a gate, moving a trigger as it entered, and this fired an explosive cartridge situated in the base of the cutter, which drove forward a chisel cutting the cable against a small anvil. On a big bomber as many as sixteen such cutters were fitted at intervals along the leading edge. The only drawback to this system was that each cutter could only work once in the course of a single flight, and afterwards the ground crew had to replace the cartridge and prime the cutter. As an article published in 1943 explained, 'It serves the double purpose of protecting the bombers against enemy balloon barrages and securing them against the misfortune of being damaged by British barrage cables if they should get off course in bad weather on their way home from the raid.'

In a bid to save precious petrol, gas bags were also seen on the streets of many cities as cars and even buses were equipped to run from hydrogen carried in these roof-top bags.

BOVRIL prevents
that sinking feeling

In December 1939 the barrage balloons still seemed comical enough and this Bovril advertisement was one of many to pick up on the theme.

Indeed, it was not only the German crews who feared the balloons over Britain as their cables were incapable of discriminating between friend or foe. Warnings were issued to the British pilots concerning the whereabouts of the balloons, but it was inevitable that 'friendly' casualties would occur. As early as January of 1940, *War Illustrated* reported that three British aircraft had already flown into the cables. No wonder that 'balloon' was considered a dirty word by the men of Fighter Command. And it wasn't only the combat and bomber pilots who had to dodge the balloons. Lettice Curtis was a pilot with the Air Transport Auxiliary, ferrying aircraft from the factories to operational airfields. 'In the UK, balloons were a major navigation hazard. The main areas between London and Prestwick which had to be given a wide berth were Birmingham and Coventry, the Liverpool, Widnes, Warrington and Manchester balloon complex, and most inconveniently Crew with its junction of six railway lines because it prevented one following the main-line, north-south railway.'

It is has been estimated that ninety-one friendly aircraft, both RAF and USAF, were ensnared by the cables' deadly embrace. Usually the strikes were fatal, but sometimes the aircraft recovered or were able to make an emergency landing. One of the worst accidents occurred on 6 October 1942, when a Dakota of No.512 Squadron struck cables over central London. Onlookers watched in horror as part of one wing was ripped off before their eyes and the stricken aircraft plunged to the ground, killing the crew of nine. The balloons were at their most dangerous to aircraft in bad weather and it was not unusual for pilots to find themselves in the midst of the balloons either through navigational error or pure misinformation. One pilot recorded, 'I had run into deteriorating weather – low cloud and poor visibility. On plotting back after landing, we realised we had flown through the Liverpool barrage at 500ft before scraping into Sealand by the skin of our teeth.'

9
MOST SECRET WAR

As well as their defensive roles, balloons have a nasty streak and many offensive and secret tasks were devised for them during the Second World War, including trailing wires, carrying bombs or incendiary devices, and even delivering propaganda material and agents behind enemy lines. The notion that balloons could deliver such items upon the heads of the enemy was, of course, nothing new. It was in 1849, in the midst of the Italian War of Independence, that the Austrians had launched a flotilla of unmanned hot air balloons against Venice, lifting 30lb bombs and shrapnel charges on the first aerial bombardment in history. Each balloon carried enough fuel to fly for thirty minutes and trailed a time fuse, but despite some initial panic the results were disappointing. General Pepe, commander of the Venetian forces, is supposed to have claimed that the aerial bombardment only served to amuse the defenders, and according to some historians the fickle winds had even conspired to return some bombs back to their senders.

Various proposals for balloon weapons had been put forward since then, although not acted upon. It took the accidental breakaway of barrage balloons to reawaken this line of thought and in November 1937, almost two years before the outbreak of war, a British newspaper report unintentionally hit the nail on the head.

> Our 'sausage' balloons have taken to escaping from their moorings, trailing long lengths of cable as they go and causing alarm, despondency, and destructive damage to our friendly neighbours across the Channel. The one that enlarged itself on 13 November plunged four towns in darkness, brought machinery to a standstill, and tramway systems to a halt, actually setting fire to a house in the neighbourhood of Calais.

The journalist concluded:

> If a single sausage can accomplish this what might a barrage do if it broke loose in wholesale style? Perhaps we have been taught a new method of using sausages in war! But it is more probable that the incident will be relegated to oblivion. It must be nearly

as galling for balloonatics to lose a sausage as it is for gunners to lose a gun. And in peacetime too!

Barrage balloons continued to break away with monotonous regularity, mainly due to the weather, and it was a problem common to every nation operating them. Unfortunately they tended to terrify the already nervous civilian population and there are many stories of people being stalked by dark shapes in the night. Eve Perry was a five-year-old living in Manchester when she had a confrontation with a balloon. 'One day as I was walking home from school, I was horrified to see an escaped balloon hovering low over my head. To a young child, it was like an enormous beast. I ran to escape but the monster followed me. I was petrified… I had nightmares about that for a long time afterwards.' For many, the image of the escapee seemed somewhat comical, and it was a device not overlooked by the makers of George Formby's 1940 film *Let George Do It*, in which our hero floats on a barrage balloon to Berlin to give Hitler a taste of the 'Formby knuckle'. Many years later the classic television comedy series *Dad's*

An unmanned balloon attack on Venice in 1849 during the Italian War of Independence.

Army picked up the theme. *The Day the Balloon Went Up* saw the Home Guard of Walmington-on-Sea in hot pursuit of a rogue balloon. Needless to say, Captain Mainwaring ends up being whipped off his feet and is unceremoniously hauled across the countryside, smashing through a haystack and ending up suspended in the path of an oncoming train.

On a more serious note, the breakaways continued to make trouble and their cables were a considerable hazard to aircraft. Fighters were frequently scrambled to bring them down as quickly as possible, and in one case a Spitfire of No.129 Squadron disappeared after chasing a balloon out over the English Channel. Many balloons also made their way to Ireland, where they were enthusiastically shot down by the pilots of the Air Corps who relished this rare opportunity to try out their skills.

On 17 September 1939 the largest breakout occurred when strong gales scattered balloons across the North Sea and Channel to cause havoc in Germany, Denmark, Finland and most embarrassingly in Sweden, where they knocked out a radio station and damaged the electrified railways. Taking a keen interest in this episode, Winston Churchill noted, 'We may make a virtue of our misfortune'. The Air Ministry was instructed to investigate the practicalities of deliberately trailing wires, but expressed concerns about the Germans copying the idea. Some experiments had already been carried out, back in 1937, to evaluate the damage a 'friendly' balloon might inflict upon the National Grid in comparison with the more vulnerable German power system, but the Air Ministry remained lukewarm about the idea and instead it was the Admiralty that took up the challenge.

Existing within the Royal Navy, a special team had been assembled under the leadership of Charles Goodeve, a young Canadian with a background in chemistry and electrical engineering; he had studied in London before the war and served as a Lieutenant Commander with the Royal Navy Volunteer Reserves (RNVR). Goodeve had already gained a reputation for himself with his work on the degaussing of ships, 'wiping' them of their positive magnetism as a protection against magnetic mines. Under the deliberately vague title of Inspector of Anti-Aircraft Weapons and Devices (IAAW&D) – abbreviated among themselves as the 'Wheezers and Dodgers' – Goodeve's team operated out of cramped quarters within the Admiralty Arch building. At first sight they were a motley crew, comprising a ragbag of engineers, scientists and RNVR from various backgrounds in civilian life, including barristers, a schoolmaster and a furniture manufacturer. A notable recruit was Nevil Shute Norway, who had been an engineer on the R100 airship and would later become famous as an author. The one quality they all brought to the job was an abundance of imagination which resulted in some of the more unorthodox secret weapons to play a part in what Churchill described as 'the Wizard War'.

One of the Wheezers and Dodgers' immediate tasks had been to come up with a viable defence against Luftwaffe attacks on shipping. These were the dark days of 1940 following the defeat of the British Expeditionary Force in France and the merchant ships were woefully ill equipped, in many cases possessing just a single machine gun to fend off enemy aircraft. A total of 745 British, Allied and neutral ships were lost between May and December of that year, with coastal vessels at greatest risk. The problem facing the Admiralty was that there simply weren't the resources, materials or time to develop elaborate anti-aircraft guns. IAAW&D needed to come up with something fast.

Several proposals were mooted, including a giant flame-thrower shooting a pillar of fire into the path of attacking aircraft. A similar scheme had been suggested to protect Fleet Air Arm shore bases against attacks by troop-carrying gliders, and a prototype was developed which spat a cocktail of diesel and tar in a terrifying ball of flame 30ft in diameter and with a range of over 300ft. That was fine if pointed directly at an aircraft on the ground, but aircraft attacking a ship presented a fast-moving low-level target. Nevertheless, an aging French trawler was kitted out with the device and the RAF provided an aircraft to make attacking runs. Unfortunately, the results were not encouraging as the pilot stated afterwards that it really wasn't that much of a deterrent. Ironically the young flight-lieutenant conducting the test flights lost his life a few days later when his aircraft struck a balloon cable in poor visibility. It may have been his death that focussed the thoughts of the Wheezers and Dodgers away from flame-throwers and on to cables.

Goodeve's team, now re-titled the Department of Miscellaneous Weapon Developments (DMWD), was called upon to evaluate an existing RAF device called the Parachute and Cable (PAC) for sea trials. It consisted of a powerful

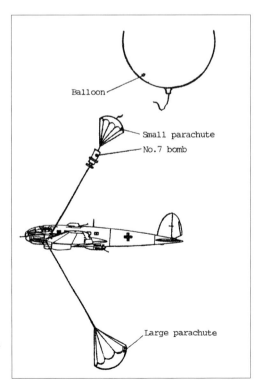

The Free Balloon Barrage was designed to ensnare attacking bombers. Air resistance on the parachute would drag the bomb into the aircraft. (Herman Van Dyk)

rocket that could thrust a steel cable up to a height of 500ft. At the top of the cable was a parachute to slow its descent and at the bottom another parachute provided additional drag when the cable was struck. The RAF had regarded PAC as a sort of emergency balloon barrage which could be thrown into the air at the flick of a switch to defend an airfield, while the Admiralty was more interested in its potential for protecting ships. The advantage over previous rocket systems was that it could be fired into the path of an aircraft without actually having to hit it. Several merchant vessels were fitted with PAC and by the spring of 1941 it had accounted for a number of enemy aircraft caught in its trailing cable, and as with barrage balloons the Luftwaffe pilots were forced to attack from greater heights thus reducing their accuracy.

Just occasionally things did not go entirely to plan. There is the report of one merchant ship sailing in a coastal convoy; equipped with PAC, it was also flying a small barrage balloon for protection. Unfortunately the rockets were accidentally triggered and they went smack into the balloon. The hydrogen exploded. The balloon's cable fell over the stern and wrapped itself around the propeller, which then acted like a winch, pulling on the cable and smashing the topmast to which it had been attached. Such incidents aside, and encouraged by the overall success of the PAC device, DMWD made further refinements, including the Fast Aerial Mine which featured an explosive charge at the end of the wire. The notion of aerial mines had obsessed many inventive minds during the First World War, but these schemes always floundered in two particulars. Firstly, if an aircraft can reach sufficient height to drop a mine – against a

A Lieutenant of the RNVR cold testing the FBB balloons in a refrigerated chamber.

Zeppelin, for example – it might just as well make a direct attack, and secondly there was always the question of where the mines would come down if they missed their target.

With London continually pounded by regular air raids into the autumn of 1940, the Prime Minister called a special meeting at Downing Street to discuss new ways of defending the capital. This wasn't to say that the barrage balloons weren't doing their job, but Churchill wanted something more flexible, a spider's web that could reach higher altitudes and be aimed directly into the path of the bombers. He revealed to the assembled experts that the possibility of carrying wires in 6in shells had proven impracticable and he wanted to know if huge rockets could do the trick. 'Just think of the difficulty for an aircraft trying to avoid a thing the size of the Horse Guards, gentlemen!' It was an officer within the Admiralty's Boom Defence operation, named Fraser, who came up with an alternative plan using balloons to carry the wires. DMWD immediately consulted the Balloon Development Establishment (BDE) at Cardington and the 'Free Balloon Barrage', or FBB as it became known, quickly took shape. This consisted of hundreds of individual rubber balloons 10ft in diameter, each lifting a yellow metal container roughly the size of a biscuit tin, and 2,000ft of piano wire with a small parachute at each end. At a predetermined height the wire would be released from a spool by an automatic mechanism and the yellow box became a live bomb. If an aircraft struck the dangling wire it would be disconnected from the balloon and, kept taut by the parachutes, dragged downwards across the wing until the bomb made contact and a tilt mechanism detonated the explosives.

Friendly aircraft needed to keep out of their way and accordingly the RAF was advised of the whereabouts of all FBB operations. As an instruction from Fighter Command noted, 'When in force, friendly aircraft are prohibited from flying at night at any height over these areas because of the danger from balloons rising after release.' But the RAF was not impressed. 'They were so against the idea of having balloons trailing wires and bombs in the same sky as their aircraft that they refused to help in any way', asserted Wing Commander Gerry Turnbull who was with the BDE during the war. 'They said, "Let the Senior Service have their toys".'

As an added safety precaution the bomb was designed to self-destruct after a given time in the air, thus protecting the general populace down below. Unfortunately, some teething troubles became apparent in early tests when leaking balloons descended before the allotted time. This would not have been an issue if the public could have been warned about the devices, but the FBB project was of necessity highly secret. And, as in all balloon operations, the weather plays a major part; despite the best efforts of the meteorologists to accurately predict wind speeds and direction, the actual conditions were often at variance with the forecasts. Instead of operating within a small, defined area the balloons tended to spread out, draping homes far and wide with wires and their nasty yellow boxes of tricks. Many householders frantically rang the Air Ministry to report that they were victims of a new secret weapon unleashed by the enemy!

Worse still, some bombs fell across railway lines or overhead electricity cables, causing considerable disruption.

In the aftermath a squad of unmarked vans would race around the countryside gathering up the contraptions before any more harm was done. On one occasion a telephone call from the constabulary at the village of Piddletrenthide in Dorset summoned the 'flying squad' of retrievers. When the men from the Admiralty arrived they found two yellow boxes lying in the yard with only short lengths of wire still attached, and the constable proudly explained that he had found the devices about a mile away and had ridden back with them hanging from the handlebars of his bike. Then there was the case of the farmer who had actually dismantled one on his kitchen table!

By the end of 1940 it was decided to test the FBB in earnest. On the night of 29 December London was subjected to a massive incendiary raid by the Luftwaffe, but what the raiders didn't know was that their arrival had been anticipated. The code word 'Albino' was issued and an army of 800 trucks and hundreds of men rolled into action. Large tents had been erected at launch sites arranged in an arc of about two miles centred on Hatfield, Hertfordshire, and 2,000 balloons were sent on their way within two and a half hours. Once again problems were immediately apparent and it was estimated that almost a third failed because either the wire had not un-spooled smoothly or the balloons had leaked. In addition, the automatic ballasting had malfunctioned on some, causing them to ascend until they burst from increased internal pressure and scattered their loads on London.

At daybreak the sorry task of picking up the pieces commenced. One balloon bomb landed in the grounds of Buckingham Palace, while others had floated further afield, reaching the south coast and even across the Channel into France. By now every yellow box displayed the warning 'Danger – Do Not Touch!' – yet this served only to whet the curiosity of the general public. In one instance a shopkeeper had collected four boxes and, as was becoming customary, transported them dangling from his handlebars. Although this test had been disappointing, another 200 FBBs were then released from Cardington in a controlled experiment to discover why so many of the wires were not uncoiling properly. It also emerged that the pressure relief valve might be malfunctioning because of the intensely cold temperatures encountered at such heights, and accordingly several officers were dispatched to a fruit research station in Kent to conduct further tests within a vast refrigerator. It was a curious situation in which these young naval men found themselves; instead of going to sea they were locked inside a cold box surrounded by crates of fruit, balloons and a set of scales to measure buoyancy. Worst of all, they became excessively drowsy after only a little time and many complained of severe headaches. After a while doctors were summoned and it transpired that they had been 'intoxicated' by fumes coming from the fruit. After a thorough analysis of the results, the FBB equipment was modified and practice launchings resumed with the assistance of Balloon Command, who had been recruited to transport the gear and launch the balloons. At least they were functioning more reliably, although the increased flight duration inevitably caused more to go astray, and in one case a French Gendarme was wounded after he tugged on the wire of a balloon to bring it down.

The next major launch of the FBB occurred near Liverpool, which was suffering heavy raids in the spring of 1941. This time only 150 balloons were released and everything went smoothly, more or less. No aircraft were snared, but a telephone exchange, a few houses, one electricity cable and a herd of cattle fell victim to the wires – relatively minor damage according to the experts and Downing Street. Plans were immediately drawn up for FBBs to protect London, Birmingham, Bristol, Portsmouth, Liverpool and Hull, but a lull in the air raids stifled all further development. Had the Luftwaffe not changed its tactics the FBB might have proven its worth – as Winston Churchill commented, 'It was surprising and fortunate that the Germans did not develop this counter to our mass bombing raids in the last three years of the war.'

The FBBs were not the only balloon weapons to be deployed by the British. On a beautiful, clear morning on 13 March 1942, at the high school in Vlissingen, situated on the island of Walcheren in the Netherlands, a group of school children on their morning break were staring at some small shiny objects high in the sky. 'They seemed to be toy balloons drifting with the wind at great height', recalls Herman Van Dyk. 'Occasionally one seemed to go up in smoke and a small cloud of objects, shining in the sun, would slowly float to earth.' Soon the heavy flak guns located at the nearby German airbase opened up, but without any visible results, and the children returned to their lessons. A friend of Herman's recorded this event in his diary, as he did with everything that happened since the start of the war, and in 2000 the two of them were reunited for the first time since their liberation in 1944. The diary shows that the second time the balloons became visible was on 4 April 1942.

> The first time that we noticed the shiny pieces floating to earth, nobody knew what they were. Having been repeatedly warned in school about incendiary cards the previous year, several of us believed that it was those. They turned out however, to be leaflets which were dropped from time to time to keep our spirits up and inform us of the real war situation. The BBC was always jammed and the German news could not be trusted.

What Herman Van Dyk and his friends had witnessed were just some of the 100,000 balloons launched by the British during the war, and while some carried propaganda leaflets others trailed wires or dropped incendiary devices. In what became known as Operation Outward, the DMWD had worked together with the BDE to devise a balloon that could carry a variety of devices deep into Nazi-occupied Europe. The clear advantages of such a scheme were that the balloons were cheap and no lives were put at risk in delivering their loads. The downside was that they were obviously at the mercy of the wind and accurate targeting would be difficult. The task of operating the balloons was passed to the Navy's

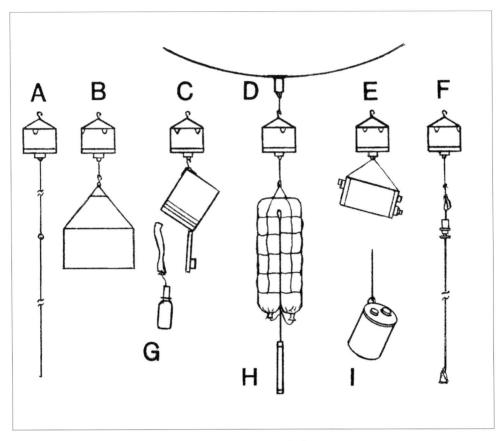

The various payloads carried by Operation Outward balloons.
  A: Wire trailing balloon.
  B: P or M type balloon carrying leaflets.
  C: Incendiary bottle container.
  D: Incendiary sleeve.
  E: Incendiary cartridge.
  F: PAC parachute and cable balloon.
  G: Incendiary bottle (Molotov cocktail)
  H: Sensitive igniter.
  I: Incendiary cylinder.
(Herman Van Dyk)

Boom Defence Department (BDD), which was responsible for the anti-torpedo and submarine nets protecting British harbours. It wasn't as unlikely an assignment at it might at first appear as the BDD had land facilities in the south-east and they had the personnel to carry out the work, mostly from the Women's Royal Naval Service (WRNS).

Two types of balloons were produced; one was a rubber balloon with a 6.5ft diameter and holding a volume of 148 cu ft resulting in a lift of 10.5lb, while the other was a larger rubberised silk balloon 10ft in diameter, a volume of

494 cu ft and a gross lift of 35.6lb. To ensure that the balloon did not expand too much a length of rope was suspended internally from the top of the balloon, and at its end a ball sat on the opening of the filling tube at the bottom. As the balloon expanded the ball was pulled slightly away from the tube and gas would escape until the balloon contracted. The balloons also carried an automatic ballasting system in the form of a cylindrical can about 6in tall. Inside this was an aneroid device, which responded to air pressure to release water ballast, thus keeping it between specified heights. Slung beneath the ballasting cylinder was the all-important payload – the business end of Outward. Almost half of the balloons trailed 300ft of steel wire, and the rest carried one of a range of incendiary devices from simple 'cards' to more sophisticated devices.

Incendiary cards had been dropped by RAF aircraft since the summer of 1940, mostly from Wellington bombers. There were several variations on these, with Incendiary No.1 consisting of a piece of celluloid with a small piece of phosphorous held in place by strips of gauze on either side. The gauze was kept wet, but once it had dried out it would spontaneously ignite. Later versions were produced which either burned more intensely or for longer periods.

The 'Incendiary Sleeve' was much larger and consisted of two burlap sleeves, each 5ft long, filled with wood chips and soaked with paraffin. An electric igniter was connected to four fuse cords leading to the end of the folded sleeves and an electrical contact would be activated when it struck the ground.

The 'Incendiary Can' functioned in much the same way as a 'Molotov Cocktail', dropping seven bottles about the size of a beer bottle in flight. Each contained a mixture of chemicals with phosphorous and sulphur acting as the igniter, and benzol and rubber as the fuel. Later on the seven individual bottles were replaced with a cluster of four. Then there was the 'Incendiary Cylinder', a single metal container 7in long, filled with benzol to be ignited by an impact fuse. In 1943 an improved version known as the 'Incendiary Canister' featured a larger container and a fragmentation explosive charge to spread the contents up to 50ft on impact.

The first Outward balloons were launched in March 1942 from BBD's depot at Felixstowe, on the North Sea coast. Balloon Command provided the hydrogen, the Naval Meteorological Office the forecasts, with the work of filling and launching the balloons carried out mostly by the Wrens. It could be hazardous work handling the volatile chemicals and many of the women experienced skin burns as a result. The balloons were only released in daylight and in agreement with the RAF none were sent up when Bomber Command's aircraft were undertaking raids. Obviously launches could only take place when the wind was blowing in the right direction, and some balloons carried radio transmitters so that their progress could be monitored. A second launch site at Dover became operational a few months later.

By the time Outward was terminated in September 1944, it was estimated that almost 100,000 balloons had been launched. To what extent they contributed to the war effort is hard to assess. Great claims have been made regarding the impact of the wire-trailing balloons, although some experts have questioned this.

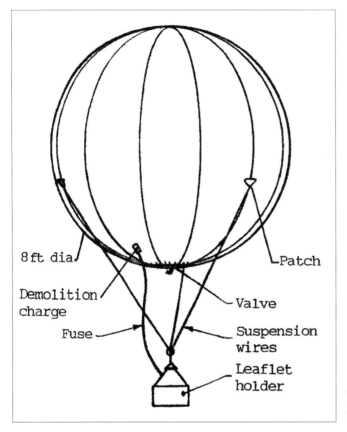

8ft dia.

Demolition charge

Fuse

Patch

Valve

Suspension wires

Leaflet holder

A schematic view of the typical British propaganda balloon. (Herman Van Dyk)

What is certain is that considerable manpower and resources were tied up with dealing with them. The Luftwaffe and anti-aircraft guns did their best – no doubt wasting copious amounts of ammunition – and those that got through had to be dealt with either by the military or the police. The incendiary cards were a particular nuisance, because they arrived in such large numbers. Many children, unaware of the danger, were burnt by the cards and this led to the Nazis labelling them *Kinderschreck*, or 'children's scarer'. A later variation on the cards was designed as a sabotage device for the resistance fighters – small enough to be easily hidden, they took thirty minutes to ignite once activated. The bigger incendiary devices usually exploded upon impact, but those that landed in soft bushes or in trees had to dealt with by disposal teams.

Although often lumped together with Outward, the British campaign of propaganda balloons actually predates it. Balloons had been used in this way during the First World War and the idea had been dusted off by the Air Ministry in 1938. Under the operational control of Bomber Command, the No.1 'M' Balloon Unit deployed rubber-proofed cotton balloons similar to the Outward ones, equipped with a release mechanism consisting of a slow-burning fuse mounted on a wooden board. The load was suspended on strings which passed through the fuse and as it burnt the strings parted releasing ballast or leaflets. A short, rapid-burning fuse linked to the balloon's envelope then ignited the hydrogen.

On the night of 1 October 1939, sixty of the 'M' balloons were launched from Toul in France carrying two different types of leaflets. One was entitled 'Das Sind Eure Führer' and detailed the personal wealth amassed by Nazi leaders in foreign banks. The other, 'Achtung!' contained the transcript of a speech made by Chamberlain declaring that Britain was at war with the Nazis and not the German people. By the end of November a million leaflets had been dispatched and Sir Campbell Stuart, who headed the Department of Publicity in Enemy Countries, assured the Cabinet that 'they present a particularly embarrassing problem to the Gestapo'.

'M' Balloon Unit continued its work in France throughout that cold winter whenever the winds were favourable, but during May 1940 they began to retreat from the German advance and by June had returned to Cardington. The propaganda leaflets, delivered by aircraft and balloon, now took on a different nature as their main function was to boost the morale of the people in the occupied countries. Operations were moved to Kent to be better positioned, but occasionally the balloons went to the wrong addresses and in

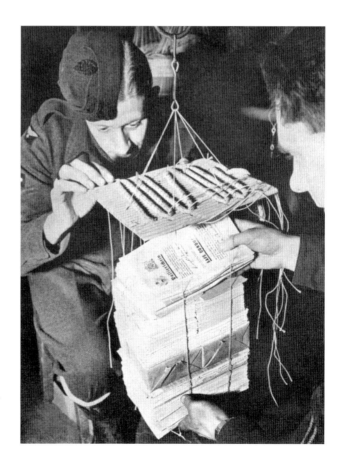

British soldiers prepare a payload of propaganda leaflets. As the fuse burnt through the strings the leaflets were dropped.

'M' balloons carrying propaganda were
released from newly liberated areas of
the Continent in 1944 and 1945.

March 1941 several dropped leaflets in Switzerland, Italy and Spain. In the latter
years of the war the material became more subversive, with the aim of softening
the spirit of resistance within the enemy troops, and after D-Day the unit
returned to the Continent and the balloons delivered Safe Conduct Passes for
surrendering German soldiers. Clearly their work was nearly done and the unit
was disbanded in July 1945.

Finally, there was one other cargo carried by balloons into occupied Europe
during the Second World War, one of which few people are aware of to this day
– a human cargo. Launched under the cover of darkness from ships in the North
Sea disguised as merchant vessels, the 'passenger' or agent would ride in a
small basket. At the appropriate location the agent would vent gas to bring
the balloon down to earth, before stepping off and leaving all evidence of
their arrival to float away downwind and undetected. Choosing a precise
destination was always going to be difficult, but the balloons were excellent
'stealth' aircraft with little chance of discovery. I once asked a retired RAF
officer who had been directly involved with these balloons why so little had been
published about them. 'It's because, even today, they are still considered a viable
means of getting agents where they are needed – unseen and unheard.'

In addition, Special Operations Executive (SOE) operatives frequently underwent parachute training from larger barrage balloons, about twice the size of the ones protecting English cities. Jumps were made from 800ft into the still air, usually through a circular opening in the bottom of the gondola to simulate low-level drops from aircraft, and often in darkness. These balloons were also used by the RAF to train considerable numbers of paratroopers, as described in Chapter 17.

10

ALL AT SEA

From the very earliest days of ballooning it was obvious to many that they could be flown from ocean-going vessels to enable an observer to see for many miles beyond the usual horizon. That this was not exploited is due to the particular obstacles associated with operating from ships, especially wooden ships, where the presence of hydrogen gas and the acids used to produce it, as well as the dangers of a balloon fouling the rigging, were not welcome. Undeterred by such details, the proponents of naval ballooning continued to put forward suggestions, although it wasn't until the mid-eighteenth century that any practical demonstrations took place. The earliest known example of a balloon launching from a ship dates back to 1849 when unmanned hot air balloons were launched from the Austrian steamer *Vulcano* to drop bombs during the attack on Venice – as described in the previous chapter. The following year messages were dispatched by balloon in the Canadian Arctic, from the Royal Navy's HMS *Assistance*, in a bid to locate survivors from Sir John Franklin's ill-fated expedition. Leaflets stating the position of the rescue ship were tied in small bundles along the length of a slow-burning fuse to ensure an even scattering over a wide area.

It took several factors to come together before full-sized, ship-borne balloons became a practicable proposition: an iron hull, steam-power to clear the decks of those cumbersome sails, and a means of communicating between the hoisted balloon and the ship below were all required. During the American Civil War the first attempts to operate from ships had been made, and towards the end of the nineteenth century military ballooning had flourished to such an extent that the navies of several countries were taking a closer look. Among the major advances were the electrolytic process of producing cheaper hydrogen and steel cylinders to store it under pressure, combined with the development of the kite-balloon, which is much more suited to the sort of conditions encountered at sea. The French Navy in particular took a keen interest and in the early 1890s several ascents were made from the deck of the battleship *Formidable*. Further experimental flights followed, including a successful attempt to locate a submerged submarine during the 1901 fleet manoeuvres.

The German navy had towed a shore-inflated kite-balloon by torpedo boat in 1897, and in Russia several cruisers and gunboats had sent up spherical balloons by the mid-1890s. Nonetheless, that great maritime nation Britain remained indifferent to them, despite plans put forward by inventor Frederick Allen Gower to use a fleet of free-flying unmanned balloons launched from a ship to drop bombs upon coastal targets. Another notable absentee in the world of naval aeronautics, since the Civil War at least, was the US Navy.

It was the Swedish who produced the first ocean-going vessel to be constructed specifically for the operation of balloons, the *Ballondepotfartyg* 1 – 'Balloon Depot Ship No.1' – from which they flew a 25,000 cu ft German-built *drachen*. Similar innovations emanated from Russia, starting in 1904 when several spherical balloons were flown from ships in an attempt to spot Japanese mines. They also flew a kite-balloon from the battleship *Rossia* in 1905 and even acquired their own balloon-ship, the *Lahn*, originally built in Glasgow in 1887 and at one time the third-fastest steamer in the Atlantic. Renamed *Russ*, she was converted for carrying up to four kite-balloons on her 450ft hull, but sadly the ship was in such a dilapidated state that she was not fit for the job. In 1907 the Italians had operated a kite-balloon from the quarterdeck of the cruiser *Elba* during manoeuvres, and during the 1911–1912 war with Turkey observation balloons flew from the *Cavalmarino*.

German naval manoeuvres with a balloon ascending on tether from the gunnery training ship *Mars* at Wilhelmshaven, 1890.

This smattering of prewar experiments was fairly inconclusive as the balloonists had, in most cases, not been given the support they needed and the vessels provided were second-hand at best. In addition, there was no real need for them as the guns at that time had insufficient range to warrant their presence, and submarines had yet to come into their own. In fact, operating the cumbersome balloons was more of a hindrance than a benefit to most naval personnel. It was going to take a world war to shake them up and in 1914 that's just what they got. As balloons went up the length of the Western Front the Royal Navy re-evaluated them in the role of directing gunfire against coastal targets, reconnoitring for the fleet and for anti-submarine escort duties. (Small non-rigid airships were also extensively used in the latter role.) In 1915 the SS *Manica*, a tramp steamer from Manchester, was refitted and dispatched to the Dardanelles complete with her Royal Naval Air Service (RNAS) Balloon Section. Further ships followed including the *Arctic*, the *City of Oxford*, and HMS *Engadine*, HMS *Campania* and HMS *Chester*.

At the height of their wartime activities the British had 131 balloon-equipped vessels to escort cargo ships travelling in convoy. Thanks to the balloon bases in Gibraltar and Malta, the Mediterranean was virtually free from U-boats, whereas in the treacherous Atlantic waters they remained an ever-present threat. For the men who manned the observation balloons their war has been described as 'unrelieved discomfort and an eternity of monotony'. Maybe so, but they could spot a submarine up to forty miles away on a clear day and few U-boats dared to come closer. In July 1917 the U 69 was destroyed in the North Sea with the aid of a balloon flying from HMS *Patriot*. Then in September 1918, Lieutenant S.G. Maudsley – of the RAF by this time – spotted a U-boat off the bow of HMS *Ophelia* east of the Orkneys. The submarine dived, but Maudsley was able to follow her track and depth charges completed the job.

Post-war, the observation balloons continued to serve as the 'eyes' of both the US Army and Navy. In early 1919 six battleships of the Atlantic Fleet operated balloons at Guantanamo Bay, Cuba. However, the following year two men were killed in accidents with balloons, which were soon replaced by the new aeroplanes. Let's not forget, however, that the US Navy – the main user of airships for convoy escort and anti-submarine patrols during the Second World War – continued to make training on both free and captive balloons mandatory for its airship personnel.

The Japanese persisted with observation balloons during the 1920s and the *Tatsuta* was equipped to operate them as the flagship of the First Destroyer Squadron in 1927. It has been suggested that the last deployment of a ship-borne observation balloon during hostilities occurred in 1925 when the Spanish carrier *Dedalo* supported the Franco-Spanish suppression of the Moroccan rebellion. Then again, given Russia's utilisation of land-based observation balloons right to the end of the Second World War, there is every likelihood that they continued with them at sea.

Gas balloons remained a vital part of the US Navy's airship pilot and ground crew training programme and remained on the LTA curriculum until 1957. (US Navy)

Throughout the Second World War ship-borne barrage balloons were deployed extensively by the British to protect estuaries, coastal waters and shipping. In January 1940 the magazine *Modern Wonders* took a look at the work of the men of the 'Balloon Navy' as they called it. 'German mine-laying aircraft hoped to be able to ring our shores with an impenetrable barrier, but they had reckoned without the latest developments of British scientists. The menace of aerial mine-laying has been checked by the work of our Balloon Navy.' The Thames in particular was protected by these balloons, not just to prevent minelaying, but also because the river was used by enemy bombers as a means of finding their objective. The larger barrage balloons, identical to the land-based ones, were flown from barges and drifters and the 1943 publication *Roof Over Britain* outlined their operations.

> Each of these vessels is mobile and keeps steam up day and night. There is a civilian crew for manoeuvring the vessel, and a crew of three or four airmen, with a corporal in charge, to manipulate the balloon. The winch is generally contained in the hold of the vessel, and as, of course, there is no means of bedding down, the balloons must always remain either flying or else close hauled.

Joseph Melford had been with the barrage balloons since 1939, initially at a land-based site near the Thames, but within six months he was transferred to one of the barges. 'That was awful', he recalls, 'because those old coal boats were filthy.'

For the crews a period of ten days to a fortnight on the boats was usual, and although they were in sight of land all provisions were brought to them by boat. Joseph remembers when the thick Thames fog sometimes meant they went hungry. 'They couldn't get the supply boat to us for several days and we were starving.'

From the Thames he was then transferred to an offshore ketch at Falmouth, where he stayed until the spring of 1943. Conditions at sea could be much rougher and it often took time for the airmen to find their sea legs. 'We used to go out on a small boat and run alongside and then transfer the crew and the balloon. When it was a bit rough out there, the balloon could be driven down until it touched the sea. Pulling it in was awful with the cable lashing across the boat. But we couldn't bed them down.' And even in the most extreme conditions he can't recall ever losing a balloon while at sea. 'Within the crew discipline was very casual, but not with the officers. I was the senior person on the ship, the corporal in charge. We had an old skipper from Devon, two naval blokes and myself and three others – they were nice characters. We cooked for ourselves and with all the chores we were never bored. Never a dull moment.' And to ensure that the crew didn't become too lax, they had to listen in to regular radio messages throughout the day and night. 'We had an RT set and they tapped out Morse code messages every quarter of an hour, and we had to record that to prove that we were always listening.'

A British ship-borne barrage balloon.

A tender delivers small barrage balloons on the Thames.

More so than with the land-based balloons the boat crews often found themselves subjected to the attention of the Luftwaffe. On one occasion a large naval ship was just being brought out of Falmouth docks after repairs.

I was just looking out to sea when three fighter aircraft appeared not very much above sea level. We said to each other, 'They're ours!' But they weren't! Next thing is they loomed up and they bombed this ship and in a very short time its stern went down. The aircraft sprayed a few of the boats with machine gun fire and they were off. They didn't hang around. When we first went out to sea we never had machine guns to protect ourselves, and suddenly HQ decided we must have them. The Lewis gun was put on board, but nobody knew how to use it, and so they sent everybody away on a training course. The course just wasn't good enough as far as I'm concerned. You stood in a line, you stepped forward, pressed the trigger and that was your training. So when some German aeroplanes came again, I shouted 'Get on the gun!' Our gunner got so excited he shot half the wheel-house down! And that was the only time we ever fired it!

Balloons and their cables also served as a valuable deterrent against direct attacks on ships on the move. As one contemporary report put it, 'In flying balloons off our coasts experts have taken all the fun out of the German sport of baiting defenceless merchant shipping.' Smaller balloons, the Very Low Altitude (VLA) smooth-sided dilatable type, distinguishable by their small triangular rigid fins and with an overall length of 34ft and volume of 2,900 cu ft at ground level, were flown from the convoys and although manned mainly by the Navy and Merchant Service, they were maintained by the RAF. When these needed repair they were replaced with new ones delivered by a special 'mother ship', which could transport several at a time in their open holds. Bigger balloons had to be towed ashore for repairs.

The Americans and Russians also had ship-borne balloons and evidence from Allied gun cameras shows that the Germans flew them to defend their ships. (Incidentally, the Russians used navigation balloons attached to buoys to mark out safe lanes through mined waters.) But undoubtedly the most famous deployment of sea-borne balloons was during the D-Day landings on 6 June 1944, and long before a single soldier had stepped ashore, balloons, of a sort, had been playing their part in other ways.

The German commanders knew that an assault on the continental mainland was coming – the only question was where it would take place. Although the Pas-de-Calais was the obvious choice with the shortest Channel crossing, the Allied commanders under General Dwight D. Eisenhower opted instead for the wide, open beaches of the Normandy peninsular. However, for the plan to succeed it was absolutely vital that they fooled the German leaders into tying up their resources in defending Calais and making them believe that any attack on Normandy was only a diversionary feint. Operation Fortitude used bogus radio traffic and thousands of inflatable trucks, tanks and landing craft to amass an entire phantom army, known as the First US Army Group (FUSAG), to be commanded by the redoubtable General Patton, no less, and positioned in south-east England ready to depart from Dover. It was the biggest and most successful wartime deception in history, but as Winston Churchill once said, 'In wartime the truth is so precious it must be protected by a bodyguard of lies.'

It was in the Western Desert, back in 1941, that decoys were first used on any great scale in the Second World War. They were assembled from whatever materials came to hand and for the most part consisted of a wooden frame covered with painted canvas. Tanks were disguised as lorries and in some cases whole new armies were assembled in the desert sands. It was the development of inflatable decoys, principally by the Dunlop company, that transformed these crude contrivances, making them lightweight and also easy to store and erect. A 'Sherman' tank, for example, could be packed into a holdall little bigger than a cricket bag, and while it would assume the size and appearance of the real thing it weighed 170lb compared with the 35 tons of its metal counterpart. They took about five minutes to inflate with a motorised air pump, could be carried by four people, and when securely pegged-down would stand up to the strongest winds – not to mention the scrutiny of the Luftwaffe's reconnaissance experts. To complete the illusion specially equipped vehicles left the right sort of track marks to simulate heavy traffic movements and even kicked up clouds of dust. Dummy aircraft and field guns were also deployed, although these required a degree of supporting framework.

The deceptions continued on D-Day itself when a small flotilla of ships headed off towards Calais towing barrage balloons fitted with 'Moonshine', a device to reflect and amplify radar signals to give the impression of a large invasion force of warships and troop carriers. Moonshine was a variation on the highly successful 'Windows', a shower of metallic strips dropped by Allied bombers to confuse the enemy radar and send their night fighters chasing nonexistent intruders. Britain had led the world in the technology of radar and it has been justifiably claimed that the early warning it provided enabled the RAF to win the Battle of Britain. Balloons were used in its development – particularly in calibration studies, as well as devising means of tricking radar. One such device was used by British submarines. Codenamed 'Peardrop', it consisted of an aluminised balloon which reflected radar signals and, when released by a submerging submarine, floated above the surface tethered by a short line to a buoy, to bounce back the German radar signals in a convincing imitation of a submarine while the real thing made a hasty exit. In October 1943 an American destroyer attacked the German U 604 and this was also seen to release radar balloons as it submerged.

When the real D-Day invasion fleet arrived at Normandy it did so under a sky peppered with silver guardians. One US soldier described the scene as his

It weighs just 170lb and folds up into a small bag, but four men can soon turn it into a very realistic decoy to deceive the enemy. Inflatable anti-tank guns, lorries and landing craft were produced in a similar way. (Dunlop)

landing craft arrived at the stretch of beach known as 'Utah', 'Barrage balloons, like big sausages tethered to earth by cables, float close overhead to protect the landing area from low-level air attack.' These were the VLA type already used for convoy protection. Inflated by RAF personnel in England they had been transported by the fleet of ships and landing craft across the Channel. There have been some suggestions that the balloons may actually have helped the German batteries to gauge their range in some instances, and that many of the landing craft crews cut their balloons adrift. But at the end of the day the balloons had done what they were intended to do, they had kept low-flying aircraft on strafing runs away from the boats and the beaches, thus saving countless lives in the process. On 16 June one Junkers Ju88 did stray too close to the balloons and it crashed into the sea in flames. The canopy of balloons continued to protect the beachheads until late October, plus other key harbours, such as Cherbourg, following their liberation by the Allies.

According to one uncorroborated source, small 2,000 cu ft balloons were 'strapped to the backs of volunteer airmen as they went ashore to provide further protection from low-flying aircraft. They flew at 100ft, but the casualty rate was high and they weren't used again!'

Barrage balloons hover overhead as vehicles and supplies come ashore in Italy in preparation for the invasion of France, 1944. (US Navy)

A modern ship-borne TCOM 'Stars' balloon operated by the US Coast Guard in drug interdiction operations in the Caribbean. (TCOM Corp)

There is another way in which balloons played a crucial role on D-Day. Throughout history battles have been won or lost because of the weather, and as it was once said, 'the weather is on the side of the attacker' and this was certainly a major factor in the days leading up to the Normandy landings. The decision of when to go rested heavily upon the shoulders of General Eisenhower, and it depended on two things: the tide and the sea conditions for the long crossing. It had been Eisenhower's intention to make the assault on 5 June, but unseasonable gales were whipping the Channel waters into a fury. After seeking the advice of the meteorological experts he gave the go-ahead for the following day, knowing that if they were wrong the invasion could fail.

Since the birth of ballooning the aeronauts have studied the atmosphere at first hand and the military have shown an interest in the results. Once manned balloons had reached the limit of human endurance, their unmanned counterparts took over the task, pioneered by the French meteorologist Teisserenc de Bort, who carried out hundreds of experiments with balloons at the turn of the century, both tethered and free, carrying mechanical instruments to record temperature and altitude. In Germany 'Met' balloons were first launched on a regular basis from Tegel in the north of Berlin – coincidentally the home of the German Balloon Corps at that time. The balloons were constructed of silk, cambric or paper, varnished with rubber solution or linseed oil, and their volume varied from 1,000 cu ft up to 17,500 cu ft depending on the height they were required to attain. The balloons would then burst from their own internal pressure and a linen cap acted as a parachute to return the instruments to the ground. Clearly the art of recovering a free balloon was at best a haphazard business and in the early 1930s Robert Bureau and Pavel Malchanov developed small radio transmitters, known as 'radiosondes', to send the information back to the ground.

Throughout the Second World War all sides continued to take readings using balloons, usually launched at intervals of six or twelve hours, and from this information the meteorologists were able to construct their isobaric pressure charts and wind speed tables. In Britain the balloons were launched by the grand-sounding 'Clerks of the Weather' or by the WAAFs or Wrens. (At the height of wartime production the output of Met balloons from the Dunlop factory alone reached a staggering 6,000 per week.) These were mostly without radiosondes and accurate wind readings were taken from the ground using one or more theodolites. In addition, captive balloons, including barrage balloons, were used to carry instruments to specific heights. Met balloons were also launched at sea and it is known that the U-boats frequently released them to gain some indication of the mid-Atlantic weather systems. As a wartime edition of *Popular Mechanics* put it, 'The world's weather is being studied more closely than ever before.'

11

BOO-BOO AND THE DOODLEBUGS

The balloon barrages, limiting the scope of enemy attacks both by night and day, have become a natural part of the war scene. It is no more quite the thing to point out to your companion the sight, only some 100 yards or so from you, of a flap-eared, pudgy, slightly vacuous monster heaving itself laboriously from common or field or park.

So commented J.C. Trewin in the March 1942 edition of *Aeronautics*. Others were perhaps a little more poetical concerning their silvery guardians. Diarist James Agate wrote, 'The setting sun turns the barrage balloons to golden asteroids.' Either way, after several years of war the balloons and all that they represented had become part of the way of life for the British, part of the scenery.

When the Americans started arriving on these shores from 1942 onwards, the balloons were often their first sight of Europe. As one American journalist put it, 'Barrage balloons are certainly the most distinctive feature of the view from a city window practically anywhere in Britain today.' With vast quantities of American equipment and soldiers amassed to swell the Allies' forces in preparation for the big assault on the Continent, Britain was wryly described as 'the world's largest aircraft carrier'. This led to the exchange that has passed into barrage balloon legend, if there is such a thing. 'If you cut the balloons loose', a member of one all-female balloon crew told an inquisitive GI, 'England would sink!'

As with so many aspects of this terrible war, feelings of fear or apprehension were often assuaged by humour and the plump barrage balloon was a natural target for comedians and cartoonists alike. But for a few people the balloons themselves were menacing, especially to the younger children, including Sally March, then eight years old. 'My mother used to take me into Bristol, but I was terrified by the barrage balloons. So she bought me a book in which they were made to look like elephants. But it didn't work!' Like many other parents Sally's mother had bought a copy of *Boo-Boo the Barrage Balloon*. In this light-hearted tale our eponymous hero is given a friendly face, marries another balloon called Belinda, and has baby twins Betty and Basil before proving his mettle by catching an enemy aeroplane in his cable. 'Boo-Boo was indeed proud and happy that he

Boo-Boo the Barrage Balloon was published to make the balloons less threatening to children.

had done his duty – and helped to save the land he loved.' This was one of several stories published to make the balloons appear a little less sinister and other titles included *Blossom the Brave Balloon* and *Bulgy*.

Although they didn't like to admit it, quite a few of the grown ups were frightened by the balloons too, and for them there was the improbable tale of *The Body in the Barrage Balloon*. Written by Colin Curzon and published in 1942, it told a far-fetched story about the murder of Squadron Leader Buttle, otherwise known as the 'Great-Blimp-in-Chief' to his men, whose body was found actually inside a balloon.

The wartime cartoonists also had a jab at them and the most famous of them, David Lowe, depicted Hitler as a 'super windbag'. He also adopted the barrage balloon to christen his most popular character, the archetypical and pompous Colonel Blimp. In 1943 the colonel graced the silver screen in Powell and Pressburger's celebrated film *The Life and Death of Colonel Blimp*, which starred Roger Livesey in a sympathetic portrayal of the old codger and Deborah Kerr playing the various women in his life. Churchill prohibited the exportation of the film, claiming that its portrayal of the Blimp character was 'detrimental to the morale of the Army', even though the Ministry of Information felt that it did more good than harm. Churchill only relented when the film became a great hit with audiences in England.

By 1944 the threat of air raids had largely abated. The Luftwaffe could no longer sustain the tremendous losses to its aircraft and more importantly its aircrew. For the beleaguered Londoners there was a sense that the bombing was finally over and that they could relax a little. Then, on the night of 12 June 1944, only six days after the D-Day landings at Normandy, a sinister new object thundered across the skies of south-east England. It was the first of the V1s. In Maidstone a bunch of night-duty policemen cheered its progress, mistakenly assuming it was an enemy aircraft on fire. It landed, if that's the word for it, on a bridge at Bethnal Green, London, killing six people and seriously injuring thirty more. Looking like unearthly crucifixes and belching a tail of flame, ten V1 flying bombs had been launched that night on a range-finding mission overseen by a lone Junkers 88. This was the prelude to what has been described as 'The Battle of London', and three days later a second attack followed – a much bigger one, consisting of 120 V1s arriving at five-minute intervals.

Designated 'V' for 'Vergeltungswaffe', or 'retribution weapon', by the Germans, the V1 was a sophisticated pilotless aircraft just over 25ft long and with a wingspan of 17.5ft. Sitting above the main fuselage and at its rear was the 11ft tube of a jet propulsion unit, known as a pulse engine. The fuel, an acetylene gas, was forced into the combustion chamber and fired by a sparking plug, heating the outer casing sufficiently to ignite the air-fuel mixture. The heated gas then emerged from the rear of the tube in a series of impulses at around forty-five per second, producing a forward thrust of 600lb. At the business end, so to speak, the warhead housed 1,800lb of high explosives. It was, claimed Churchill, 'science perverted to destruction'.

The V1s were soon nicknamed 'Doodlebugs' or 'Buzz Bombs' by the British because of their loud throbbing sound. H.E. Bates, famed for his *Darling Buds of May*, was a roving correspondent working for the Air Ministry at the time and he described the noise as being very like 'the clattering harshness of a cheap and gigantic motor bike'. Once the V1 had reached its intended destination that hideous noise would end abruptly as the device tilted earthward and the fuel-starved engines cut out. My mother was in London at the time of the flying bombs and she once told me that it was the sudden heart-stopping silence that you most feared, waiting for that terrible moment of impact. Within a week civilian casualties amounted to a staggering 756 killed and 2,697 injured, and the flying bombs continued to come by day and by night, rain or shine. In one incident on 18 June a bomb fell on a crowded chapel at the Wellington Barracks in Buckingham Gate killing 121 people and injuring a further 141. That same day another bomb had struck the High Street in Lewisham killing fifty-nine and injuring over 300.

The Government had expected something like this, although ironically it was the existence of the bigger V2 rockets that had been identified first from aerial photographs of the Penemunde site in north-western Germany. Faced with the dilemma of whether it was more harmful to morale to keep it from the public or to come clean, the Home Secretary, Herbert Morrison, made a statement to the House of Commons. 'It has been known for some time that the enemy was making preparations for the use of pilotless aircraft against this country and he has now started to use this much vaunted weapon.' The cat was well and truly out of the bag, but as he went on to say, 'It is important not to give the enemy any information which would help him in directing his shooting, by telling him where the missiles have landed.' Accordingly, any news reports merely stated that a raid had occurred in 'southern England'. Summing up, he added, 'All possible steps are, of course, being taken to frustrate the enemy's attempt.'

This included a frontline of fighter aircraft patrolling the Channel coast; then came the searchlights and four rows of 8-gun AA batteries – more than 1,000 guns at its peak, including many manned by women, and finally the balloon squadrons hastily relocated from all over the country to form a concentrated belt of cables, a thicket of steel, stretching from Cobham in Kent to Limpsfield in Surrey. Many of the balloon teams had driven through the night with special police escorts and one of the first to arrive had travelled down from Glasgow. Getting so many fresh sites up and running, often in the middle of nowhere, was an enormous logistical exercise with telephone lines installed, roads, hard standing and anchorage points laid, and hydrogen and supplies put in place. The location of the balloon sites needed to be far enough out from London so that impacted bombs would not fall on built-up areas, and the airfield at Biggin Hill in Kent became the Balloon Centre.

By the beginning of July around 1,000 balloons were in place, and at its height this became the greatest concentration of wartime balloons ever seen with 1,750 barrage balloons covering 260 square miles. H.E. Bates described them as

The menacing shape of a V1 flying bomb or Doodlebug sits at the end of its launch ramp. This example is situated at the Imperial War Museum's Duxford site. (John Christopher)

'the only materially beautiful thing produced by the whole campaign. The sight of up to two thousand of them glowing in the southern sun, smooth and silver against the blue sky, was an incongruous thing in this odd campaign of hideous robot combat.'

At 380mph the V1s flew too fast for most aircraft, with the exception of the Tempest V, which could attain 416mph, and it was the Tempest Squadrons of 150 Wing that led the air battle. They were ably assisted by the new Spitfire XIVs of 91 and 322 Squadron and also the Mustangs of 316 Squadron – the latter being mostly flown by Polish pilots. Originally the tactic was to shoot them out of the sky, but on 23 July Australian Flying Officer Kenneth Collier of 91 Squadron demonstrated a new tactic. Out of ammunition, Collier closed in on the flying bomb and used the wing of his aircraft to flip it off course. Another variation was to position the fighter's wing just above the Doodlebug's, thus starving it of lift and tipping it over. But the fighters had very little time, perhaps only six minutes flying from the coast before coming up against the balloons. Members of the Royal Observer Corps were stationed on the fringe of the balloon barrage to fire red warning rockets to turn away any aircraft straying too close.

There was one vital advantage in the defenders' favour: the flying bombs flew at relatively low altitudes and they came in a straight line from the launch sites to their main target, London. This air corridor became known as 'Doodlebug alley', and it was a dangerous place to work. Snag a flying bomb and it might explode upon impact, or stagger on dragging the cable behind it like a 'fish taking the bait' until it dropped into the open countryside, or it was just as likely to fall

A balloon team celebrates its second Doodlebug kill in two days. (Imperial War Museum)

Balloons of the No.2 Mobile Balloon Flight were first deployed in Burma by the British, to guard the Bailey Bridge over the Chindwin River near Kalewa.

straight down onto the balloon site itself. One airman and three WAAFs were killed when a V1 ran down the cable at Brasted, at Biggin Hill airfield three men died when the Nissen hut they were sleeping in suffered a direct hit, and at Tatsfield a flying bomb struck a balloon cable and exploded on buildings just a few hundred yards away. As the number of cable strikes increased so did the demand on replacement balloons. One site received its third, which they christened *Doodle Anne II*, after they had brought down V1s on two successive days.

The onslaught of the V weapons had not only been an assault against people and property, dreadful as that was, it was also part of the propaganda war. For many Germans the advance of the Allies following the Normandy landings, combined with the damage being inflicted by bombing raids on their cities, contrasted starkly with the Nazi's earlier promises of military invincibility and a thousand-year Reich. Propaganda Minister Joseph Goebbels played upon the impact of the V weapons for all it was worth, stating, 'London is chaotic with panic and terror. The roads are choked with fleeing refugees.' Did the German people really believe that these were the long-promised wonder weapons that would turn defeat into victory in a matter of months? In Britain, Winston Churchill remained defiant. 'If the Germans believe that the continuance of this present attack, which has cost them very dear in every branch of production, will have the slightest effect on the course of the war or upon the resolve of the nation or upon the morale of the men, women and children under fire; they will only be making another of those psychological blunders for which they have so long been celebrated.' Bold words, but the bombardment did have an effect on the spirit of the Londoners and it is estimated that one million people fled from the city. Because of the glancing angle at which the V1 struck, the widespread surface blast caused enormous damage to property in addition to the high casualties. At the peak of the attacks over 24,000 homes were damaged every day – that's a rate of 1,000 every single hour – stretching the Civil Defence services way beyond endurance.

It was the Allies' advance in September of 1944 that brought the main onslaught of the Doodlebugs to an end as the launch-sites in northern France were overrun. Only a few irregular raids continued in the ensuing months with V1s launched from new mobile sites further east or from specially adapted carrier aircraft over the North Sea. Between June 1944 and March 1945 a total of 9,251 V1 flying bombs had been plotted on their way to London, and of these 278 were stopped by the balloons, saving countless lives.

But worse was still to come. On 8 September 1944 the German scientists unleashed the V2s against Britain. These were supersonic ballistic rockets that arched sixty or seventy miles up into the stratosphere to fall back to earth too fast for any warning. There was no defence against the V2, certainly nothing a barrage balloon could do, and thankfully this development had come too late to change the outcome of the war. Time had run out for the Nazis and the last V2 was launched on 27 March 1945, claiming the life of a young housewife in Orpington – the last British civilian to be killed by enemy action.

For the men and women of the barrage balloons the end of the V1 campaign had already signalled the end of their war. The No.1 Balloon Training Unit at Cardington had been closed, back in November of 1943, by which time 10,000 balloon operators and 12,000 driver/operators had been trained for other duties. On 5 February 1945 Sir Archibald Sinclair, the Secretary of State for Air, announced the stand-down of RAF Balloon Command when he addressed a special parade held at the Command's headquarters. For thousands of women with the WAAF, demobilisation brought an abrupt end to their new way of life. But as Dorothy Melford, the fabric worker who had become a corporal on the balloon sites, recalls, 'It was time to move on. I was twenty-three when I came out and I didn't have any clothes to wear. I had gone in as a teenager, and worn nothing but uniform. All I had was a sixty pounds gratuity in a Post Office savings account.'

It was also time to assess the effectiveness of the balloon barrage over Britain and the conclusions were somewhat mixed. In October of 1945, the Under-Secretary of State for Air informed Parliament that 'twenty-four piloted and 278 non-piloted' enemy aircraft had been destroyed by the balloons. However, this tally of strike rates misses the point. The balloons had served primarily to deter low-flying bombing attacks and more importantly they positioned the enemy aircraft where the AA guns and the fighters could most effectively deal with them. Yet it is a cruel irony that by pushing the bombers higher these silver sentinels may actually have contributed to the indiscriminate bombing of cities. This was especially devastating in areas such as London's East End where streets of densely packed housing stood cheek-by-jowl with the docks – the main target.

There is also the question of friendly aircraft brought down as the Under-Secretary was to admit: 'Unfortunately, ninety-one of our own aircraft collided with cables, causing thirty-eight to crash.' (In fact, these figures were probably far short of the actual totals.) I believe that on balance, by the end of what had been a cruel and vicious war, the balloons had served their country well. The fact that they stopped so many Doodlebugs from getting through was certainly their greatest achievement. They also served to bolster public morale on the Home Front by providing a highly visible symbol of Britain's air defences, and that will always be to their credit. In addition, there were the ship-borne balloons and those that flew during the North African campaign and in other countries.

More than fifty years later there are few relics of the balloons remaining. The hangar at Pawlett in Somerset still stands tall and proud, albeit somewhat rusty. Another two at Pucklechurch, to the north of Bristol, are now part of an industrial complex, and at the Imperial War Museum's Battle of Britain exhibition at Duxford a balloon winch has been lovingly restored. There is, however, one modest tribute to the balloons situated in London's Cleveland Square, a large open area surrounded by the tall Georgian houses which made it so well suited for siting a balloon, especially with Paddington railway station just a few hundred yards away. This is a private square so you can't get in without permission, but in the middle of the gardens is a small plaque which reads: 'The balloon bed, site of a barrage balloon during World War II which helped protect the square against enemy action.' And while the memories of the surviving men and women who served with the balloons may have dimmed, history's enduring image of the Home Front will always be of wartime skies peppered with these silvery guardians. Without the balloons Britain may indeed have sunk.

Britain was not the only participant in the Second World War to deploy balloons and other countries with a tradition of military ballooning were also active. These included Germany, the Soviet Union and the USA in particular, while a handful of other nations used them to a lesser degree. In many cases their method of deployment varied little from the previous war and when the Nazi's Blitzkrieg rolled through Poland at such devastating speed, several Polish observation balloons were encountered. These tended to be much slimmer in profile than the British barrage balloons, although they shared the same 'Y' tail configuration. Either German in origin or at least influenced by the German designs of that period, they were expandable balloons with an elasticated horizontal panel running down each side instead of an internal ballonet system to cope with pressure changes. The fins were air-inflated via an external air scoop. Old First World War balloons were often dusted off and pressed into service once more as observation balloons, although France, for instance, still had the know-how to build its own. An example of one of these was under evaluation at Cardington in

August 1937, when it broke free and proceeded to drag its cable across the country all the way to Bury St Edmunds.

In Germany the defensive balloons were known as *Sperrbalone*, *sperr* meaning barrier just as barrage does, and during the First World War experiments had been carried out with aprons of cables much like the British system. However, by the start of the Second World War their value was not given much consideration in the face of widespread technological progress in warfare, although balloons were photographed flying over Hitler's chancellery in 1939. There are examples of manned balloons being used for observation purposes, but when the Germans went on the defensive later in the war the *Sperrbalone* were more widely deployed in a protective role and by the beginning of 1944 some 1,757 balloons were flying over Germany and its territories. These were mostly located in cities, or around important industrial facilities and ports, including the shipyards and the U-boat pens, while smaller groupings deterred low-level attacks on bridges, dams, power stations, electrical transformers and so on.

Several escaped German balloons fell into the hands of the British and in general terms they were found to be designed on the same principle as the British ones, although much more slender in profile. Three main types were identified and these were christened by the Allies as the 'Essen' type, which was 108ft long, the 'Hamburg', which was produced in 90ft and 70ft versions, and the smaller 'Normal' in three main sizes, 56ft, 40ft and 35ft long – the latter of these mainly

This prewar Czech observation balloon is probably a relic of the First World War and did not represent much of a deterrent to the Blitzkrieg. The observer's basket is just visible to the left of the picture.

intended for ship-borne deployment at sea or in harbours. It was felt by the experts that the German balloons had a tendency to ride nose-up into the wind because of their more elongated shape and the position of the attachment points much nearer to the back than on the British design. There was also evidence that many of the balloons were fitted with more than just one cable and that in some cases balloons were flown in tandem, one above the other, to achieve greater heights and thus provide greater protection.

By 1943 most Allied air attacks were taking place well above 10,000ft, although one important low-level raid was launched against the Polesti oil field, located in the foothills of the Transylvanian mountains in Rumania, the primary source of oil for German forces in the Mediterranean. The Allies decided that a knock-out blow could significantly shorten the war in Europe, and although Polesti was known to be heavily defended with AA batteries and a large number of balloons, a low-level attack was required to ensure accuracy and to catch the defenders off-guard. In the event a total of 179 US Army Air Force B-24 bombers took part in the attack on 1 August 1943, but bad weather and fearsome anti-aircraft fire took their toll and several aircraft succumbed to the cables. One B-24 was severely damaged when a cable bit deeply into the wing's leading edge forcing the aircraft to climb the cable until it hit a contact bomb, killing eight members of the crew in the ensuing crash. Fifty-four of the aircraft, almost one-third, did not return.

A rare photograph of a *Sperrbalone* team in action. The Germans frequently favoured these smaller and more mobile balloons in their defence plans.

'Das Auge der Artillerie' – the caption on this photograph of a German observation balloon team in action in 1940 translates as 'The eyes of the artillery', proving that the Germans also used observation balloons in the early stages of the war.

Characteristic of the German balloon barrages was their apparent mobility. They would frequently appear at a location for a short time, then disappear only to be seen there again at a later date. This shifting pattern of balloons caused problems for the Allied planners and on one occasion the BBC broadcast a coded appeal for information on the balloons protecting Dresden. Jimmy Yule, an inmate in the notorious Colditz Castle POW camp, was able to coax some valuable information out of one of the more chatty guards, and this was relayed back to London via another coded message concealed within a prisoner's letter.

In Russia the General Staff of the Red Army had put out a call at the beginning of the 'Great Patriotic War' for aeronauts to join specialist observation balloon divisions to undertake 'the most difficult and responsible direction of the battle in order to defeat and destroy the fascists'. Before the outbreak of hostilities they had several balloon regiments with an estimated 850 observation and barrage balloons. The tradition of using manned balloons to direct the artillery was deeply embedded in the military's thinking and they were used for this purpose throughout the war. However, they suffered terrible losses in the first battles of 1941 and only gradually were the numbers built up again until they reached 3,000 balloons. A substantial balloon barrage of at least 500 balloons is known to have protected Moscow, including many in tandem, and on the night of the opening attacks in July 1941 two German bombers were brought down by the cables. Similar barrages flew at Leningrad, Murmansk and other cities.

Women serving in the Red Army were treated with complete equality and as well as operating balloons many became officers, some serving as observers. One of these was Lieutenant Aleksandra Dyeisovia Kosmyenko, a graduate of the Leningrad Military Academy who had volunteered in 1939 and was later commended for her valour. 'On 12 January 1942, on the greatest day of our great city of Leningrad's history, Comrade Kosmyenko was spotting for our gallant corps and was observed to report such accurate coordinates that our artillery units made nine direct hits on enemy tanks', wrote the commander of the 67th Army. 'She herself advanced with the infantry corps and personally killed sixteen enemy troops, blew up three tanks and saved a platoon commander when he had been shot twice.' No wonder that she was being nominated for the Order of Lenin as a true hero of the motherland.

A 1942 image of Russian forces transporting hydrogen in 'nurse' balloons.

The Russians adopted some novel measures to deliver the hydrogen gas to the balloon units. It was sometimes transported in 'nurse' balloons moved by soldiers on foot, often for considerable distances, and airships were also used. They would be fully inflated and heavily laden to take the gas to its destination where a quantity would be removed and the airship lightened for the return flight. In 1945 an estimated 700,000 cu ft of gas – the equivalent of about 350 barrage balloons – and 320 tons of cargo was delivered by this means. The extreme winter weather in Russia also caused great difficulties and in the storms of October 1941 the 1st Barrage Balloon regiment lost forty balloons in a single night. In one incident later that year an officer called Veligura was whisked aloft after trying to secure a balloon and drifted for 110km in the strong winds before landing safely. Just as with Thaddeus Lowe years before, he was arrested as a spy until he could prove his story. Right until the dying days of the war, observation balloons kept up with the thick of the action. During the Battle for Berlin in April and May 1945, Soviet observation balloons flew near Templehof at the edge of the city, and several captured German balloons were used.

The Russians also used captive balloons extensively for parachute training for its troops and it is said that 2,278 jumps were being made per day by 1944. Furthermore, some sources have suggested that the Red Army utilised free balloons to infiltrate 'guerrillas' behind enemy lines.

It was, ironically, the country with the most balloons that never saw them pitted against enemy aircraft attacking its territory. Interest in barrage balloons in the USA can be traced back to 1923, when the General Staff invited the chiefs of the various services to consider their use in protecting important locations. The consensus of opinion was favourable and the Air Service set about developing balloons and methods of operation, although there also began an untidy squabble between the services over who would actually operate them.

Initially, just a handful of balloons were constructed for evaluation and it wasn't really until 1940 onwards that any serious progress was made. In October of that year a programme was envisioned in which 4,400 balloons were to be produced over the next three years and several training camps established. However, this was beset with organisational problems until 1941 when it was decided that the Coast Artillery would take responsibility for the balloons, with the Air Corps providing initial development and assistance with the training of personnel. Interestingly, in June of 1941 an officer was sent to learn from the experience of the British and perhaps the main lesson he brought back was that it sometimes takes a war to get things done! To improve cooperation between the Air Corps and Coast Artillery a Joint Barrage Balloon Committee was established in November 1941. When the Japanese attacked Pearl Harbour one month later, some 300 balloons were ready for deployment and the main rubber companies, including most notably Goodyear and Firestone, had been given substantial orders for more. In March of 1942 the US War Department was reorganised and all barrage balloon operations were transferred to the Army's Corps of Engineers.

SOMETHING BIG – like lifting an ELEPHANT

A NEW, strange feature of the American Scene—those Flying Elephants in the neighborhood of vital war plants . . .

At night they are moored from ten to twelve thousand feet up—the better to clip your buzzards' wings, Tojo. With the mooring cable, a barrage balloon weighs about 1,350 pounds. It takes a lot of LIFT—12,000 cubic feet of HYDROGEN—to do this job! . . . Hydrogen has only 60/1000 the weight of air.

Along our West Coast, Shell is supplying the hydrogen . . . Scientists at the "University of Petroleum," Shell's research laboratories, got hydrogen as a by-product when they discovered how to make acetone and methyl ethyl ketone from petroleum gases.

The acetone and methyl ethyl ketone now do duty in smokeless powders and cordite . . . in paints and lacquers for our tanks and guns . . . in making rayon fabrics for parachutes and safety "glass" for bomber windows. And the hydrogen lifts those Flying Elephants!

Practically every advance of Shell Research now goes direct to the war factories or war fronts: *100-octane aviation gasoline*, first produced in commercial quantities by Shell; *Butadiene*, for synthetic rubber, first regularly supplied in quantity to our rubber manufacturers by Shell; nitration grade *Toluene* for TNT—Shell was first to get it from petroleum.

• • •

Tomorrow, new products—growing from these and scores of other Shell research accomplishments—will be at your service in your everyday peacetime life.

 First oil refinery to win the Army-Navy "E"—
Shell's Wood River Refinery

SHELL RESEARCH—Sword of Today
Plowshare of Tomorrow

Shell published this wartime advertisement in the USA to highlight their role in supplying the hydrogen for the 'flying elephants'.

Front view of a Goodyear-built barrage balloon reveals the distinctive lobe design favoured by the Americans.

Most of the American balloons differed from the British type. They were 'dilatable' and several models and sizes were produced, reflecting the number of different manufacturers involved. The main types in production were the low-zone balloons such as the D-5 with an operational ceiling of 7,500ft, of which Goodyear built nearly 500, and the D-7, which was in essence an American-built version of the British MkVII. Of particular interest is Goodyear's D-BB-6L model, known as the 'Strato-Sentinel', which was capable of flying at 20,000ft – much higher than any other barrage balloon. Displacement at ground level was 49,000 cu ft and at full dilation this increased to 71,000 cu ft.

Balloon battalions were deployed to protect navy yards, some aircraft works including Boeing at Seattle, the Pacific coastline and further afield at the Panama Canal, on Hawaii and around the perimeter of Pearl Harbour. (At one stage the Air Corps Board even considered using smaller balloons to protect columns of foot soldiers, but the idea was rejected because the balloons might act as markers for the enemy.) By the end of 1943 it was clear that the threat to the American homeland had diminished and the balloons began to disappear as the battalions within the USA were deactivated. Emphasis turned to the smaller Very Low Altitude (VLA) balloons, which were used to defend shipping, and served during the Allied landings in the Mediterranean and at Normandy where the 320th

Coast Artillery Barrage Balloon Battalion was made up entirely of black enlisted men. The last of the balloon units was decommissioned in Hawaii in December 1945.

In the Pacific the Americans had encountered few Japanese balloons, although they were spotted over Tokyo on the Doolittle raid of 18 April 1942. Others were seen protecting Wewak, the New Guinea harbour, in 1943. However, it would later emerge that the Japanese had a much more sinister role in mind for their balloons.

12

THE FU-GO
BALLOON BOMB

If the barrage protecting London had been the balloon's 'finest hour', then surely the attack on North America by the Japanese was its darkest. Conceived entirely independently of the balloon-bombs used in Europe, the 'Fu-Gos', as they were known, were the first intercontinental missiles. Designed to cross the wide expanse of the Pacific Ocean, they rode the high-altitude jet stream winds to deliver incendiary devices, bombs and terror deep into the heart of the American homeland. That they failed is due in no small part to a concerted cover-up by the American authorities and some bad timing on the part of the Japanese. Instead of setting the western seaboard's extensive forestry areas alight the Fu-Gos, by virtue of the seasonal nature of the jet stream, arrived mostly in the winter months – the very time when the trees were damp or blanketed in snow. But when the snows melted in the early spring and the hikers returned to the forests, the veil of secrecy devised to protect the public brought tragedy.

On 5 May 1945, Reverend Archie Mitchell, minister of the Christian Alliance Church in Bly, Oregon, decided to take his wife and five children from the parish for a picnic in the peaceful Gearhart Mountain area of Lake County, Oregon. It was a glorious morning with sunshine streaming through the canopy of trees as the excited children, all aged between twelve and thirteen years old, clambered out of the car along with Mrs Mitchell. While her husband found a more convenient spot in which to park the car, the others trekked into the woods until the laughter and shouting stopped abruptly. They had come across what looked like a parachute tangled up among the trees. Mrs Mitchell called to her husband, but before he could reach them curiosity had overcome one of the children, who pulled at the strange device. Suddenly an explosion shattered the peace of the forest. Reverend Mitchell ran to the scene only to find that his wife and all five children had been killed. The force of the blast had ploughed up the ground and the device, whatever it was, had been totally destroyed. He was so dazed by the blast and the shock of seeing everyone dead that he hardly noticed two forest workers standing at his side, and together they covered the bodies.

Originally the only publicity concerning this incident stated that an 'unidentified object' had exploded, killing six people. But a few weeks later the truth began to emerge as the authorities recognised the need to warn the civilian population of the danger. The news blackout was lifted and the Undersecretary of War revealed that North America had been under attack from a swarm of deadly Japanese balloon-bombs. Released from the fetters of censorship the newspaper editors spread the extent of the startling story: 'Japs Put 9,000 Balloon Bombs in Air Against US.' And this assault had been going on for several months. Since late 1944 bizarre occurrences had been reported from various remote areas of the west. Explosions had been heard in the woods, strange flashes filled the sky and flying objects had been seen drifting overhead. On 4 November the first positive identification of a balloon was made when a US Navy patrol boat came across a large fragment of what appeared to be cloth floating off the coast of California. The debris was hauled in and upon examination some Japanese markings revealed the balloon's origin, although the nature of the equipment it had carried remained a mystery. Over the following weeks several more balloons were found in areas including Wyoming, Montana and Alaska, and it became clear that this was a concerted assault on the USA by a new weapon.

Deeply concerned by these events the government was anxious that news of the silent intruders might trigger widespread speculation and panic among the general population. While the threat from the incendiary and explosive devices was evident enough, they also had to consider the possibility that the Japanese might use the balloons to deliver bacteriological agents, spreading disease throughout the USA – just as they had in 1942 when almost 100 Chinese inhabitants of a remote town near Shanghai died after a plague agent was dropped by aircraft. It was also known that the Japanese military had been conducting experiments with plague-infested fleas, gas gangrene and anthrax. Therefore the immediate response was to play down any publicity surrounding them and consequently only a smattering of isolated reports made it into the newspapers.

Gradually a handful of balloons was recovered intact, because either their bombs or self-destruct devices had failed to detonate, and the military began the delicate task of sifting through the evidence they offered. While the engineers and ordnance experts dissected the hardware, there remained the crucial question of where the balloons had come from. That they were Japanese in origin was beyond doubt, but surely it was impossible for balloons to have travelled over 6,000 miles across the Pacific. And if not from Japan itself, then where? Various alternatives were considered, including the extraordinary possibility that they had been launched from submarines off the western seaboard, from American beaches, or even from the internment camps where thousands of Japanese-Americans had been confined for the duration of the war.

Incredibly, the preliminary assessment revealed that the envelopes were constructed of no more than layers of paper held together with a vegetable glue. With a diameter of 32ft, each balloon envelope held about 19,000 cu ft of hydrogen, providing a lifting capacity of around 800 to 850lb at sea level. Suspended beneath the envelope via nineteen shroud lines was the payload, consisting of a sophisticated automatic altitude control system and a nasty cluster of bombs, including 11lb thermite incendiary bombs and, in most cases, a 33lb high-explosive anti-personnel bomb. The ingenuity of the Japanese was to be marvelled at, but what baffled the Americans most was the amount of ballast carried, thirty-two sandbags in total with each one weighing around 7lb. This was way too much for a one- or two-day flight of perhaps a few hundred miles.

Apart from the equipment itself the balloons held other clues – clues as tiny as little grains of sand ballast – and samples were immediately sent to the US Geological Survey. Ground down from local rock over the aeons, no two sands contain exactly the same mix of minerals and each individual grain carries its own messages, tiny signposts to its origin. The geologists began by painstakingly sorting the individual grains into little piles of similar colour. From these it was possible to determine what minerals were present in the samples and, equally important, what minerals were not present. For instance, while there was no granite, which is a very common mineral in most sands, and also no coral, which eliminated warmer waters, the sand did contain certain rare volcanic minerals. From this geological fingerprint the scientists began to build their evidence and additional pointers came in the form of microscopic animal and plant fossils. Ironically the final pieces of the jigsaw were found in geological surveys conducted by the Japanese themselves before the war, as well as from studies of fossils conducted at the end of the previous century. Only the beaches on the east coast of Honshu, the main island of Japan, seemed to offer a match with both the right mineral and fossil content. It seemed incredible, but here was clear evidence

A few of the Fu-Go balloons landed intact and this example was reinflated for inspection by the lighter-than-air experts. (US Air Force)

that the balloons had flown right across the Pacific Ocean! It wasn't until after the end of the war that the facts behind this most secret of weapons were revealed.

The Imperial Japanese Army already had a track record of using balloons, mostly for observation purposes, so when a programme to develop new weapons was launched in 1933 it was not too radical a step for a balloon-bomb to be considered. Known as the 'Fu-Go' weapon – the term appears to be taken from the first two letters of the Japanese word for balloon, *Fusen* combined with *Go*, the equivalent of 'number' – it was originally envisaged as a relatively small balloon of just over 13ft in diameter and capable of releasing a bomb about seventy miles behind enemy lines. This concept wasn't taken any further, but other balloon-borne applications were investigated, including the dropping of propaganda leaflets and also larger balloons to carry soldiers deep into enemy territory under the cover of darkness. However, it wasn't until the Second World War that the balloon-bomb concept was revived.

On 18 April 1942 American bombs fell on Tokyo, shattering any illusions that Japan itself was beyond the reach of the enemy. The 'Doolittle Raids' – named after their leader Lieutenant Colonel Jimmy Doolittle – were in retaliation for Japan's devastating attack on Pearl Harbour only four months earlier. Launching from the carrier USS *Hornet* 650 miles away from Japan, sixteen B-25 Mitchell bombers had inflicted only minor physical damage, although the psychological effect on the civilian population and its military leaders was indescribable. Japan would be avenged and its national honour restored only by striking at the very heart of the American continent, and the search began for a method of taking the war to the other side of the Pacific. As with the Germans, the Japanese considered building a long-range bomber big enough to reach America on a one-way flight. Such an aircraft would take time to develop and a stopgap measure was implemented to launch small mini-bombers from the decks of submarines off the American coast. In September 1942, a single Yokosuka E14Y1 aircraft set off some fairly insignificant forest fires in Oregon, after which attention turned once more to the long-range balloon.

By the spring of 1943 a 19½ft-diameter balloon had been produced with an anticipated range of around 2,000 miles – too short a distance to cross the Pacific, certainly, but then again the subs would play their role. The plan was for the balloons to be inflated on the deck of a submarine and then sent adrift with an automatic altitude control device and a single 11lb incendiary bomb which was released approximately ten hours later. The only limiting time factor was the great difference between day and night temperatures and its effect on buoyancy, creating too many problems for longer flights encompassing both day and night. While the Japanese Navy readied two of its submarines, the army prepared 200 paper balloons and their payloads, but by the summer of 1943 the tide of war was already turning against the Japanese. The submarines were urgently needed elsewhere and the plan was shelved.

Against the background of the American's relentless push towards Japan, demands to bomb the USA became increasingly fervent. If the submarines were no longer available then the range of the balloon-bombs must be extended so they could be launched from Japan itself. The estimated journey time for a balloon flight to the USA was around six to eight days, travelling at around 60 to 70mph, which was really stretching the flight endurance of existing balloon technology. A way had to be found to reduce that time and meteorological experts were brought in to gather data on the little-known transpacific wind patterns. From measurements obtained with radiosonde balloons it was discovered that at certain times of the year high-altitude winds of up to 200mph existed. This river of fast moving air at 30,000ft or so – now known as the jet stream – is caused when air from the Arctic moves southwards in the northern hemisphere's winter and pushes against the warmer equatorial air. The Americans later encountered these winds for themselves on high-level bombing raids against Japan, and it was the discovery of the jet stream that eventually led to the successful circumnavigation by the *Breitling Orbiter 3* balloon team in 1999. But back in wartime Japan, of more importance was the fact that the jet stream could whisk a balloon-bomb across the Pacific in a much more manageable time. To put the theory to the test, the paper balloons previously prepared for the submarine assault were taken out of storage and launched during the winter of 1943–44. Each one was equipped with a small radiosonde device to transmit data back to listening stations in Japan. Their aim was not to reach the USA, but to collect hard evidence concerning wind speed and direction and the results were most encouraging.

Work now began in earnest on a practical balloon-bomb. The engineers had to overcome the effect of day and night temperature variation, from more than +30°C to -50°C, causing the balloon to climb or sink wildly. The release of excessive gas pressure build-up during the day was solved simply enough by fitting a pressure-relief valve at the base of the envelope, although this meant the balloon would become progressively less buoyant as the flight went on. Conversely, the loss of altitude in the cold of night was countered with a sophisticated altitude control system consisting of a series of sensitive barometric aneroids and a small wet-acid battery connected to a series of small detonators which, when triggered, would release bags of sand ballast. So equipped, the balloon would follow a mild roller-coaster ride maintaining an altitude of between 30,000ft and 38,000ft. And, if the engineers and meteorologists had made their calculations correctly, the bombs would be released over their intended target once all the ballast had gone.

By early 1944 extensive manufacturing facilities were set up to meet the military's demand for 10,000 Fu-Gos in time for the winter's jet stream season. Engineers and scientists from all over Japan brought their expertise to bear upon the many problems this entailed. The balloon envelopes themselves were to be constructed from a paper made from the fibres of the kozo bush – a non-vital material at a time of increasing shortages. For strength the fibre had to be of a uniform consistency, but the paper had to be lightweight – a difficult challenge for the traditional hand-made paper industry of Japan, and a major breakthrough came with the introduction of mechanical processing. Several layers of this paper were laminated together, up to three or four for the upper hemisphere of the envelope, using an adhesive made from potato starch which at the same time acted as a sealant to gas-proof the paper. Once dry the laminated sheets were carefully inspected for flaws, patched if necessary, and then cut into 600 individual panels for each envelope. Completed envelopes were taken to theatre buildings and sumo-wrestling halls throughout Tokyo and air-inflated under pressure for twenty-four hours to test for leaks.

An enormous workforce was required to assist with the delicate assembly work and thousands of Japanese schoolgirls reported for duty at the factories after their short wartime school day was over. To prevent accidental damage from abrasions they had to wear gloves and socks, fingernails had to be closely trimmed and sharp objects such as hairpins were strictly forbidden. It was meticulous work, for even the slightest leak could reduce the flight endurance of a balloon.

Launching the fragile balloons was equally critical. Light surface winds were required for them to be safely inflated and then ascend to the altitude of the faster winds. On 3 November 1944 the balloon assault on America was set in motion. It was an auspicious day for the Japanese, the birthday of a former emperor, and an ideal time for the jet streams. Amid tight security each balloon was laid out on a circular launch bed formed by nineteen anchor points in the ground, to

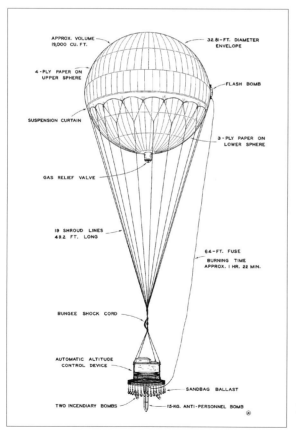

Diagram of a Fu-Go paper balloon. (Smithsonian)

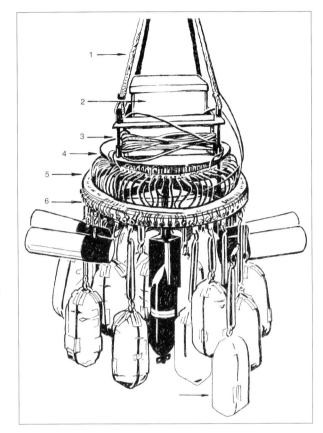

The business end of the Japanese
flying bombs – the Fu-Gos.
   Suspension lines
   Wet-cell battery
   Aneroids in box
   Bakelite plate
   Fuses
   Aluminium ring with
blowout plugs
   Sand ballast

which suspension bridles were attached. With the gas tube in place the envelope was only partially inflated with hydrogen gas from cylinders to allow for gas expansion as air pressure reduced with altitude. A simple wooden framework held the payload in position as the paper envelope lifted upright. The inflation tube was then removed and the gas valve fitted in its place at the base of the envelope. It took approximately thirty to sixty minutes to prepare each balloon and once the signal had been given they were released to drift away, the flaccid envelopes looking like pale jellyfish silently climbing at between 600 and 1,000ft per minute into the clear air.

To monitor the position of the balloons, lightweight radiosondes were occasionally carried instead of bombs. Their information indicated a reasonably constant speed and direction for the ten hours or so before they were usually out of range. A release mechanism was incorporated in these balloons to drop the equipment into the sea long before it might reach enemy hands.

The Japanese Navy had produced its own version of the Fu-Go, later known as the Fu-Go B-Type. Made of rubberised silk these were of similar size to the paper balloons, but instead of controlling altitude by releasing gas or ballast the navy's sealed balloons were strong enough to tolerate varying internal pressures. These balloons were often used to carry the radiosondes, but because of the heavy drain on valuable resources the B-Type was produced only in limited numbers and it was eventually abandoned in favour of the paper A-Types.

It is estimated that 9,300 Fu-Gos were launched between November 1944 and April 1945. Only a small percentage is believed to have reached the intended destination, with an estimated 285 accounted for by the US authorities. Once the Americans had determined that they were indeed under attack from these balloon-bombs they reacted in several ways. Firstly, it was important to deal with balloons that had landed, whether to put out any fires or to make safe those still intact. Then any incoming balloons had to be detected and if possible intercepted. Next came the location and destruction of the launch sites in Japan. And finally, all reports of the balloons had to be suppressed; not only to keep the public in the dark – although the authorities were mindful of the mass hysteria caused by Orson Welles' infamous 'War of the Worlds' radio broadcast in 1938 – but it was imperative to withhold news that would enable the Japanese to monitor their success.

Finding balloons that had landed was not easy. They were spread over a vast area from California in the south all the way up to Alaska and Canada. The authorities were kept busy responding to sightings or taking care of downed balloons that had failed to self-destruct, and in many cases these still carried their unexploded bombs. To aid in the hunt all national and local government agencies, including forest rangers, were ordered to report any sightings of the balloons or the recovery of equipment.

Although the military authorities still had little idea of the scale of the attack, or even its true nature, the Fourth Air Force, responsible for the air defence of the west coast, was put on alert. On 19 December the first interception of a balloon was attempted and although the target was never located these sorties continued for several months, eventually resulting in two Fu-Gos being brought down over land. The US Navy had its own share of aircraft, particularly the Corsairs and Hellcats, and several balloons were shot down before they reached the American continent. On 13 April 1945, Navy aircraft accounted for nine inbound balloons off the Aleutian Islands, with many more escaping to continue their journeys. The balloons were flying too high to be easily spotted, and the interception rate remained low despite efforts to establish extended radar protection.

Sometimes the best form of defence is attack. Based on the evidence of the geologists, American reconnaissance aircraft were flown over several locations on the eastern side of Honshu. As expected their photographs verified the presence of a number of launch sites, complete with partially inflated balloons and what appeared to be hydrogen generators. B-29s were sent to bomb these areas in May, but it was already too late to make much difference. By now the Fu-Gos had stopped coming for other reasons. The seasonal jet stream was dissipating and with so few reports of any damage being inflicted in the USA the Japanese had lost faith in their 'Windship Weapons'. Whether the balloon assault would have continued into another winter if the war had continued is uncertain.

Ironically, the bomb that had killed Mrs Mitchell and the five children from her husband's church was probably one of the last Fu-Gos sent to America. A bronze plaque now marks the spot in the Gearhart Mountain area of Lake County, Oregon, 'Dedicated to those who died here May 5, 1945 by Japanese explosion... The only place on the American continent where death resulted from enemy action during World War II.' But the saga of the Fu-Gos doesn't quite end there. Author Robert Mikesh has studied the subject for over thirty years and he believes that the danger remains even now. 'Anybody walking through the north-west woods who finds some unexplained object should look at it a little cautiously. The possibility exists that there are some undetonated weapons still out there.' And indeed, on New Year's Day 1955 the Department of Defence announced that a bush pilot flying for Wien Alaska Airlines had spotted a dull white object on the ground near the Scheenjek River. When an Air Force H5 helicopter was dispatched to the remote spot the crew found remnants of a paper 'chute' and a gondola. Upon inspection at Wright-Patterson Air Force base it was discovered that this definitely was a Fu-Go and that the explosives were still potent. Almost sixty years later, the menace of the Japanese balloon-bombs still goes on.

13

COLD WAR ENCOUNTERS

At precisely 5.39 a.m. on 16 July, 1945, the dark skies of the New Mexico desert were instantaneously lit by the 'blinding dawn' of the nuclear age. The detonation of the first atomic bomb had been codenamed 'Trinity'. The bomb itself was an innocuous squat device, just 5ft round and weighing 5 tons, cradled in a harness of cables at the apex of a 100ft-high steel tower. Surrounding the tower were several barrage balloons rigged at 500ft, suspending from their bellies sensitive gamma ray detectors to measure the yield of the bomb in the milliseconds before they were vaporised.

Such was the searing heat at ground zero at the moment of detonation that the surrounding sand was turned to glass. Watching from the protection of a bunker several miles away was the scientist who had headed the Manhattan Project, Robert Oppenheimer, and under his breath he muttered to himself a line of the Bhagavad Gita, 'I am become death, the shatterer of worlds.'

The highly classified work of the Manhattan Project had begun as a desperate race to beat the Germans in the construction of a nuclear bomb. But now that the fighting in Europe was over, the priority turned instead to ending the bitter war with Japan. The new US President, Harry S. Truman, had been pressing the Japanese to surrender and in a bid to avert a long, drawn-out and bloody invasion he threatened Emperor Hirohito and his military leaders with 'a rain of ruin from the air, the like of which has never been seen on this Earth'. Subsequently on 6 August 1945, just three short weeks after Trinity, the B29 bomber *Enola Gay* dropped the 'Fat Boy' bomb on the industrial city of Hiroshima, and three days later Nagasaki was also bombed. Then, on 14 August 1945, the Japanese people heard the voice of their Emperor for the very first time as he made a public radio broadcast to the nation announcing that all active resistance would cease. The unthinkable had happened – Japan had surrendered.

The Second World War was finally over, and the smoke had hardly cleared when Soviet leader Josef Stalin instigated his scheme for the domination of those European countries under the Communists' sphere of influence. Looking to his former allies, the Americans, Stalin was not prepared to play second fiddle in the new world order, and vowing to redress the obvious imbalance in military strike power which the atomic weapons had created, he forced the pace in the production of a Soviet bomb. As the two superpowers eyed each other up through a filter of disparate ideologies, it was the former British Prime Minister, Winston Churchill, who in 1946 summed up the mood of the time and described the new political landscape in Europe by saying that 'an iron curtain' had descended across the continent. In the ensuing atmosphere of mutual distrust and fear, there began a deadly game of poker which would take the world to the brink of destruction.

In 1948 one of the first flash points occurred in the divided city of Berlin. Following a decision by Great Britain, the USA and France to combine their 'zones of occupation' within Germany into a single body, the Soviets declared that all previous arrangements regarding the administration of the German capital no longer applied and that the Western Powers ceased to have any jurisdiction over the city. Then on 24 June the Soviets imposed a blockade cutting off all road and rail links with the west. Faced with the possibility of abandoning the Berliners, the Americans and British chose instead to fly in essential supplies until the matter could be resolved. At the peak of the Berlin Airlift, which continued until the following May, some 2,500 tons of food were being delivered on a daily basis. With a continuous stream of aircraft arriving at

At Yalta the three Allied leaders, Churchill, Roosevelt and Stalin, had laid the foundation for a post-war world and the ensuing Cold War. (US Library of Congress)

four-minute intervals, the pilots faced the hairy task of reaching Berlin via a long and narrow air-corridor passing over East German territory, all the while running the gauntlet of the Soviets' orchestrated programme of deliberate harassment. To disrupt the flights they resorted to electronically jamming radio channels, directing powerful searchlights at the cargo planes to blind the pilots, and even sending Mig fighter jets to buzz them. And on some occasions barrage balloons were allowed to drift into the air corridor.

So it was that the humble balloon, that most archaic throwback to former centuries, continued to serve its military masters in one way or another. And, unabated, the 'wicked wit of man' devised ever more outlandish roles for their lighter-than-air craft, especially within the murky world of espionage and covert operations. But nobody could have predicted the bizarre turn of events that were to unfold following a chance discovery in the desert not too far from the location of the Trinity tests.

On 14 June 1947, a ranch foreman named Mac Brazel came upon an area of wreckage or debris on a remote part of the Foster Ranch where he worked, situated approximately seventy miles north-west of the unremarkable town of Roswell, New Mexico. This debris consisted of what he described as 'rubber strips, tinfoil, a rather tough paper and sticks'. No mention of flying saucers or aliens. But whatever it was that Brazel had stumbled upon on that fateful day, and what took place afterwards, has since become a minefield of facts, half-truths, claims and counterclaims spanning more than fifty years. Unravelling the true story is no easy task so long after the event, especially as Brazel and other key characters are deceased. And invariably, where the world of conspiracy theories and secret government operations overlap, the waters have become increasingly muddied. Theory has built upon theory, layer upon layer, to such an extent that it would take an archaeologist to unearth the truth, so deeply is it buried. So grab your spade and let's start digging.

Appropriately enough, it was on Independence Day, almost three weeks after the initial discovery, that Mac Brazel decided to return to the site and gather up some of the debris. That summer the USA had been gripped by a spate of sightings of mysterious flying objects – some accounts suggest as many as 800 in what became known as the 'great UFO craze of 1947' – and upon reflection Brazel thought that perhaps it might be best to hand his find over to the Chaves County Sheriff in Roswell. The dutiful sheriff immediately notified the nearby military base at Roswell Army Air Field (RAAF), home to the elite 509th Bomb Group, the only nuclear strike force in the world and including the *Enola Gay* of Hiroshima fame. The Air Force responded quickly by sending three intelligence officers, including Major Jesse Marcel, to investigate the scene.

And that would probably have been the end of the matter, except at noon the following day the Public Information Officer at RAAF, Major Walter Hunt, put out an extraordinary press statement announcing the recovery of wreckage from a 'flying disk'. Hunt is no longer alive, and therefore it remains a mystery as to what possessed him to make such a sensational statement. Besides, it should be

Wreckage of what appears to be
a not so simple weather balloon
is displayed for the press at Fort
Worth on 8 July 1947. (US Air
Force)

remembered that at that time a 'flying disk' didn't necessarily equate with aliens
and national anxieties about invading hordes from the skies had as much to do
with little 'red' men as the green variety. Could he have been deliberately playing
on the wave of UFO mania to draw attention away from something else?
Certainly the Air Force did not expect the statement to have such an immediate
effect, with the telephone switchboards at the airbase jammed with calls from the
media and the public alike. Four hours later Colonel Blanchard, Hunt's
commanding officer, took control of the situation and ordered an immediate
retraction of the press release. He was too late, as demonstrated by the banner
headline in the local newspaper the *Roswell Daily Record*, which proclaimed
'RAAF Captures Flying Saucer on Ranch'.

Colonel Blanchard then ordered the debris to be flown to Fort Worth AAF in
Texas, where Brigadier General Roger Ramey, commander of the Eighth Air
Force at Fort Worth, inspected it and consulted with his weather officer on the
base who correctly identified the fragments as nothing more than bits of a
'weather balloon'. In an attempt to defuse the growing wave of hysteria, Ramey
then called a second press conference on 8 July, where the newsmen
photographed the debris being examined by a contrite Major Marcel. Ramey
asserted that the announcement about a flying disk had been nothing more than
a simple 'misunderstanding' and accordingly the *Daily Record* now sang a different
tune, 'Ramey Empties Roswell Saucer'. And there the story apparently died a

natural death. There was no Roswell 'incident' in 1947. The American public soon lost interest in this event and it gradually faded from memory until a little over thirty years later.

In 1978 an article was published in the *National Inquirer* in which Jesse Marcel, one of the three intelligence officers originally sent to the site, now claimed that he had in fact recovered UFO debris back in 1947. Several UFO researchers took a keen interest in Marcel's claims and in 1980 two authors, Charles Berlitz and William Moore, published their book, entitled *The Roswell Incident*. They were convinced that the weather balloon story given out by the Air Force was nothing more than a cover. After interviews with several witnesses they maintained that the government had not only retrieved a flying saucer at Roswell but also alien bodies. In some of the more extreme accounts these witnesses had the crash site teeming with armed military police pouring over the wreckage, and one version even suggested that President Truman had arrived with an entourage of experts desperately trying to translate the last words of a dying alien. The general gist of all this was that a saucer and alien bodies were transferred to a hangar at the Roswell airbase before being moved on to a highly secret government installation where they remain to this day.

The Roswell 'incident', as it was known thereafter, continued to gather momentum with a flow of new witnesses coming forward to talk about their experiences to authors, journalist and TV hosts. Meanwhile, the US Air Force (USAF, formerly the USAAF), stuck to the weather balloon story despite mounting pressure from the likes of Congressman Steven Schiff of New Mexico. A champion of the Freedom of Information Act, he began lobbying Washington to fully investigate this matter until in September 1994 the USAF published its answer. In a document entitled 'The Roswell Report: Fact Versus Fiction in the New Mexico Desert', it finally came clean – the weather balloon story had been a lie. Mac Brazel's debris had come from a balloon all right, but it was no weather balloon. This was a highly sensitive military programme codenamed Mogul, a project so shrouded in secrecy and compartmentalised in structure and execution that very few participants had known its real purpose.

This could explain why Walter Hunt, the Public Information Officer at RAAF Roswell in 1947, had not initially identified the debris as coming from a standard weather balloon. The sort he was probably familiar with on the airbase would have been relatively small and equipped with radiosonde transmitters to return their data to the ground. It is my belief that Hunt may have realised that the Roswell debris was sensitive and accordingly he made his famous flying disk statement to draw interest away from the real purpose of the balloon launches. By deliberately associating them with the crankier element, he hoped to deter further serious interest or investigation. That he spectacularly failed to do so is in no doubt. However, Hunt was not in a position to know about Project Mogul and it wasn't until 1994 that the USAF's Roswell Report lifted the lid.

Mogul had been conceived by Dr Maurice Ewing of Columbia University, New York. During the Second World War he had conducted research for the US Navy into what was known as the 'sound channel', demonstrating that an underwater explosion could be heard thousands of miles away with microphones placed at a predetermined depth. Ewing deduced that if sound waves could be transmitted by currents deep in the ocean, then it was possible that an equivalent sound channel in the upper atmosphere might also exist. Knowing full well that the Soviets had the capability to build a nuclear bomb, the Americans hoped that Mogul would provide them with a means of listening for test detonations on the other side of the world using low-frequency acoustic microphones at high altitudes.

The configuration for Mogul's constant-level balloons was quite distinctive. It consisted of a 600ft 'train' of up to two dozen or more standard 350 gram neoprene (and later polyethylene) weather balloons. They were spaced at 20ft intervals and beneath them a string of 'rawin' ('radar wind') targets was suspended, plus a return parachute and an array of test equipment, including microphones, transmitters, dry-cell batteries and containers holding ballast. Individually these components were unclassified items and therefore unlikely to attract particular interest if they fell into the wrong hands.

The project was coordinated by the Air Material Command (AMC) based at Wright Field in Ohio, and preliminary test flights were made from Bethlehem, Pennsylvania, in April 1947. When these failed due to high wind speeds at that location, the team relocated to Alamogordo Army Air Field (now Holloman AFB) in New Mexico – about eighty miles and the other side of the Saccramento Mountains from the ranch where Mac Brazel worked – and most Mogul launches over the next four years originated from there. (In the following year some also flew in the Pacific to monitor the Sandstone atomic tests at Entiwetok Atoll.)

On 4 June 1947, Mogul test flight No.4 launched from Alamogordo and the string of balloons floated high over the mountains before the tracking signal was lost. According to the 'Roswell Report', Brazel's description of tinfoil, tape and sticks was 'consistent with a balloon device and most likely from one of the Mogul balloons that had not been previously recovered'.

There was one particular detail concerning the debris which the report hoped to clear up. Some of the eye witnesses claimed that the wreckage had been embellished with mysterious markings, some form of hieroglyphics in pink or purple. The kite-like radar target devices consisted of a balsa wood framework covered with metallic paper, but curiously they had been assembled using a plastic adhesive tape featuring stylised flower designs. This was because they had been constructed under contract by a toy factory and post-war material shortages meant the company had used some leftover tape that was to hand.

The USAF concluded that their research had uncovered no evidence that the event which took place at Roswell in 1947, 'involved any type of extraterrestrial spacecraft'. End of story. Except that no effort had been made to explain why so many people thought they had seen aliens, dead or alive or both, at the Roswell site. Several had spoken of these creatures as having common characteristics – four-fingered hands, hairless pear-shaped heads with only minimal features, and one-piece suits. Some actually went so far as to compare them to dummies or dolls.

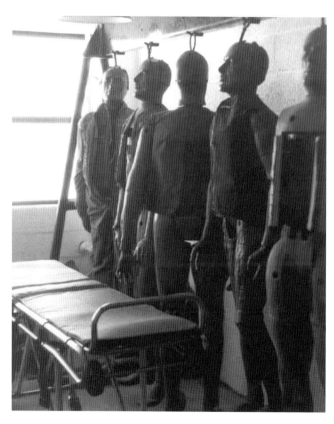

Sierra Sams – manufactured by the Sierra Engineering Company of Sierra Madre. Were these anthropomorphic test dummies the cause of so many claimed sightings of alien bodies? (US Air Force)

Clearly tired of the whole affair, the USAF issued yet another 'final' report, released a week before Roswell's fiftieth anniversary in 1997, emphatically entitling it 'The Roswell Report: Case Closed'. Despite the audible groans of the ufologists, it revealed yet more secret military balloon programmes. Between 1954 and 1959 Project High-Dive had been concerned with testing a revolutionary ultra high-altitude parachute, but because the initial tests were so dangerous they used lifelike anthropomorphic dummies carried aloft beneath balloons. Some of these dummies, says the Air Force, landed in the Roswell vicinity. 'We would send over helicopter recovery crews with a number of body bags and pack them in the bags as soon as we got there', recalled one of High Dive's technicians. The dummies – known as 'Sierra Sams' because they were manufactured by the Sierra Engineering Company of Sierra Madre – were bald, almost featureless and dressed in standard USAF one-piece jumpsuits. Sometimes a converted ambulance would be used for the recovery work and this frequently features in the accounts of the eye-witnesses. But the conspiracy theorists remained unconvinced because the High Dive experiments did not begin until a full seven years after the Roswell 'incident'. And what about the evidence of their star witness, Glen Dennis?

Dennis had been working at the Ballard Funeral Home in Roswell in 1947, and he stated that on 6 July he drove an injured airman to the hospital at Walkers airbase. It was at the hospital entrance that he looked into the back of a military ambulance where he saw debris, some of which featured hieroglyphics. When entering the hospital a highly agitated nurse sent him away and an angry red-haired Air Force captain threatened him, warning him to keep quiet about what he had seen. The following day the nurse told him that alien post mortems had been conducted in the hospital the day before, but apparently the doctors had abandoned the work because the odour of the corpses was overpowering. The USAF's response to the Dennis story is that it is no more than a confused mix of details brought together from two separate Air Force accidents, one in 1956 and the other three years later. Psychologists describe this amalgamation of memories as confabulation, when a person mixes real memories with their own interpretations and other accounts of events to produce what to them is a genuine and vivid recollection of events.

In June 1956, a KC-97 aircraft had crashed in the desert killing eleven crew members; military personnel had immediately surrounded the crash site to keep the public away while the burnt and mangled bodies of the crew were removed to Walkers airbase. However, because of the strong smell of burnt flesh and aviation fuel the post mortems were stopped, the bodies were resealed in body bags and then sent to the Ballard Funeral Home, where refrigeration was available. This is where Dennis worked.

The second accident occurred when High Dive had reached the stage at which dummies could provide no further data, and the tests continued with human guinea pigs. Under the codename Excelsior, USAF personnel were preparing to make the long lonely leap from the edge of space and training for this project took place under the strictest security. Captain Joe Kittinger volunteered for the mission, and along with two other pilots, Captains Dan Fulgham and William Kaufman, ascended in an open gondola on 21 May 1959 on a low-altitude training flight. Unfortunately, when the balloon landed near Roswell, the gondola rolled end over end until it came to rest upside down with Fulgham's head trapped between its edge and the ground. He and Kaufman were taken by helicopter direct to Walkers airbase, by which time Fulgham's head had swollen like a balloon to twice its normal size, and wrapped in bandages his presence in the hospital was bound to attract attention. The wreckage was collected by a converted ambulance and also taken to the base where it was parked in exactly the same position where Dennis claimed to have seen alien wreckage. Meanwhile a red-haired Kittinger, uninjured in the accident, was arranging the return of their equipment back to Wrights Paterson airbase and he probably did ask people not to discuss what they had seen.

Mark Rodeghier of the Centre for UFO Studies remains unconvinced by the report, and he summed up the feelings of the ufologists, describing its findings as 'preposterous' and 'another government whitewash'. 'If the Air Force, in good faith, treated the events as occurring in 1947, they would have been stuck without an explanation.' Then again, the USAF was on a hiding to nothing as it is near impossible to prove that something hadn't happened. It had already

On 16 August 1960, Joe Kittinger takes his 'long lonely leap' from an altitude of 102,800ft. (US Air Force)

admitted to earlier cover ups and had not done itself any favours by producing one secret military balloon project after another. Yet there was more to come. Flying saucers really had landed in the desert. From 1966 until 1972 the balloon unit at Holloman airbase, New Mexico, had conducted tests for NASA's Viking, Surveyor and Voyager space programmes. These included taking the saucer-shaped Viking Mars lander to 100,000ft, and releasing it to freefall back to the desert. The landers were stored in hangars at the base and they may have sparked stories of flying saucers as the Viking nose cone in particular does bear an uncanny resemblance to some of the dioramas on display at Roswell's UFO attractions.

The 1997 'Case Closed' report concludes that 'from being the rather benign description of the "event" and the recovery of some material as described in the original newspaper accounts, the "Roswell Incident" has since grown to mythical (if not mystical) proportions in the eyes and minds of some researchers'. It has to be said in conclusion that there is not one single photograph of extraterrestrial debris, saucers or aliens – apart from some discredited autopsy footage – and not one piece of physical evidence to examine under a microscope. As Deon Crosby, Director of the International UFO and Research Centre in Roswell, admits, 'I wish we had a piece of debris. We don't. I wish we had a photograph of the crash site before the retrieval. We don't. I wish we had a photograph of the bodies. We don't have any of these things. What we have is many hundreds of

Flying saucers really did land in the New Mexico desert. A mock-up of the Viking Mars lander is prepared for a drop experiment from a balloon in August 1967. (NASA)

By cruising at the same speed as the wind the USS *Valley Forge* aircraft carrier creates calm conditions for the launch of a high-altitude Skyhook balloon in 1960. Note how the smoke from the ship's funnel goes straight upwards. (US Navy)

witnesses.' But why should he worry? The town has become a Mecca for UFO tourists and it is estimated that around 20,000 people a year will pour into the museums and gift shops.

Did aliens crash in the desert? Is this merely an enduring Cold War myth born out of the fears and anxieties of the time, or maybe it is all an elaborate government conspiracy? USAF Colonel Richard Weaver, author of the 1994 'Roswell Report', told CNN, 'I don't think the government is capable of putting together a decent conspiracy.' Other theories abound and include one recently published in *Popular Mechanics* which suggests that the military were testing secret wartime German or Japanese saucer technology. Certainly everyone agrees that something did crash near Roswell in the summer of 1947. For my part, I firmly believe that it was a balloon, but then that probably makes me part of the conspiracy too.

Does the USAF think that the whole matter has now been put to rest? 'Of course not', commented one Defence Department spokesman. And a sceptical Mark Rodeghier of the Centre for UFO studies agrees: 'We look forward in eager anticipation to the next "final" Air Force report.'

14

SPY IN THE SKY

On 19 August 1960, a Soviet show-trial sentenced American pilot Gary Powers to ten years' detention after his U2 high-altitude reconnaissance aircraft had been brought down by ground-to-air missiles near the armaments centre at Sverdlovsk. But long before Powers' plight had hit the headlines, the USA had been operating a secret overflight programme using spy balloons.

In the latter years of the Second World War a new type of high-altitude balloon had been made possible by the work of Dr Otto C. Winzen, an American scientist who had developed the synthetic lightweight material polyethylene. With the prospect of military aircraft flying ever higher, and even manned spaceflight just on the horizon, there was an urgent need to gather data on conditions in the upper atmosphere. Polyethylene balloons provided the ideal means to do this as they were relatively cheap to manufacture (the seams could be heat welded instead of glued as with the old fabrics) and they could carry large payloads to considerable heights. Previously, high-flying research balloons had been hampered by the weight of their rubberised cotton fabrics resulting in an altitude 'ceiling' or limit of around 70,000ft. (If you made the balloons bigger they didn't fly any higher because of the subsequent increase in envelope weight.) Experimental flights commenced in 1947 with the polyethylene 'Skyhooks' – a term coined by the US Navy's Office of Naval Research (ONR) – attaining altitudes of 100,000ft or so. However, as is often the case, the dividing line blurred between purely scientific research and the needs of the military and both the USAF and US Navy were to be closely involved in every aspect of these high-altitude studies.

Big enough to be easily seen by an observer on the ground, the vast polyethylene envelopes shimmered with a reflective metallic appearance, often changing colour as they caught the last rays of the sun. These were single balloons as opposed to Mogul's long string of smaller balloons, and although shaped like an inverted teardrop they were easily mistaken for a disk when seen from the ground.

It is not surprising that the first major spate of flying disk or saucer sightings coincided with their launches. In January of 1948, just months after the first

Skyhook launch, a flying disk was reported high above Kentucky. The tower crew at Godman Field could see the object and called up a group of four incoming F-51 Mustangs of the Kentucky Air National Guard to investigate. One aircraft, short on fuel, continued on its way, while the other three began to climb with their flight leader Captain Thomas F. Mantell in the lead. He radioed back to Godman tower, 'I have an object in sight above and ahead of me, and it appears to be moving at about half my speed or approximately 180 miles an hour.' The tower asked him to describe it. 'It appears to be a metallic object, or possibly a reflection from a metallic object and it is of tremendous size.' As Mantell climbed beyond 20,000ft his two wingmen peeled off – none of the aircraft had carried sufficient oxygen for such a high flight. 'I am trying to take a closer look', came Mantell's final message before he blacked out through hypoxia. His F-51 continued to climb for a while and then began an arching turn to the left, accelerating into a steep dive. Mantell may have regained consciousness as the aircraft plummeted, but it was too late and the strain tore the F-51 into several pieces before it hit the ground.

This episode contained all the ingredients to become an enduring part of UFO mythology, including a cover up by the authorities. USAF officials stated at the enquiry that Mantell had most likely been chasing the planet Venus which was bright enough to be seen even in daylight, and only later was it revealed that he had probably been attempting to intercept a Skyhook launched from Camp Ripley earlier that day. Curiously though, the launches had not been kept especially secret, and indeed several magazines published articles about them at the time. As early as May 1948 the cover of *Popular Science* featured what appeared to be a colossal aerial jellyfish and asked, 'Are secret balloons the flying saucers?' Inside, a seven-page article described the balloons in considerable detail. 'Twenty miles above the Earth, the US Navy is hanging its laboratories in space. Balloons that swell to seventy-seven times their starting size provide the floating platforms.' It went on to explain that this was Project Skyhook. 'No explorations initiated in this postwar period are more pregnant with meaning for the future than this one, carried out by General Mills, Inc, of Minneapolis…' The amount of information given in this article, including several photographs of the radiosondes and instruments, is somewhat surprising in the context of supposedly secret operations. Was it part of a cover up to reinforce that these were indeed harmless 'weather' balloons? When it described the payload the article had hinted at matters more clandestine. 'Radiosondes, parachutes, tiny radio transmitting stations, radar reflectors, cosmic ray counters, special telemetering equipment, and other devices, about which the government maintains secrecy, have been sent aloft under a single plastic bubble.'

By early 1951, 270 Skyhooks had been launched, most of which were employed in legitimate scientific research, in particular in the field of cosmic ray studies, but as the chill wind of the Cold War intensified the Pentagon and CIA had other missions in mind. The vast interior of postwar Russia, with its great industrial and military complexes, remained a closed book to the outside world with the USAF's reconnaissance aircraft flights restricted to the fringes, with only occasional and very limited deeper incursions.

This veil of secrecy was regarded in different ways by the opposing superpowers. The Americans, fearing the unknown, assumed the worst and they felt threatened. Whereas for the Soviets, secrecy equated with security and strength as their apparent military might was mostly built on a bluff. As Churchill had put it, the Soviet Union was 'a riddle wrapped inside a mystery inside an enigma'. And set against this atmosphere of mutual mistrust, each side continued to feed upon its opponent's every action to reinforce its own entrenched position.

With the death of Stalin in March 1953, the White House sensed a slight thawing in relations and in July of 1955 the 'big four' world leaders met for a summit meeting in Geneva. President Eisenhower, British Prime Minister Anthony Eden and French Premier Edgar Faure attended, along with the Soviet Premier Nikolai A. Bulganin, although it was quite clear that it was his fellow delegate, Nikita Khrushchev, who already held the strings of power. On the second afternoon Eisenhower astounded the assembled leaders when he presented his 'Open Skies' proposals, and directly addressing his comments to the

When President Eisenhower's 'Open Skies' proposals met with a brick wall from the Soviets, he was left to agonise over the use of unmanned surveillance balloons over Soviet territory.

Soviet delegates, he outlined a course of action for the two nations. 'To give each other a complete blueprint of our military establishments… To provide within our countries facilities for aerial photography to the other country – we to provide you the facilities within our country, ample facilities for aerial reconnaissance, where you can make all the pictures you choose and take them to your own country to study; you to provide exactly the same facilities for us and we to make these examinations, and by this step to convince the world that we are providing as between ourselves against the possibility of great surprise attack, thus lessening danger and relaxing tensions.'

The British and French leaders approved the bold plan, even Bulganin appeared agreeable, but Khrushchev dismissed it all as an espionage plot by the Americans. Eisenhower later commented, 'Khrushchev's own purpose was evident – at all costs to keep the USSR a closed society.' In waving aside the accusations of spying, Eisenhower conveniently failed to mention that the USA already had surveillance measures in hand.

Five years before the summit a meeting of the Air Force Scientific Advisory Board had discussed ways of extending photographic coverage of the USSR. They found that no aircraft yet built could fly high enough to undertake such a mission, and satellite technology was still several years in the future. The answer lay in the new Skyhooks. Hiding behind a string of codenames – one for every step in development – including Projects Gopher, Grandson and Greyback, within the all-encompassing Project Genetrix – the President gave the balloon reconnaissance programme a priority level equal only to that of the development of the hydrogen bomb. The plan was to launch camera-carrying balloons from five locations – Gardermoen in Norway, Evanton in Scotland, Giebelstadt and Oberpfaffenhofen in West Germany and Incirlik in Turkey – to be borne by the silent winds high over the Iron Curtain and across the expanse of Russian and Chinese territory before recovery over the Pacific. A protracted period of development and testing of the balloons and systems was conducted in the early 1950s and the reconnaissance balloons were designated as WS (Weapons System) 119L.

Two sizes of balloon were made available, the 128TT with a volume of 800,000 cu ft and a float-altitude of between 75,000 to 85,000ft, and the smaller 66CT balloons which could only reach up to 60,000ft. (Why these heights were chosen is unclear, as balloons capable of attaining 100,000ft were available.) The all-important payload was made up of several elements – two ballast containers filled with fine steel shot, a control box containing the electronics and a transmitter to indicate the balloon's position, plus a 57in-high large camera box (about the same size as a domestic fridge). This housed the DMQ-1 and later the DMQ-2 camera packages, and was wrapped in a thick layer of polystyrene to protect the equipment from the cold and keep it afloat in the sea. This equipment was suspended from a 'spreader' or load bar and a long extendible metal rod was added to aid recovery, though unfortunately this made the balloons more visible to Soviet radar. Between the load bar and the envelope was a large parachute to bring the 1,400lb payload down safely.

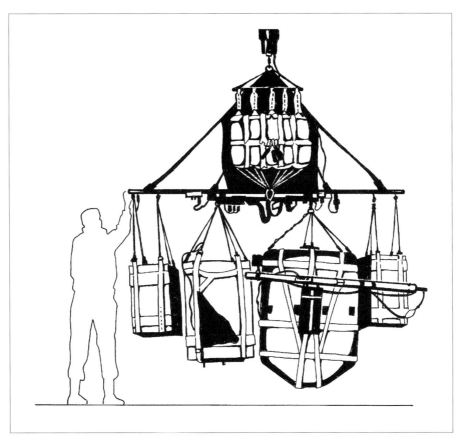

WS-119L payload. Showing from left to right the ballast box, control box, camera gondola, and second ballast box. The long pole is to assist with water recovery.

Despite ongoing progress with Genetrix, President Eisenhower remained very nervous about its deployment, and the Open Skies proposals put forward at Geneva had been one way of putting the Soviets to the test. Their rejection served to strengthen the case for the balloons and, in January 1956, the Genetrix overflights began. An elaborate cover plan known as 'White Cloud' was already underway, beginning with twenty weather research balloons launched from Hawaii and Alaska during the first half of 1956. These served to deliberately blur the distinctions between Genetrix and genuine weather balloons, and press coverage of White Cloud was encouraged. The Radio Free Europe propaganda balloons were also active around this time, to further confuse matters (see Chapter 15). And in parallel with Genetrix, the Moby Dick programme had been instigated by the USAF back in May 1951, ostensibly to obtain more detailed information about the behaviour of the wind at high altitudes. The first Moby Dick balloon had lifted off on 19 February 1953 from the Naval Air Station in Vernalis, California. This project was not classified as secret as it helped to establish the weather balloon cover for future and more sensitive flights, and –

'hey presto!' – in 1956 it was announced that the Moby Dick studies were being extended to Europe and the Far East.

The first wave of Genetrix balloons lifted off on 10 January 1956 – eight from Incirlik and one from Giebelstadt. The decision whether to launch from individual sites depended on the wind direction and weather conditions. Clearly the German and Turkish sites had some advantage in being so close to the Soviet Bloc countries. The maximum altitude for the balloons was set at 55,000ft and the automatic ballasting systems ensured that they would not descend below 40,000ft while traversing the Soviet Union, although why this operational height was chosen is puzzling since it put the balloons within range of Soviet defences. The cameras, activated by light-sensitive photo-cells, were set to ensure an overlap on the images, and other timers were set to separate the payload and dump ballast if the balloon did not climb high enough, or to drop ballast to maintain the minimum altitude during the remainder of the flight. A final timer triggered the high frequency recovery beacon at the end of the flight, and the times for these depended on the launch location and the anticipated wind speeds. A balloon from Turkey, for example, was expected to reach the Pacific in perhaps fifty hours, while one from Scotland might take double that time.

By 13 January the first of the balloons arrived at the recovery zone and began transmitting its whereabouts to the crews of the C–119 aircraft. They activated the radio-controlled gondola release mechanism which separated the payload at 50,000ft, sending it floating down by parachute while the balloon shot upwards and burst into thousands of harmless fragments. At 9,000ft the payload was hooked aboard the specially equipped aircraft.

More launches followed in quick succession as the game plan was to send as many balloons as possible before the Soviets realised what was happening. Inevitably, some balloons went astray, coming down in Sweden, Norway and even in Kent, England, but most reached Communist airspace. Each gondola carried a multilingual placard stating, 'This box came from the sky. It is harmless. It has weather data in it. Notify the authorities. You will receive a valuable reward if you turn it in as it is.' For illiterate finders the message was conveyed in pictures and for the Russians another placard was later added.

It came as a surprise to the US that the Soviet radar was able to detect the balloons; their only difficulty was in dealing with them. The Mig fighters could reach them, but only just, and at those altitudes they were at the limits of controllability. Besides, it was incredibly tricky for a fast jet travelling at 300 knots to make contact with a relatively slow-moving balloon. Anti-aircraft guns could also reach them, but the shell fire tended to disperse making accurate targeting almost impossible. However, as the Genetrix balloons continued to drift across their airspace the Soviets observed them carefully. It was soon noted that when the balloons cooled, at dusk and at dawn, they were at their lowest and most vulnerable as well as being at their most visible in the low sunlight. The shoot-down rate gradually improved, although considerably more balloons were being lost to the weather at the launch sites and recovery zones, or they simply wandered off course. 219 balloons were launched in the first two weeks of the operation, of which around three-quarters went missing.

As the White House braced itself for a torrent of protest, the Kremlin remained curiously quiet. In part this may have been due to the Soviets' success in tackling the balloons, and of the 112 balloons launched between 26 and 30 January, not one made it through. The silence couldn't last, and on 4 February 1956 the diplomatic storm broke with a protest delivered to the US Ambassador in Moscow. This described the 'spheres' as 'a gross violation of Soviet airspace… contrary to obligations assumed by the US government in accordance with the UN charter and incompatible with normal relations between states. The Soviet Union presents a decisive protest and demands that the government of the United States takes measures for the prompt cessation of the impermissible activity of the American military organs.' They were also upset about the propaganda balloon campaign being waged in Europe.

In response the Americans put their fingers in their ears and hummed. Eisenhower, in truth, felt that balloon reconnaissance was a 'dirty trick' and he worried that this highly visible form of peacetime espionage could seriously worsen relations with the Communists. Nonetheless, the cover story was trotted out and the Soviets were chided over their 'apparent confusion' with harmless weather balloons. An Air Force press release even had the gall to ask the Soviet government to return any gondolas that had come into its possession! This enraged the Soviets and their response was to display a number of the gondolas, together with approximately fifty balloon envelopes, at the residence of the Soviet Foreign Minister in Moscow. On 9 February, journalists were invited to inspect and photograph them while a meteorologist expert explained why these could not be Met balloons. They were then condemned as a hazard to aircraft and as an American attempt to conduct a policy to take the world to the brink of war. In this way the Soviets succeeded in getting a halt to the programme, and although the USAF proposed sending balloons at higher altitudes the President decided that enough was enough and Project Genetrix was terminated on 1 March 1956.

Compared with the political damage incurred, Genetrix had done little to probe the darkness of the unknown Soviet territory. Of the 448 balloons released in total, sixty-six had made it to the recovery zone, and of these only forty had returned photographs. On the plus side these images covered the equivalent of 8 per cent, or over one million square miles, of Soviet and Chinese territory. And while that may not sound much, it was 8 per cent more than nothing and in financial terms this was deemed a very cost effective exercise. On the other hand, the balloons had actually caused the Soviets to sharpen their air defences, especially in improving high-altitude aircraft and the surface-to-air missiles which eventually brought down Gary Powers.

There are several footnotes to this story. The day before the 9 February Moscow press conference, a Soviet Met balloon had been found by the US Army in northern Japan. It was tiny in comparison with the Skyhooks, only 5ft high, but it was exactly the sort of ammunition the US had prayed for. Better still, it was confirmed that other Soviet Met balloons had been found in Alaska over the previous three years. With tongue pressed ever so lightly in cheek, the US handed a note to the Soviet Ambassador, stating, 'It is illogical that the Soviet government should desire one rule for itself and another for the rest of the world', and demanded the return of Genetrix gondolas in exchange for their balloons.

In July of 1958, a limited balloon reconnaissance programme was resumed with Operation Melting Pot. Launched from aircraft carriers in the Pacific, the WS-461L balloons achieved much greater altitudes at 100,000ft, well beyond the reach of Soviet defences, and they travelled east to west in the higher winds. Once again some carried meteorological packages, while others an improved panoramic camera, the HYAC-1. Unfortunately the timers on the backup automatic cut-down device had mistakenly been set for faster wind conditions than were actually encountered and the balloons started falling within Communist territory. Eisenhower was furious at the blunder as once again he awaited a Soviet protest, which eventually came in September and was greeted with the old tried and tested weather balloon story. So the Soviets put the equipment on display and the Americans halted the overflights. They concentrated instead on the U2 aircraft and also the new spy-satellites under the cover of the USAF's Discoverer scientific programme.

Nearly fifty years later the threads of the Project Genetrix story were picked up by the British press, who got very excited when newly released government documents revealed that balloons had launched from Scotland – something already described in some detail by Curtis Peebles in his 1991 book *The Moby Dick Project*. The real story, the one that should have been on every front page, was America's secret plans for balloon 'weapons of mass destruction'. If balloons could carry cameras deep into the heart of the Soviet Union, the military planners argued, then they could carry other payloads. In peacetime these might include propaganda material or counterfeit money to destabilise the economy, but in a throwback to the Japanese Fu-Go the proposed wartime payloads included incendiary bombs to set forests ablaze, plus nerve gas and biological weapons including anthrax spores, undulant fever, smallpox and yellow fever. Soviet agriculture was also to be targeted with wheat and potato blight, plus infectious livestock diseases such as foot and mouth.

Development of these 'dirty' weapons began in 1953 with the idea of a cluster of bombs carried by balloon, then dropped on their targets releasing a cloud of destruction over an area equivalent to the footprint of a low-yield nuclear bomb. The Air Research and Development Command named the project Flying Cloud, with a weapons designation of WS-124A. Forty-one test flights were conducted within the USA in 1954, concerned in particular with the ability to accurately predict the balloon's course. This was going to be vital as a misguided balloon could cause devastation to a friendly country. But despite USAF claims that the system had a 24 per cent success rate at hitting an intended target area, their figures were not accepted by the Air Weather Service. At any rate, Flying Cloud was cancelled mainly due to the rapid proliferation in the number and destructive force of nuclear weapons. It was recognised that a war with Russia would be a fast-track to thermonuclear Armageddon with little time for the launching of balloons. But many years later these plans would come back to haunt the Pentagon in their new war against terrorism.

15

MIGHTIER THAN
THE SWORD

Locked in a nuclear standoff, the Cold War protagonists waged a propaganda war instead to win the minds and hearts of the people. In the USA the National Security Council instructed the CIA to 'initiate and conduct psychological operations designed to counteract Soviet-inspired activities', and against a background in which the free flow of information, both within eastern Europe and from outside, was tightly controlled, Radio Free Europe (RFE) was established in 1948. Ostensibly, at least, funding came from appeals and contributions, but in fact it was provided by the CIA. The role of RFE was to broadcast foreign-language programmes direct to those countries under Soviet control. While the rhetoric reflected certain Western positions, it was to be without any direct connection to the US government.

The CIA's Special Procedures Group devised a scheme to augment the RFE radio broadcasts with a flood of propaganda leaflets delivered by balloon under the codename Project Ultimate. By the conclusion of this programme, a staggering total of around fifty million 'friendship' leaflets had been floated eastwards. The first test launch occurred in August 1951 from a site just three miles from the Czech border, and carried leaflets printed by the Free Europe Press featuring inspiring slogans such as 'A new hope is stirring… Friends of Freedom in other lands have found a new way to reach you.' The hydrogen-filled Met balloons were 4ft in diameter, and each one was capable of carrying around 3,000 leaflets. With up to 2,000 balloons launched each night when conditions were suitable, a total of eleven million leaflets were delivered to the citizens of Czechoslovakia.

In practical terms the tests were deemed a great success. Experiments were made with different types of balloons, including a tetrahedron or pillow-shape which was simple and cheap to manufacture with just a hot knife both cutting and sealing lengths of polyethylene tubing at either end. If one end is sealed at 90°, from the other a tetrahedron is formed with greater volume for a given amount of film, and tying one corner provides a perfect anchor point. An ingenious ballasting system was devised with the leaflets loaded in a cardboard carton which was held upright by the weight of dry ice; as the dry ice evaporated the carton would tip over releasing the leaflets. Eventually the balloon launchers were able to accurately anticipate the drop zone by calculating the weight of the dry ice, the lift of the balloon, its payload and the direction and speed of the wind.

Operation Prospero saw the next phase of launches. Starting on 13 July 1953 and continuing over the next four days, 6,500 balloons carrying 12,000,000 leaflets were launched from the small Bavarian town of Tirschenreuth to ride with the wind into Czechoslovakia. For the first time this was done in conjunction with RFE broadcasts announcing the launch and backing up the message on the leaflets with special radio programmes criticising recent currency reforms. Suitably warned, the Communists responded by sending aircraft and anti-aircraft guns to the border to take pot shots at the intruders, and in Prague the police loudspeakers ordered civilians to hand in any leaflets to the authorities. Clearly, thought the CIA, this coordinated onslaught of propaganda must be working and this paved the way for further launches.

In 1954 Operation Veto saw further broadcasts and balloon leaflets aimed at Czechoslovakia. Attempting to cultivate a popular appetite for the liberation of Czechoslovakia, these referred to a 'People's Opposition' which, according to RFE, was not a formal organisation but a spiritual one made up of every Czech and Slovak who was opposed to the Soviet's influence. In a remarkably long text

In the propaganda war the secret weapons were not always so secret. This Free Europe Press leaflet describes in some detail how balloons were being used to spread the word beyond the Iron Curtain. (Valhalla Aerostation)

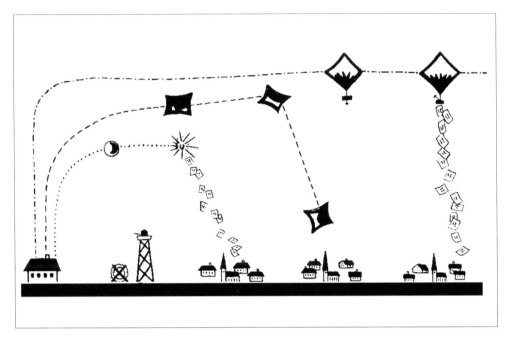

Three types of balloon delivery were employed, as this diagram published by the Free Europe Committee shows. The balloons either burst with increased internal pressure to drop their leaflets, some descended to earth with the leaflets on board, or they released them via a timer. (Valhalla Aerostation)

the leaflets listed a non-violent programme of ten demands – such as 'Housing for Families, not the State' and 'Who Does the Harvest Belong To?' – and as a symbol of opposition small stickers with the number '10' were included to be applied to Communist Party posters.

Later that year Hungary received its first swarm of balloons in Operation Focus, timed to coincide with local elections in November. Once again a set of demands – this time twelve – laid out the manifesto of a National Opposition Movement, and small '12' stickers were included. Using its new powerful transmitter in Portugal RFE backed up the launch with broadcasts as the Voice of Free Hungary.

In 1955 the final phase of RFE's balloon releases targeted Poland with Operation Spotlight following the high-profile defection of Josef Swialto, a colonel in the Polish secret police. Swialto's statements before a Congressional Committee, in which he exposed in detail the techniques employed by the Communists, was recorded and broadcast via RFE and the balloons delivered a lengthy compilation of the testimony. It is believed that Swialto's revelations resulted in a massive purge by the authorities and that thousands of Party members and government officials were dismissed.

Periodically the Communists condemned the activities of RFE, but following the Hungarian uprising in October 1956 in which over 10,000 people were killed as they rebelled against Soviet rule, the protests reached new heights.

Imperialist money, claimed an editorial in *Pravda*, 'had been used to conduct an unbridled, slanderous claim against people's Hungary... Numerous propaganda balloons had been released, radio broadcasts had been made, and the reactionary underground has been established and strengthened... creating lawlessness in Hungary.' When the Czechoslovakian authorities claimed that a fatal airliner crash had been caused by balloons straying into its path, the programme was in danger of backfiring. The Eastern Bloc media had an orgy of counterpropaganda and the CIA decided to pull the plug on the balloons and concentrate instead on RFE's broadcasts from improved transmitters.

However, it wasn't only in Europe that the Americans perceived a threat from communism. When Fidel Castro overthrew the Cuban dictatorship of Fulgenico Bastista in December 1959, the Americans hailed him as a hero, but their attitude soon changed when Castro seized American property on the island and began to openly espouse communism. Once it became clear that Castro was accepting economic and military support from the Soviet Union, President Eisenhower imposed an economic embargo on the island and the CIA began scheming his 'removal'. Just as with RFE they began by establishing an 'independent' radio station, Radio Swan, which broadcast a familiar mixture of news, music and propaganda.

When John F. Kennedy took over the Presidency in January 1960, he inherited a CIA plot to train and infiltrate anti-Castro exiles back into Cuba to stir up a rebellion. Pressure was mounting from exiles themselves and he approved the infamous landing at the Bay of Pigs which took place on 17 April 1961. The result was a fiasco, the exiles were routed by Castro's forces and there was no popular uprising. Feeling humiliated in the eyes of the world, Kennedy's administration became obsessed with ousting the Cuban leader. As the President's brother and US Attorney General, Robert Kennedy, stated, 'No time, money, effort or manpower is to be spared' in getting rid of Castro. Consequently Project Mongoose – the largest covert operation ever undertaken by the CIA – was put in motion. At its head was Brigadier General Edward Lansdale, who devised an operational plan to 'help the people of Cuba overthrow the Communist regime from within'. Lansdale advocated the starting of an American-backed revolution within Cuba supported by sabotage and economic warfare. More controversially, he called for the open use of US military forces, which only served to inflame the situation causing Castro to request additional military support from the Soviet Premier, Nikita Khrushchev. Shortly afterwards the Americans began receiving reports of increased Soviet shipping to the island and in August 1962 surveillance photographs showed that SAM missiles were being sited in Cuba. Kennedy's worst fears were confirmed in October when new photographs revealed the installation of offensive nuclear missiles. The two superpowers were locked in a face-off and for thirteen days the world stood poised on the brink of nuclear annihilation.

During the crisis the CIA continued to plan the assassination of Castro as well as all possible 'diplomatic, economic, psychological and other pressures to overthrow the Castro-Communist regime without overt employment of US military'. Sometimes their far-fetched schemes bordered on the absurd. It was suggested putting chemicals in Castro's shoes so that his body would absorb them and react by making his beard fall out – no beard, no Castro – or somehow introducing hallucinogenic chemicals into his cigars to make him appear incoherent. In parallel, the war of words was to continue against his regime and, as only recently revealed in a secret CIA memorandum directed to Lansdale on 17 September 1960, propaganda balloons had been considered as the means of spreading the word.

This eight-page document outlines a scheme to launch helium balloons from a ship, situated in international waters, which was to be chartered by a Cuban exile 'with the private financial means to establish the facility without causing questions as to how the funds were raised'. It goes on to say that this 'sponsor' will also be put in touch with a cleared firm that specialises in balloon technology to provide the balloons and helium, install launching equipment on the ship, and to train members of the crew in launching techniques.

Guidelines for the content of the propaganda leaflets followed predictable themes: 1) A return of the revolution to its original acceptable aims; 2) The betrayal of the revolution by Castro and the communists; 3) Exposing the contradictions between promises and performance; 4) The take over of Cuba by

Not only did the CIA want Fidel Castro's hair to fall out, but they concocted plans to bombard Cuba with balloon-borne leaflets to encourage a popular uprising.

Soviet Bloc communists; 5) An appeal to the masses to cooperate with the resistance; 6) Calling upon the population to commit specific acts of administrative harassment, passive resistance and simple sabotage to thwart the actions of the Communist regime, and to generally promote the *gusano libre* (free worm) symbol which, it was claimed, was synonymous with resistance against the Castro regime.

Technical studies verified the feasibility of the operation. The plan was for a vessel to cruise at night in a westerly direction approximately ten miles off the northern coast of Cuba. The balloons would be carried over the island by the prevailing low-altitude winds in the area, and after releasing their load via an automatic timing device the balloons would then fly on to disappear over the sea. It was anticipated that four launch stations could provide a capability of eighty balloons per hour.

> Depending on the type of paper used as well as the format and size of the leaflets, it is estimated that each balloon can deliver on target a payload of between 2,000 and 4,000 copies of a given leaflet. Assuming two balloon launching operations per month and the release of approximately 500 balloons per operation, it is estimated that between two and four million leaflets can be dropped over Cuban targets each month.

In addition, a variety of 'novelty items' such as *gusano libre* pin badges, toy balloons and stickers, as well as small, lightweight gramophone records might also be dropped, the numbers depending, of course, upon their weight.

Naturally the CIA had a firm eye on the issue of 'plausible denial' and the document addresses a number of potential problem areas. For instance, what if the Cubans accused America of harbouring or abetting criminals who violate Cuban airspace causing a menace to aviation? And what if a child were injured or buildings damaged by falling objects? The document reports that the risk to aircraft was explored 'during extensive tests conducted by the CIA during the 1950s, which proved it was impossible to fly a propeller-driven aircraft into an unmoored balloon'.

As the Cuban Missile Crisis intensified Mongoose was put on hold. That the CIA had ever imagined that littering the streets of Havana with leaflets and toys could rouse the people into an uprising against Castro is not perhaps so far-fetched when viewed in the context of the Alice in Wonderland world of covert operations in which even a man's beard was regarded as a viable target. Yet there is one further twist to this tale of Cold War intrigue. When this memo to Brigadier General Lansdale was finally made public in the summer of 1993, as a result of legal action taken under the US Freedom of Information Act, it was the very last of the papers relating to the Cuban Missile Crisis to be disclosed. What was it that made this document more sensitive than any of the other 3,500? Why had it been kept under wraps for thirty years? It was, and I quote the State Department, because 'disclosure could vitiate the potential usefulness of this and similar proposals in the future', and that 'intelligence sources and methods' must be protected under the National Security Act. They had wanted to keep it secret because the humble balloon was still considered a viable operational tool by the intelligence and military agencies, which goes some way to explaining why certain other covert operations are still shrouded in secrecy.

And as well as delivering propaganda and cameras, the Cold War warriors were using balloons to carry a special kind of human cargo – spies!

16
REBIRTH

The abandoned bomber-training base at Brunning, Nebraska, is a lonely and remote spot devoid of obstructions and far removed from prying eyes. It is an unlikely place to start a revolution.

The Montgolfier brothers may have captured the lifting power of hot air to show us the way to the skies, but it was the hot air balloon's sturdier and more robust cousin, the gas balloon, that had explored it and mapped its furthest reaches. Almost without exception, gas balloons, whether inflated with hydrogen or coal gas – or possibly with helium if you were American, seriously rich or served in the US Navy – had dominated the lighter-than-air scene for almost two hundred years. Even in the twentieth century, or at least for the first two thirds of it, those aviators determined to become airborne by buoyant means still selected the gas balloon to accomplish their lofty ambitions. That is, they did until the events at Brunning on 21 October 1960.

Designated the ONR X 40 Raven 1, the balloon resembled an inverted onion or teardrop – a shape determined by experimentation and now universally adopted by the hot air fraternity. Unlike a conventional gas balloon there was no net and instead the load was carried by the envelope itself. This was constructed from a strong nylon known as Flare-cloth, made by Chase-Foster, with a minimum tensile strength of 30lb/in and weighing less than 1 ounce per square yard. As a woven fabric it was, however, extremely porous and a layer of 0.0005in Mylar plastic was laminated onto the inside of the cloth. At the top or crown of the envelope was an opening 9ft across, kept closed during the flight and released by an explosive squib to spill air speedily after landing to prevent the balloon from dragging. At the bottom end of the envelope was a 12ft band of a glass cloth in case the burner flame radiated excessive heat sideways, and at its base was the open mouth where a ring acted as a transmission member between envelope and payload. The envelope itself was 39ft in diameter and held 27,000 cu ft of air – fairly big in comparison with a gas balloon – but it should be remembered that the lift of hot air is only 17lb per 1,000 cu ft compared with 65lb for hydrogen.

The payload itself was disarmingly simple. Suspended by four cables from the load-ring was a simple rectangle of plywood which sufficed as the pilot's seat, with two small fuel tanks mounted either side and a tiny burner overhead. The choice of fuel had been between petrol, paraffin and propane, all of which possess similar heat output per pound. But the first two were abandoned as the fuel needed to be pumped and the burner preheated, much like the Primus stoves used by campers, whereas propane in liquid form would be delivered to the burner under its own pressure. Initial indoor tests had gone well and everything was ready for the test flight.

The inflation took longer than anticipated with an aircraft heater fired into the flaccid envelope for a full thirty minutes before it stood upright. The pilot was none other than Ed Yost, who had been working for General Mills on the various Cold War balloon projects, including the CIA's Radio Free Europe balloons. He clambered into his seat and the burner was ignited. Cautiously Yost cranked the fuel valve a full twenty-two revolutions and with the burner firing away continuously the balloon remained wedded to the concrete. The team looked at each other in dismay, then realising that the slight breeze was cooling the envelope they began to walk the balloon downwind and before they had gone 50ft it became airborne. The burner remained at full power throughout the flight

American Ed Yost takes the first modern hot-air balloon for a flight from an abandoned airfield at Brunning, Nebraska, on 21 October 1960. But the US military were interested in more than just fostering a new aviation sport. (US Air Force)

as the balloon ascended to 500ft and levelled out of its own accord before gradually descending to the ground after twenty-five minutes. As a flight it had remarkable parallels with the original Montgolfier excursion of 1783, and in its way it was an equally momentous occasion. But why was a department of the US Navy so interested in reinventing the hot air balloon?

Gas balloons had been used to take agents into occupied Europe during the Second World War and this practice continued well into the Cold War era. The British Wing Commander Gerry Turnbull had worked on these clandestine balloon operations and before his death in 2000 he occasionally talked about them. He was once asked if he had got to know the agents he transported or whether he had heard from any of them later on. 'Of the ten I got to know well, nine of them were immediately rounded up, thanks to Philby', he replied. (Philby had headed a group of double-agents in the UK under the control of the KGB.) This was one of the few occasions when Turnbull had spoken openly about this matter because, as he asserted, he was governed by the Official Secrets Act and balloons were still considered a viable means of infiltrating agents.

As for the hot air balloon, Ed Yost says that he had been tinkering with the idea for his own amusement back in 1954, when he had built a couple of small prototypes in his backyard. The larger one had a volume of 16,000 cu ft and he fired it up with a plumber's blowtorch or 'pot' as the Americans know them. When this balloon lifted 40lb of sand ballast Yost built a bigger balloon, 27,500 cu ft in volume, fitted it with a rudimentary seat and flew it tethered in Huron, South Dakota. 'I took pictures of the darn thing, and took them back to Washington', he later recalled. For 'Washington' read 'Pentagon' where, officially at least, the USAF and US Navy, under the auspices of their Office of Naval Research (ONR), saw the balloon as a means of rescuing downed airmen.

Their vision ran something like this: A pilot shot down over Vietnam would eject from the aircraft and, instead of deploying a conventional parachute, a small hot air balloon would unfurl enabling him to hover in the area rather than fall to the ground. Presumably this would give sufficient time for a rescue aircraft to arrive on the scene and snatch him in mid-air, in much the same way as the Genetrix payloads had been retrieved. Under the title PASS, for Pilot Aerial Survival System, it all sounded plausible enough, in theory, but somehow it just didn't ring true. Firstly there was the artist's impressions of an ejecting pilot firing up a small burner to convert his parachute into a balloon – an unlikely scenario given the practicalities of inflating a balloon on the ground at the best of times. Then there was the problem of pilots floating about over hostile territory, waiting for a pick-up. Surely this left them more vulnerable than ever, just dangling there for all the world to see and moving at the sort of pace that made them easy prey for the enemy. But for me the most suspect aspect of it all was the ONR's brief in the first place; to develop a hot air balloon that could carry a man, fly for three hours, reach 10,000ft and be reusable. Three hours? That's a very long time.

The contract was awarded to a new company, Raven Industries, based at Sioux Falls in South Dakota and formed from a team of researchers from General Mills,

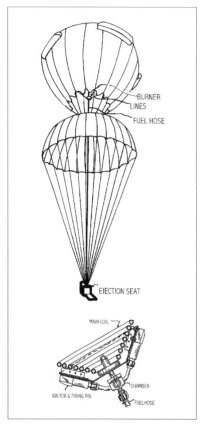

Design for a self-inflating balloon escape system, with a close-up of the burner mechanism. (Larry Nelson)

with $47,000 of finance from the ONR. Following the moderately successful first flight of the ONR X 40 Raven 1, several improvements were made. Most importantly, the burner was upgraded with a simple on/off valve for the propane supply and instead of burning unpressurised vapour, liquid propane was introduced into a jacket surrounding the burner flame – later upgraded to a coil of stainless steel tubing – where the heat pressurised it for a far greater intensity of output. Three handling lines were added to the equator to assist with the inflation and an improved inflation fan fitted with a small burner was introduced to speed up the process. By the autumn of 1961 over thirty flights had been made, all successfully, and Raven was able to report back to the ONR that their requirements had been met. 'A low-weight manned flight system capable of safely carrying one man for three hours, at altitudes up to 10,000ft had been repeatedly flown.'

Very early on in the development programme, after only four flights or so, the balloonist Don Piccard had been hired by Raven to promote the sporting side of their new 'Vulcoon', as it was christened from a combination of the words 'Vulcan', and 'balloon'. This hasty appointment so early in the developmental stages raises the question of why a branch of the US Navy had set up a company to develop this new 'sport'. Could it be that they wanted a cover for secret balloon operations, by the CIA possibly, and saw that if the hot air balloons became commonplace their special operations in more sensitive parts of the world might attract less suspicion? This is conjecture, admittedly, although it is undeniable that the business of launching balloons, for whatever purpose, would become far easier and cheaper if hot air became the lifting medium instead of gas. And if these experiments initiated a new popular sport, then so much the better.

In 1961 the British broadcaster and journalist Anthony Smith was looking for a balloon to conduct flights in Africa, much in the vein of Jules Verne's epic tales. 'I was dithering whether to use a gas balloon, much favoured by every European balloonist, or one of the new American contrivances. Don was full of enthusiasm, of course, for selling a hot air balloon to me', he recalls. 'By no means had Raven, by then, manufactured a balloon suitable for my purpose.' The Americans, for their part, reckoned that they could overcome all the shortcomings of their hot air balloons. 'What better way, I now realise, for hot air ballooning to become a popular pastime than for a journalist film-maker and author to promote it?' Smith chose the more reliable gas balloon for his expedition and his books went on to inspire many members of the British Balloon & Airship Club which he founded in 1965. Meanwhile, the hot air balloon continued to evolve rapidly and in 1963 Yost and Piccard proved their concept by successfully flying across the English Channel. The cheapness and practicality of the propane-powered balloon made the sport accessible to many, but I wonder how many of this new breed of aeronauts realise the unpalatable truth that the hot air balloon, conceived as a child of warfare by Joseph Montgolfier, has enjoyed its greatest resurgence as a direct result of the Cold War and the needs of the military and intelligence community.

Still, you can't blame the child for its parents, and while hot air ballooning has become an enjoyable pastime for some, we would do well to remember that for others it is not so much a great adventure as a desperate and dangerous flight to freedom. In pride of place at the Checkpoint Charlie Museum in Berlin sits a ramshackle cluster of inverted propane tanks mounted on a platform just 4.5ft square. In 1979 this contraption had carried eight people – the youngest just two years old – across the Iron Curtain to the West. It had been an astonishing feat of bravery as the Strelzyk and Wetzel families had derived their knowledge of ballooning only from a few books. Fearing discovery at every turn they had scoured the department stores throughout Eastern Germany buying up lengths of fabric here and there, but never too much so as to attract the suspicion of the authorities. This was especially tricky as their first attempt had ended disastrously a few months earlier when their balloon had come down 600ft short of their goal, dumping them on the wrong side of the border and within no-man's land. Abandoning the equipment they then began a frantic race against time to construct a replacement before the police could trace them. Working secretly on an antique sewing machine they completed a 108,000 cu ft balloon in three months, and then the wait began for the wind to blow to the West.

At the Checkpoint Charlie museum in Berlin an exhibition celebrates the brave flight of the Strelzyk and Wetzel families who flew their precarious home-built balloon to freedom in 1979. Not all politically motivated aeronauts fared so well and some would die in the attempt. (Phil Dunnington)

At 2.40 a.m. on 16 September all was ready and the multicoloured balloon slowly lifted off from a remote location near Poesnnek, illuminated against the black sky by the glare of the single burner. Every moment was fraught with danger. As they climbed into the night sky powerful search lights fingered the darkness, revealing that they had been spotted. Peter Strelczyk took the balloon up to 7,900ft. It was bitterly cold and they were terrified. At any moment the fuel system could have frozen solid, sending them plunging out of control. As they began to descend the burner spluttered on the last meagre drops of propane and still at 6,500ft they were suddenly engulfed in darkness, falling out of the sky at 1,000ft per minute. The balloon skimmed some trees before slamming into dense bushes; it bounced upwards one last time and then came to rest, with only Günter Wetzel sustaining slight injuries. The flight had lasted twenty-eight minutes and after travelling for twenty-three miles they had landed near the small town of Nalia, in West Germany.

The success of the Strelzyk and Wetzel families inevitably attracted imitators. In 1983 the Czechoslovakian cycling champion Robert Hutyra, along with his wife and two children, escaped in a home-built balloon to Austria. But another attempt went tragically wrong when W. Freudenburg was killed in 1989 by falling from a balloon. It was stated by East German sources that clothing and other items found at the site indicated that a woman had also been present on the flight, but had not been found.

In the four decades since Ed Yost's flight at Brunning the sport of ballooning has flourished all over the world and there are more balloons flying now than ever before in this unique craft's two-hundred-year history – most of them borne aloft by hot air. Whether it would have flourished like it did without the interest of the ONR is hard to say, but I for one will be eternally grateful for the pleasure their aerostatic offspring has given me. And as for the various military applications for balloons, the story is far from over.

17

FAREWELL BOO-BOO
AND BULGY

It was the day the balloon came down. On 31 March 1995 the RAF's Balloon Operational Squadron was disbanded, bringing an end to more than a century of British military ballooning. The Closing-Down Ceremony, at Hullavington Barracks in Wiltshire, was conducted by Air Vice Marshal D. Cousins and Squadron Leader C.R. Pickthall, who had commanded the Unit since 1990. He said afterwards, 'The balloons will be missed and the Service will have lost a very cost-effective tool and an extremely reliable servant, which has helped the UK Armed Forces for many years and whose history is older than that of the RAF itself.'

I suspect that most people reading of this ceremony in the following morning's newspapers were surprised to learn that the RAF had still been operating balloons at all. In fact their use for parachute training had begun in 1941 after Churchill had called for large numbers of men to be trained in preparation for the liberation of Europe. Not enough aircraft were available for the task and so the MkXID kite balloon was recruited. In appearance this resembles the standard wartime barrage balloons, although it is more than double the size with a volume of 45,000 cu ft and capable of lifting a cage plus four jumpers and their Parachute Jump Instructor (PJI). The balloons soon proved to be an ideal platform, allowing the novice to make their first descent in controlled conditions, and ever since then these balloons have remained the mainstay of parachute training in the UK, even during the preparations for the Gulf War when the C130 aircraft were busy elsewhere.

The Balloon Unit, later renamed the Balloon Operational Squadron (BOS), was the last remnant of RAF Balloon Command and had moved from Cardington to Hullavington in 1966. Its abiding motto was, 'In silence we serve', and this the BOS continued to do as an independent unit deploying three mobile balloon crews operating in most corners of the UK.

Thousands of servicemen had their first taste of parachuting from the RAF balloons, and one of these was Trooper David Williams, who recalls that unforgettable 'bottle-job' of leaping from a balloon at Hullavington:

I was to be fourth out of four to jump, so I was first in. The static line was clipped to the gondola cable stop. Two minutes left to remember all drills and actions covered in the last two weeks. The PJI gave the command to the winch master, 'Four to 800'. Four recruits to 800ft. We were off. The upward motion of the gondola was as sickening as the humour… 800ft above the ground is high enough to be unnerving. It was so quiet and you are still connected to the ground by that steel cable. The moment of truth had arrived and my turn to jump – my three companions had been and gone. I was called forward. Contrary to popular legend, PJIs do not force or push you out. You go yourself and it's more difficult. 'Go!' Arms snapped down on my reserve chute on my chest, a shuffle forward and an exit like a champagne cork. 'One thousand, two thousand, three thousand.' That's the theory – the chute opens and you land. The reality I'm told is different. The drills were fine, except that I shouted them all out in less than a second and that was before I had even left the gondola. Below me was an instructor yelling at me through a megaphone. And before I knew it I had landed in the classic textbook manner. As I scrambled around on the ground untangling myself the Flight Sergeant stood above me. 'Well done Williams. That wasn't so bad was it?' 'Bloody marvellous sir, can I go again?' Total fear to total elation in split seconds. The balloons are there to test the nerve and mettle of the Airborne recruit; a pure and simple bottle-job.

Then there were the night ascents. Bob Baker was part of the support team for a detachment from No.1 Parachute School, based in London at the time, and occasionally he got to go along on the parachute continuation training, either from Hercules aircraft or from balloons. This included a night drop at RAF Henlow in Bedfordshire.

All drops were undertaken in complete darkness. There was no moon about, and it was a freezing night. The parachutists had torches attached to them to permit the drop zone staff to see them. As I was to fly on the last drop I went and got my parachute and just flung it on my back and did the straps up to hold it there, without fitting it properly. I had already completed a parachute course and so I should have known better. I entered the basket as before, when the dispatcher was happy he signalled the winch operator and off we went. In the darkness there was no real perception of movement or height gain during the climb. It was then that the dispatcher told us that for some reason the winch driver was paying out the cable far too fast, and that we were climbing slower than he was letting it out. This situation did not seem too worrying at first, just more interesting. Then the dispatcher decided to tell us the implications of the situation. Because the balloon was leaving cable on the ground, and we were not going up as fast as we should, there was the possibility that when they stop paying out the cable, and the balloon reaches the top of its climb there may be a sudden jolt. One of two things would happen, either we would bounce and stay where we were, or there would be a bounce, a snapping noise and we would be free flying. He would dispatch us quickly so as we would all remain inside the airfield, including myself, before he would exit the basket. Just what you want to hear when you know your parachute harness is not done up properly, and there was not a lot that could be done

Up until 1995 the RAF continued to use descendants of the wartime balloons for parachute training, such as this 45,000 cu ft balloon seen here without its cage attached. (John Christopher)

now, except wait. Then the bounce happened. We waited our fate. Luckily the cable did not snap – the parachutists jumped according to plan and we returned to earth safely.

Just like their wartime counterparts there were occasional breakaways to contend with and, as Bob recalls, sometimes even worse.

One Sunday morning back in the early 1960s I was standing just outside with my father and his friend when suddenly there was a tremendous explosion, the like of which I hadn't heard before. At the time I lived within half a mile of the perimeter fence of RAF Abingdon where the No.1 Parachute Training School (PTS) was based. We all ran up the garden to look around for something obvious, like a column of black smoke, but there was nothing. Apart from many birds in the air nothing seemed out of the ordinary. Then we realised that the barrage balloon was missing. We drove around to the road adjacent to where the balloon should have been – all the residents were in their gardens in a sort of dismay and every window was smashed. What appeared to have happened was that the balloon had been swaying in the wind, hit one of the light stanchions and the hydrogen had exploded with the force of a small bomb. There was nothing left to see of the balloon other than bits of silver material blowing across the ground.

In addition to parachute training, BSO also had responsibility for maintaining 100 inflatable tanks – mostly Russian models – armoured personnel carriers and field-guns, which were used as training aids. (This 'rubber regiment' was subsequently transferred to RAF Benson in Oxfordshire.) At times the balloons were borrowed for other duties, much of it classified, including development work with the Blue-Joker balloon-borne low-level detection radar system in the 1950s, in support of the Bloodhound missile trials in Wales and also with the Atomic Weapons Research Establishment tests in Australia and on Christmas Island in the Pacific. More recently, in 1994, balloons assisted in tests with the army's Starstreak Hyper-Velocity anti-aircraft missile, suspending a 350kg target at a fixed height and range.

There was a general misconception that the balloons were leftovers from the Second World War, but in reality their rubber-impregnated fabric of Egyptian cotton had a useful lifespan of only about eight years before it became too porous, mostly through ultraviolet degradation. Synthetic materials have been considered, but they are too prone to static for hydrogen operations and non-flammable helium is about six times the cost of hydrogen. By the early 1990s there were several factors contributing to the demise of the BOS – not least of these was that the higher quality Egyptian cotton was no longer being manufactured. It came down to the 'bean counters' and to save costs parachute training was contracted out to aircraft operators. On April Fool's Day, 1995, the last of the balloons was hauled down, deflated and cut up into pieces as souvenirs – a symbolic finale to a distinguished career.

Jumping from a balloon into still, quiet air remains a rare experience for most latter day parachutists, and although the RAF may have given them up the big balloons are still flying in Belgium, in Russia, and for the Royal Thai Army Special Forces. Some of these balloons are constructed by the British company Advanced Inflatables, who say that they are more reliable, safer and more economical when compared to large transport aircraft. Their envelopes are made from a UV-stabilised polyurethane-coated nylon and hence are inflated with helium. The Thais offer sport parachutists the opportunity to gain their 'three-elephant' balloon wings and every year hundreds of them travel to the Special Warfare Centre at Lopburi just to jump from a tethered balloon. I think the RAF missed a trick there.

18

A BETTER MOUSETRAP

At the dawn of the twenty-first century you might be forgiven for thinking that the only descendants of the barrage balloons still flying are the advertising blimps beloved by car showrooms and discount furniture warehouses. But you couldn't be further from the truth, and the humble balloon keeps bouncing back! The new generation might feature sophisticated electronics packages instead of observers standing in overgrown laundry baskets, but they still perform a mostly familiar list of functions, including providing Met information, as a platform for surveillance and communications equipment, as weapons and decoys, moving and sheltering equipment and troops, delivering propaganda and finally – a sign of our modern times – defending *against* and even working *for* the terrorists.

Without any doubt the real workhorse of the lighter-than-air world is the radiosonde. More than 1,800 Met balloons are released every single day all around the world – that's an incredible one million or so per year. They are made of high-quality neoprene rubber and are designed to burst at predetermined altitudes, dropping their payloads back to earth by parachute. In flight the electronic packages transmit information on wind speed, atmospheric pressure, temperature and humidity, to create a three dimensional picture of the atmosphere up to 100,000ft, unlike satellites which only look downwards. Accurate meteorological information is important to all branches of the military and many forces obtain data by releasing their own balloons, especially from naval vessels. In some cases automated systems have been developed, but it is still common for personnel to release Met balloons by hand. Meteorologists have been supplying information to the armed forces for over a hundred years, and since 1962 the British Met Office has been sending forecasters from its Mobile Met Unit (MMU) to support military zones. These men and women are either commissioned or enlisted into the RAF Reserves and they are responsible for on-the-spot forecasts for not only the RAF, but also the Royal Navy and the Army as well as units from NATO and other allied forces. In recent years they have been operational in Yugoslavia, the Middle East and in Afghanistan.

A US Navy ensign releases a radiosonde met balloon – just one of thousands launched worldwide on a daily basis. (US Navy)

Following the Second World War the Met Office also used kite-balloons to monitor low-level weather conditions, because they can be flown at specific heights. These operations were halted in 1980 because of the cost, then reinstated in 1995 as part of the Meteorological Research Unit at Cardington. Twice daily the balloon undertakes the 'BALTHUM run' to measure Bearing, ALtitude, Temperature and HUMidity, and the data is transmitted direct to the Met Office HQ at Bracknell. The balloon is a 25,000 cu ft MkVIII built by Airborne Industries, which can be run up at a respectable 300ft per minute and usually loiters at 4,500ft. With the main customers being the RAF and the UK's Civil Aviation Authority, the Met Research Unit is owned by the Ministry of Defence.

Tethered balloons can be used as a platform for a wide range of surveillance and communications payloads and, although experiments have been conducted into new shapes, including the Vee-balloon developed by Goodyear in the early 1960s, the conventional kite-balloon has won through. In the USA they were given a new lease of life, in particular with the introduction of the latest materials, and in the mid-1960s the Advanced Research Agency of the US Department of Defence fostered further development under the codename Egyptian Goose. The Schjeldahl Company in Minnesota was contracted

The Met Research Unit balloon is closely related to the barrage balloon and carries sensitive instruments to measure the weather conditions at altitude. (Met Office)

to develop the 250,000 cu ft 'Family II' tethered balloon system to provide 'heavy lift station keeping' with payloads of 750lb hoisted up to 12,000ft for acoustic, radar and optical surveillance in addition to communications relay. In the 1970s Martin Marietta (formerly the General Electric Electronics Systems Division) produced the Seek Skyhook for the USAF. Four balloons were built, each equipped with a parabolic radar antenna rotating at 5rpm giving a detection range of over 150 miles from a height of 12,000ft. Meanwhile, in 1972 Westinghouse formed the TCOM company to develop a range of tethered balloons, from its 15M, the equivalent of a small barrage balloon and capable of taking a 154lb payload to 1,000ft, up to the 71M which lifts a hefty 3,527lb payload all the way to 15,000ft. The 71M is capable of staying airborne for thirty days in wind speeds up to 70kt, although TCOM says it is 'survivable' at 90kt.

US Customs took delivery of these low-altitude surveillance systems in 1986, with a string of radar balloons stretching from the Bahamas to the Pacific coast forming a key part of the USA's anti-drug National Air Interdiction Strategy. In 1993 a two-day Congressional hearing found the Tethered Aerostat Radar System to be technically and economically effective, working out at about half the cost of airborne early warning (AEW) aircraft. 'For all intents and purposes, the air war has been won along the southern border', claimed Customs

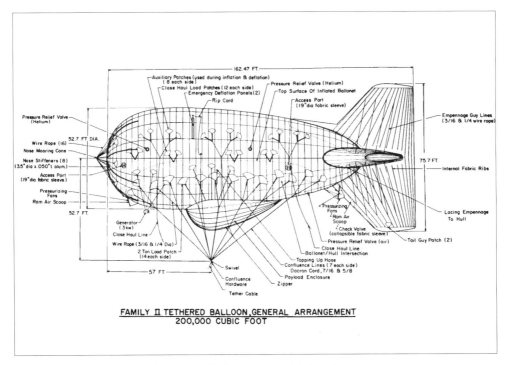

Anatomy of a 200,000 cu ft tethered balloon. (TCOM Corp)

This massive 250,000 cu ft tethered balloon or 'aerostat' is used to hoist a sophisticated electronics radar and surveillance payload aloft. (TCOM Corp)

Commissioner Carol Hallet. But the scheme isn't without its critics, who point to poor performance figures and blind gaps known as 'gates' by the smugglers. There are also the weather limitations, especially with turbulence or lightning strikes, and several balloons have been carried away by strong winds. *Time* magazine has described the radar balloons as the 'thin grey line', suggesting that, 'There is no evidence that the balloons have led to any increase in drug seizures.' But the balloons are only part of the bigger picture protecting the southern border, and without them it has been suggested that 60,000 troops would be needed to do that job.

Both Saudi Arabia and Kuwait have used the TCOM tethered surveillance balloons, and similar balloons have been operated in Korea, Nigeria and Iran. The Kuwaiti balloon was in service for six days before the Iraqi invasion of 1990, during which it was destroyed. Nonetheless, the system had given warning of the approaching invasion force which was instrumental in the Emir's escape, and as a result a replacement system was ordered. A further nine balloons have been supplied to foreign customers during the 1980s, although their identities have not been revealed. It is known that during the Falklands War in 1982 a tethered balloon was deployed by the British Navy as an aerial radar platform to detect low-level attacks by Argentinean fighters and missiles. More recently surveillance balloons were also deployed by Western forces during the Iraq conflict.

The Israelis favour unmanned intelligence gathering and they have a home-grown tethered balloon company named Rafael which produces the Stratus 'communication-intelligence collection system', with a high-resolution camera providing 360° coverage and a vehicle-detection range of 6.5km. As recently as 2001, the Israeli Defence Force operated small, remotely controlled airships to beam back images from Palestinian areas and as Dan Meridor, a minister with responsibilities for defence within the Prime Minister's office, put it, 'We have a handicap – we can't afford to lose people. Unmanned is important.'

Another role for which balloons are ideally suited is raising radio antennae. Back in the 1940s the US Army Signal Corps was issued with a balloon-in-a-can, the M-278A manufactured by the Dewy and Almy Chemical Company and designed to carry antennae. The long list of instructions on the label includes thawing the balloon under your armpit if the rubber is stiff from the cold. Also in the 1940s, *Popular Mechanics* published a drawing for a stratospheric balloon trailing a 200ft antenna to broadcast propaganda from the heavens. Certainly by 1984 USAF had a tethered balloon antenna system for VLF communications in the event of an emergency, and their Geophysical Laboratory has tested a balloon-borne antenna carried to 1,000ft to provide emergency radar cover. In addition, the Air Launched Balloon System (ALBS) delivers a 'quick reaction tactical communications relay platform' via a combination of balloon and parachute.

To overcome their inevitable subservience to the wind, work began in the 1960s to develop a motorised or powered balloon, such as Raven's High Platform II which could operate for periods greater than six months. In 1969 the USAF began the POBAL programme to evaluate station-keeping balloons, and the US Navy had a long-endurance surveillance platform known as the High Altitude Powered Platform (HAPP). Other military projects not kept secret include the Silent Joe project, to carry microphones, radar and a radio transceiver on a powered balloon, and it is said that nine of these were deployed over Vietnam to detect enemy truck convoys and troop movements. Currently there is a great deal of interest in stratospheric communications/surveillance platforms in the shape of enormous unmanned solar-powered airships which, it is claimed, could remain on-station for up to three years at a time. Strictly speaking these airships fall outside the remit for this book, but you can bet that the military are taking a very keen interest in this line of development.

Some communications balloons have already flown beyond the stratosphere. On 12 August 1960, the USA's Echo I was launched within the nose cone of a Delta rocket. Inflated in orbit, it was a vast 100ft-diameter Mylar balloon – so big that the engineers had bobbed about in small helium-inflated balloons to inspect it in its hangar. On the first transmission via Echo I President Eisenhower made a most generous declaration, 'The satellite balloon which has reflected these words may be used freely by any nation for similar experiments in their own interests.' Just as well, really, as they had no way of stopping them. This was a 'passive satellite' simply bouncing transmissions across the world. Brighter than the North Star, it stayed up for eight years and in 1964 it was joined by Echo II,

Balloon in a can issued by the Signal Corps US Army. (Valhalla Aerostation)

Static inflation test of the 135 ft diameter Echo II satellite balloon in 1961. If you look
carefully the figure of a man can be made out at its base. (NASA)

bigger still with a diameter of 135ft. Smaller balloons have also served as communications satellites – usually around 30ft across and with filmy skins which
disintegrate when exposed to sunlight, leaving a wire mesh sphere to bounce
back the signals.

The realm of the upper atmosphere and the edge of space is beyond the
constraints of sovereign airspace and political control, and accordingly the
military are keen to exploit this ultimate 'high ground' – a place from which
they can scrutinise every square inch of the planet's surface while virtually
immune from attack. And when mankind first reached out into space,
whether in the name of scientific progress or the development of high-flying
military aircraft, it was balloons that paved the way. The USA in particular
has maintained a significant programme of high-altitude research into such
areas as the upper atmosphere, meteorology, astrophysics, pollution drift and so
on. The main exponent of scientific balloons is, of course, NASA, whose
main launch facility is at Palestine, Texas, although some launches take place in
other parts of the world, especially where southern hemisphere flights are
concerned. By the 1970s NASA was launching over 500 high-altitude balloons
yearly, including the larger constant-level balloons. However, in a world
where 'overt' and 'covert' are sometimes flip sides of the same coin, a careful
look at the participants in many of these projects reveals some familiar names,

including the ONR and the USAF, indicating that they serve both the civilian and military sectors just as many satellites or even the Space Shuttle does. Balloon launches also take place at the Air Force Missile Development Centre at Holloman AFB, New Mexico, on what are usually described as government 'research programmes'.

Beside their benign surveillance and communications roles, balloons have also been directly involved in weapons programmes, including the USAF's 1960 tests of a combination balloon/parachute system for the recovery of missiles. This involved an on-board 9ft-diameter balloon that could be inflated from a tank of compressed helium in one-tenth of a second. The USAF's Gas Explosion Simulation Technique (GEST) programme of 1973 simulated nuclear blasts, using tethered detonatable gas balloons, to study the movement of the explosive plasma and the surrounding air. And under Ronald Reagan's Star Wars programme, balloons had a military role in space itself. The US Senate 'Inquiry into Missiles and Satellite Programmes' found that metallic balloon satellites can be made to simulate Inter-Continental Ballistic Missile (ICBM) nose cones and therefore provide a permanent, realistic target for development and training activities in support of anti-ICBM systems. They could also be used to frustrate ICBM defence systems, serve as decoys for military satellites, or in sufficient numbers, saturate the enemy's ICBM warning radars.

One example of these decoys came in the shape of Minuteman missiles developed by the USAF as Inflatable Erectable Decoys (IEDs). These looked like inverted ice-cream cones but carried an electronic package to make them appear to radar as the real thing. Another way of dealing with enemy radar is to jam it, and the Off-Board Balloon Jammer (OBJS) is a missile-launched electronics payload with radar jamming and surveillance equipment deployed beneath a 26ft-diameter balloon, inflated in-flight by compressed helium. Operating at 27,000ft for up to six hours it is nearly radar transparent, claims the manufacturer Southwest Research Institute in San Antonio, and other applications could include 'radio relay equipment, infrared sensors and autonomous weapons systems'.

On the subject of decoys, that old favourite the inflatable rubber tank is still trundling along. During the Kosovo conflict the US Defence Department grudgingly admitted that the Serbs had lived up to their reputation as masters of camouflage and many of the 'smart bomb' video-game images screened at Pentagon briefings were in fact zooming-in on fake bridges, inflatable tanks and black logs attached to old truck wheels to appear like artillery guns. When a Pentagon spokesman was asked if the number of decoys being struck was out of proportion compared to the millions of dollars in weaponry thrown at them, he replied, 'I don't know how extensive the decoys were… Clearly we did hit decoys. It's a standard operating procedure to use decoys in situations like this.' Not wishing to give precise figures, he added, 'I think the only conclusion that matters here is that we struck enough targets to win.'

The British army continues to deploy highly realistic inflatables both in the battlefield and during training. These are made by companies such as Advanced

Inflatable Products, whose range includes the T80, T72 and BRDM. Occasionally the dummies break cover and hit the headlines. In 1993 questions were asked in the House of Commons following the disappearance, presumably stolen, of £8,000 decoy tanks from an army training area. The UK Secretary of Defence replied that, 'Eighty-eight tanks were deployed to add realism to exercises involving units of the RAF, the USAF and the Royal Netherlands Air Force. Of these three were not recovered... The local police are investigating.' A similar situation occurred during exercises in 2002 when a tank went AWOL in 80mph winds. Sergeant Major Brian Pratt was quoted as saying, 'If anyone's seen my tank, please give us a bell!'

Goodyear Aerospace took the inflatables concept to the extreme with the Inflotaplane, developed for the ONR. This consisted of a bundle of fabric surmounted by a small engine which inflated to become a one-man aircraft. Raven Industries also developed an inflatable aircraft in the form of the Small Thermal Airship (STAR) which had its maiden flight in January 1975, although a similar hot air airship built by Cameron Balloons in the UK had flown two years earlier.

Balloons, both spherical and kiting, have been utilised by the military to hoist various other loads into the sky. Variations on the tethered concept include the

This army of inflatable rubber tanks is remarkably lifelike. The Chinese company which constructs these '80' tanks also produces decoy missile launchers, aircraft and other vehicles. (Sharp Simulation Equipment)

Boomerang project, in which test flights were conducted for surface-to-air recovery with a C-130 snatching a load from a 'U'-shaped balloon. And in the commercial sector several countries, including the USA and the Soviet Union, have had some success with tethered logging balloons in otherwise inaccessible locations, and similar systems have been considered by the military for ship-to-shore transportation of heavy loads or equipment. It is interesting to note that in 2002 a NATO White Paper concerning 'Elements of the Rapid Force Deployment Concept' referred to the Ultra Large Airship (ULA) projects being developed by several companies, including CargoLifter in Germany (now defunct) and the UK's Advanced Technology Group. A Pentagon spokesman has verified that the US Department of Defence is taking a look at the ULA concept as a means of deploying troops and equipment 'anywhere and anytime in the world'.

And if those troops need shelter they can inflate a building, and if they need light there are 'powermoons' – a system that uses internally illuminated helium balloons to turn night into day. These tethered balloons come in various sizes, for instance the Solarc 500 has a volume of 2,300 cu ft, measures 16ft in diameter and carries a 4,000-watt mercury-vapour light to between 40 and 150ft. Used widely by the film industry where conventional outdoor lighting rigs can be very expensive, they have also been evaluated by the emergency rescue services in Hessen Rheinland-Pfalz, Germany. They found the softer blanket of light, with almost no shadows, much more appropriate than the hard glare of spotlights.

One balloon application which by its nature is anything but secret is delivering propaganda, although the payloads aren't always leaflets. In 1961 balloons were used to deliver food parcels in China as far as 1,000 miles inland. Both sides in the Korean conflict have used balloons to carry their 'messages' and the South Koreans took the idea one step further with a balloon-borne pornography delivery service. Cigarettes, soap, tights and photographs of women in bikinis were floated into the Communist north, along with leaflets promising defectors free houses, cash, good jobs and hearty meals. In a rare example of civilians employing propaganda balloons, in 1989 a group of relatives of American soldiers missing in Vietnam raised $2.2 million to launch helium balloons from out in international waters. They believe that some of these men are still held prisoner and the leaflets carried messages encouraging their liberation with the promise of a generous reward.

Then 11 September happened. And in the aftermath we are all coming to terms with a new threat, that of international terrorism, and one in which the balloon might play both a defensive and offensive role. With 'homeland defence' the new buzz-phrase in political and military circles, it could just be that a new generation of Boo-Boos and Bulgys will rise to the occasion as a defence against low-flying aircraft used as weapons. Several balloon manufacturers are keen to exploit this new market, and one of these is Don Cameron in the UK. 'Whether we can persuade the military and security services that a modern version of the old-fashioned gasbag has a role to play in the defeat of terrorism remains to be seen. We believe the record from the Second World War speaks for itself and that barrage balloons do offer proven protection against aerial attackers.'

Even before the terrorists took centre stage, some experts had expounded the virtues of the modern barrage balloon providing an extra measure of protection against low-level aircraft and SAM missiles. Major Franklin J. Hillson of the USAF wrote, 'In our search to build a better mousetrap, we often neglect the lesson of history... More technology always seems to be the answer, but a simple solution to the low-level threat is the barrage balloon – naturally suited to defend small, important areas.' He argued that while technology changes, some things remain the same and just as a balloon and wire could deter a Gotha over London many years ago so can they thwart an attacking aircraft today. In addition to the defence by cables we are also likely to see a string of radar balloons, like the ones guarding the US southern border, popping up along both the Atlantic and Pacific seaboards and over specific potential targets. And in November 2002, the US Missile Defence Agency announced that it was looking for contractors to start work on an unmanned high-altitude airship (HAA) to carry 40ft radar dishes watching over a 750-mile-diameter area against ballistic missile attacks. In 2003 the Agency put its money where its mouth is and awarded a $40 million contract to Lockheed-Martin as the next phase to produce a technology concept demonstrator to be launched in 2006. Officials say that up to ten of these could be lining the coasts of the USA by 2010.

Ultra Large Airships (ULAs) are also receiving more serious consideration and in April 2004 the USA's Defence Advanced Research Projects Agency

A mobile tethered system with a relatively small balloon of 19,000 cu ft. (TCOM Corp)

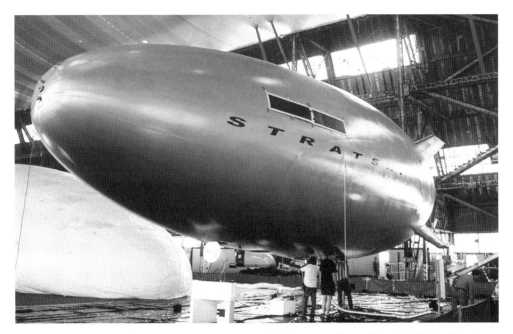

Several companies and government agencies are looking to a future breed of high-altitude unmanned airships to provide communications links and surveillance platforms. This is a one-tenth scale test version of the StratSat being developed at Cardington by the British company Advanced Technologies Group. (Ute Christopher)

(DARPA) published a 'Draft Program Solicitation' for a Heavy Lift-Air Vehicle Design to be known as 'Walrus'. This, in Pentagon speak, is 'a large lifting air vehicle capable of transporting a Unit of Action (UA) from Fort-to-Fight as a complete integrated package of personnel, equipment and supplies.' And we are talking very big here, with a payload of 500 tons being transported up to or over 6,000 nautical miles. While these projects are actually airships, not balloons, and are therefore outside the remit of this book it is an indication of the military's desire to think 'outside the box' and the politicians' willingness to invest the big money.

Perhaps the biggest problem in combating the terrorists is anticipating their choice of weapon, and incredibly an attack by balloon could be on the cards. The story begins in March of 2001 when a thirty-nine-year-old, named Steven Smiley, attracted the attention of the Los Angeles police after releasing four helium-filled bin bags carrying flares and an explosive powder. These devices detonated when the flare burnt through to the explosive, and one landed on the local sheriff's station four miles from Smiley's home. Confirming that there were no injuries, a police spokesman commented, 'Smiley had a fascination with explosives, was creating them in his own house and letting them float in the neighbourhood, not knowing where they would land.' This demonstrates just how easy it is to improvise a simple balloon bomb, something the terrorists already have in mind.

When the Aum Shinrikyo or 'Supreme Truth' Cult released sarin nerve gas into the busy Tokyo underground in March 1995, twelve innocent people died and over 5,000 were hospitalised. This attack heightened international awareness of the dangers of the wrong weapons getting into the wrong hands. According to a senior military analyst, quoted in the Japanese journal *Mainish Weekly*, further attacks upon Japan have taken the form of balloons which have been found with crude timers and plastic dispenser tubes dangling underneath. 'These devices have absolutely no markings except 2-20-95, the date of the first gas attack in Tokyo.' The tubes contained no trace of gas, but they may have served as a warning of what the Aum Cult is capable of. Should this all sound a bit fanciful, it is worth remembering that the Japanese had the technology to send biological and bacteriological payloads on the Fu-Gos back in the 1940s. The US security agencies certainly take such risks seriously and the National Guard has added certain 'scenarios' to its training manuals. According to *The Washington Post* these include storylines in which 'animal rights activists let loose balloons loaded with botulism germs, and the gay rights parade which also involved balloon weapons, this time filled with the nerve agent ricin in powder form'.

Just eighteen months before the 11 September attacks gave the Western world its abrupt wake-up call, evidence emerged that some extremists were looking at including balloons in their deadly arsenal. In March 1999 the *Sunday Mirror* reported that Moslem cleric Hamza al Masri had called on fanatics in London to create 'another Lockerbie' by launching balloon bombs at major airports such as Heathrow. The report suggested that prototypes of these aerial mines had already been tested in Afghanistan.

Then in 2002, US troops in Kabul made a startling discovery in the abandoned office of an Islamic relief agency. Drawings of anthrax-carrying balloons were found, along with sketches of fighter aircraft shooting them down. According to CBS News this was 'clearly a blueprint for an anthrax attack'. The man running the agency was Bachirudden Mahmoud, a Pakistani nuclear scientist who had played a key role in the development of Pakistan's nuclear bomb and is a known associate of Al-Qaeda. Two journalists who had visited a hidden Al-Qaeda camp near Jalalabad reported that they had seen 'thirty boxes of sarin gas in cardboard boxes with Russian lettering on the side'. Tragically, the day after their reports were filed the men were taken from their cars and shot. Are these events connected? It remains to be seen.

For every military application that you can think of for the balloon, there are sure to be others that remain classified. Clues as to what these 'black projects' might entail can be found in this history of the balloon at war. So keep watching the skies – and remember, they may be watching you!

BIBLIOGRAPHY

Bates, H.E., *Flying Bombs over England*, Froglets Publications, 1994.

Brewer, Griffith, *Theory of Ballooning*, Royal Naval Air Service, 1918.

Ballooning and Its Application to Kite-Balloons, Air League of the British Empire, 1940.
   (11th Revised Edition)

Broke-Smith, Brigadier P.W.L., *The History of Early British Aeronautics*.

Chamberlain, Geoffrey, *Airships – Cardington*, Terence Dalton, 1984.

Coombs, L.F.E., *The Lion Has Wings*, Airlife, 1997.

Coppens, Willy, *Days on the Wing*, John Hamilton, *c*.1925.

Cornish III, Joseph Jenkins, *The Air Arm of the Confederacy*, Richmond Civil War
   Centennial Committee, 1963.

Cross, Robin and de Gex, Jenny, *Unsung Heroines – The Women who Won the War*,
   Sidgwick & Jackson, 1990.

Cruickshank, Charles, *Deception in World War II*, BCA, 1979.

Dwiggins, Don, *Riders of the Wind*, Hawthorn, 1973.

Escott, Sqd. Ldr Beryl E., *The WAAF in World War II*, Alan Sutton, 1995.

Evans, Charles M., *War of the Aeronauts*, Stackpole Books, 2002.

Fisher, John, *Airlift 1870*, Parrish, 1965.

Griehl, Manfred and Dressel, Joachim, *Zeppelin! The German Airship Story*, Arms &
   Armour, 1990.

Haining, Peter, *The Dream Machines*, New English Library, 1972.

Hall, Norman S., *The Balloon Buster*, Corgi, 1967.

Haydon, F. Stansbury, *Military Ballooning during the Early Civil War*, John Hopkins
   University Press, 2000.

Hildebrandt, A., *Balloons & Airships*, EP Publishing, 1973.

Hodges, Goderic, *Memoirs of an Old Balloonatic*, William Kimber, 1972.

Jackson, Donald Dale, *The Aeronauts*, Time Life, 1981.

Kilduff, Peter, *Over the Battlefronts*, Arms & Armour, 1996.

Kirschner, Edwin J., *Aerospace Balloons – From Montgolfiere to Space*,
   Aero, 1985.

Lachambre, A & H., *Les Ballons a la Guerre*, Paris, 1888.

Layman, R.D., *To Ascend from a Floating Base*, Associated University Press, 1979.

McDermott, Vincent, *Kite Balloons in the Royal Naval Air Service 1914–1918*, 1998.

Mikesh, Robert C., *Japan's World War II Balloon Bomb Attacks on North America*,
   Smithsonian, 1973.

Morgan, Janet, *The Secrets of Rue St Roch*, Penguin/Allen Lane, 2004

Morris, Alan, *The Balloonatics*, Jarrolds, 1970.

Nicholson, Mavis, *What Did You Do in the War, Mummy?*, Chatto & Windus, 1995.

Nockolds, Harold, *The Story of the RFD Group – Rescue From Disaster*, David & Charles, 1980.

Ogly, Bob, *Doodlebugs and Rockets. The Battle of the Flying Bombs*, Froglets Publications, 1992.

Pawle, Gerald, *The Secret War 1939–1945*, Harrap, 1956.

Payne, Lee, *Lighter Than Air*, Orion, 1991.

Peebles, Curtis, *The Moby Dick Project – Reconnaissance Balloons Over Russia*, Smithsonian, 1991.

Petschull, Jürgen, *With the Wind to the West*, Hodder & Stoughton, 1980.

Pushman, Muriel Gene, *We All Wore Blue*, Robson Books, 1989.

Reit, Seymour, *Masquerade, The Amazing Camouflage Deceptions of World War II*, Robert Hale, 1979.

Reitsch, Hanna, *The Sky My Kingdom*, Bodley Head, 1955.

Rolt, L.T.C., *The Aeronauts*, Alan Sutton, 1985.

Selle de Beauchamp, *Des Memoirs d'un Officier des Aerostiers aux Armees de 1793 á 1799*, Paris, 1853.

Shock, James R, *The US Army Barrage Balloon Program*, Merriam Press, 1999.

Tissandier, Caston, *D'un Aérostier Militaire de l'Armée de la Loire*, Paris, 1891.

Villiers du Terrage, *Baron Marc de. Les Aérostiers Militaires en Egypt*, Paris, 1901.

Walker, Percy B., *Early Aviation at Farnborough – Balloons, Kites & Airships*, Macdonald, 1971.

Roof Over Britain – The Official Story of the A.A. Defences, 1939–1942, HMSO. 1943.

Magazines and journals include:

Aerial Wonders, Aeronautics, The Aeroplane, Aeroplane Monthly, Aerostat, Aerostation, Air International, Airship, Aviation News, Ballooning, Balloon Life, Buoyant Flight, Flight, Flying, Gasbag/Airshipworld, Icare, Illustrated London News, Modern Wonders, Popular Mechanics, Popular Science, Royal Air Force Magazine, The Times, Trailrope, The War Illustrated, War in the Air.

INDEX

Ae-Ballon, 73
Advanced Inflatables, 203
Advanced Technology Group, 213
Afghanistan, 9, 204
Air Launched Balloon Systems, 208
Air Material Command, 171
Air Ministry, 111, 118, 121, 126, 143
Air Raid Precautions, 95
Air Transport Auxiliary, 115
Air Weather Service, 185
Alamogordo Army Air Field – see Holloman AFB
Albatross, 70, 75
Aldershot, 53-54, 57
Alexander, Major E.P., 37
Algerian campaign, 40
Allen, James and Ezra, 32, 37
Al Qaeda, 9, 216
American Expeditionary Force, 73-74
L'Archimede, 48
Arctic, 132
Armand Barbés, 45
d'Arlandes, Marquis, 12-13
Arlington, 33
Ashanti Expedition, 53
Ashmore, Major-General E.B., 81-82
Assistance, HMS, 130
Atlantic, 29, 32, 33
Atomic Weapons Research Establishment, 203
Auxiliary Air Force, 92, 98

B-24, B-25 and B-29 bombers, 150, 160, 164
Baker, Bob, 201-202
Baldwin, Stanley, 85
Ballondepotfartyg 1, 131
Balloon Command, 93-94, 99, 102, 106, 122, 125, 147, 200
Balloon Development Establishment, 88, 121, 123
Balloon Operational Squadron, 200
balloon fender, 110-111
Balloon Squadrons, 92, 93
Balloon Training Unit, 88, 147
Banbury, Arthur V., 73

barrage balloons, 8, 81-115, 117-118, 137-138, 141-156, 204, 213-214
Barrow-in-Furness, 95
Bates, H.E., 143-145
BE2c aircraft, 84
Beaumont, Captain F., 53
Beauregard, General, 34
Bechuanaland, 55-56
Berlin, 40, 139, 153, 197
Berlin Airlift, 168
Berlitz, Charles, 170
Biggin Hill, 144, 146
Biot, 27
Birmingham, 93, 115, 123
Bismark, 48
Blanchard, Colonel, 169
Bloodhound missiles, 203
Boer War, 57-59
Bomber Command, 106, 125-126
Bonaparte, Napoleon, 26-28
Boom Defence Department, 124
Boxer uprising, 58
Brady, Mathew, 34, 38-39
Brazel, Mac, 168, 170-171
Breitling Orbiter 3, 161
Bristol, 93, 106, 123, 141, 148
Bristol, 58
Britain, Battle of, 94, 137
British Expeditionary Force, 65, 118
British Navy – see Royal Navy
Brunning, Nebraska, 193-194
Bryan, George Randolph, 34-35
Bulganin, Nikolai A., 179-180
Bull Run, Battle of, 32
Burma, 146
Bury St Edmunds, 149
Butler, Major General Benjamin F., 32

C-119 aircraft, 182
C-130 aircraft, 213
Campania, HMS, 132
Camp Ripley, 178

Cameron Balloons, 212, 213
Caquot, Captain Albert, 67
Caquot balloon, 67-68, 70, 73, 89
Cardiff, 93
Cardington, 88, 92-93, 95, 103, 105-106, 121-122, 147-148, 200, 205
CargoLifter, 213
Castro, Fidel, 189-192
Cavalmarino, 131
Cavandish, Henry, 10
Céleste, 42, 44
Chamberlain, Neville, 94, 127
Charles, Professor Jacques Alexandre César, 11-15, 17
Chase, Salmon, 30-31
Chester, HMS, 132
Cheves, Captain Langdon, 36
Churchill, Winston, 118, 121, 123, 136, 142-143, 146, 167, 200
CIA, Central Intelligence Agency, 186-194
City of Oxford, 132
Civil Aviation Authority, 205
Clouston, Flight Lieutenant A.E., 88-89
Cold War, 9, 166-197
Collier, Kenneth, 145
Commonwealth, HMS, 58
Compagnie d'Aérostiers, 20-26, 28, 31, 51
Comstock, Captain Cyrus, 37
Constitution, 33, 36
Conté, Nicola Jacques, 17-26
Coppens, Willy, 75-76
Corsairs, 164
Coutelle, Jean Marie, 17-26, 51, 54
Coventry, 93, 108, 115
Coxwell, Henry, 40, 53
Crew, 93, 115
Crosby, Deon, 174-176
Crusader, 53
Cuba, 132, 189-192
Curtis, Lettice, 115
Curzon, Colin, 142

Dad's Army, 117-118
Dagron, 46-48
Dakota aircraft, 115
Dartois, Camille, 42
decoys, inflatable, 136-137, 211-212
Dennis, Glen, 172-173
Department of Miscellaneous Weapon Developments, 119-123
Department of Publicity in Enemy Countries, 127-128
Derwentside, 95
Detachable Parachute Link, 91-92
Dewy and Aimy Chemical Company, 208-209
D-Day, 128, 136-140, 143
Donauwerth, 24
'Doodlebugs' – see V1
Doolittle, Lieutenant Colonel Jimmy, 160
Dornier 17, 109
Dover, 90, 94-95, 125, 136

'drachen' – see kite balloon
Dresden, 151
Duchess of Connaught, 58
Dunlop, 86, 100-102, 136-137, 140
Duruof, Jules, 42-43

Eagle, 33
Echo I and Echo II, 209-210
Eden, Anthony, 179
Egypt, campaign, 26
Egyptian Goose, 205-206
Eighth Air Force, 169
Eisenhower, General and President, 139, 179-181, 189, 209
Engadine, HMS, 132
Enola Gay, 168
L'Entreprenant, 19-23, 31
Enterprise, 19, 31
Evanton, 180
Ewing, Dr Maurice, 170-171
Excelsior, 173
Excelsior, 33
Exeter, 113

Fairey aircraft, 90, 113
Fair Oaks, Battle of, 35, 36
Falmouth, 134
Family II, 205-206
Fanny, 33
Farnborough, 60, 90
Fast Aerial Mine, 120
Faure, Edgar, 179
Fazakerley, 102
FE2b, 81
Felixstowe, 102, 125
Fighter Command, 115, 121
Firestone, 153
First US Army Group, 136
First World War, 8, 52, 65-82, 88, 120-121, 126, 132, 148, 149
Fleet Air Arm, 119
Fleurus, Battle of, 19, 22-23
Fletcher, Derek, 95
Flyer, 60
Flying Cloud, 184-185
Focus, 188
Fokker D-7 aeroplane, 76
de Fonvielle, Wilfrid, 42
Formby, George, 117
Formidable, 130
Forth of Firth, 93
Fort Omaha, 73
Fort Worth, 169
Fourth Air Force, 164
Fox, Ann, 106
Franco, General, 86
Franco-Prussian War, 39, 51
Franklin, Benjamin, 15, 25
Franklin, Sir John, 130
Free Balloon Barrage, 8, 119-123
Free Europe Committee, 188

Free Europe Press, 187
Freudenburg, W., 198
Fu-Go balloon bombs, 157-165, 184
Fulgham, Captain Dan, 173

Gambetta, Léon, 45-46, 48
Gardermoen, 180
Gas Explosion Simulation Technique, 211
Gaylussa, 27
Général Cambronne, 50
Général Chanzy, 48-50
General Mills Inc, 178, 195-196
General Myer, 52
General Post Office, 93
Genetrix, 180-183, 195
George VI, 94
George Sand, 45-46
George Washington Parke Curtis, 33
Gibraltar, 10, 132
Giebelstadt, 180, 182
Giffard, Henri, 62
Glasgow, 93
Godalming, Surrey, 100
Goddard, Eugene, Louis and Madame, 42, 44, 52,
    63
Goebbels, Joseph, 146
Goode, Lieutenant, 68
Goodeve, Charles, 118-119
Goodyear, 153-155, 205, 212
Gopher, 180
Gower, Frederick Allen, 131
Grandson, 180
Greely, Brig. General Adolphus V., 52
Greyback, 180
Grover, Captain G.E., 53

Haggett, Rex, 110-113
Hallet, Carol, 208
Harwich, 93
Hearson, Air Commodore J.G., 88
Heath, Major G.M., 58
Heinkel He111, 95, 110-111
Hellcats, 164
Hercules, 9, 201
Herbert, Craig, 66
Heron, 55
High-Dive, 172-173
Hillson, Major Franklin J., 214
Hinman, First Lieutenant, 71-73
Hirondelle, 44
Hirohito, Emperor, 166
Hiroshima, 168
Hitler, Adolf, 86, 89, 110, 142, 149
Hodges, Goderic, 66, 71, 82
Holloman Air Force Base, 171, 174, 211
Home Guard, 118
Hook, 94
Hornet, USS, 160
Hosche, General, 24, 26
hot air balloons, 10-16, 34, 77, 193-199
Hull, 93, 123

Hullavington, 200
Hunt, Major Walter, 168-170
Hussein, Saddam, 9
Hutyra, Robert, 198

Incirlik, 180
India, 58-60
Inflatable Erectable Decoys, 211
Inspector of Anti-Aircraft Weapons and Devices,
    118
Imperial Airship Service, 82
Imperial Japanese Army, 160
Intrepid, 33, 36
Iraq, 208
Israeli Defence Force, 208
Italian War of Independence, 116-117
Ivy, William, 52

Jacobs, Eileen, 102
Jacobs, Hans, 109
Le Jacquard, 48
Japanese navy, 163
Jean Bart, 50
Johnston, General, 34
Joint Barrage Balloon Committee, 153
Jourdain, General Jean-Baptiste, 18, 20, 24
Junkers Ju88, 95, 138, 143

Kaiser, 64, 81
Kaufman, Captain William, 173
KC-97, 173
Kennedy, John F., 189
Kennedy, Robert, 189
Kent, Flight Lieutenant J.A., 110
Kentucky Air National Guard, 178
Kerr, Deborah, 142
Khrushchev, Nikita, 179-180, 189
King, Samuel, 32
Kitchener, Lord, 65
kite balloons, 61-77, 81-114, 131, 200-203, 204-
    208, 213-214
Kittinger, Captain Joe, 173-174
Knight, Dame Laura, 108
Korda, Alexander, 86
Korea, 208, 213
Kosmyenko, Lieutenant Aleksandra Dyeisovia, 152
Kosovo, 211-212
Krupp, 48-49
Kuwait, 208

Lachambre, 52
Ladysmith, 58
Lahn, 131
Lansdale, Brigadier General, 189-191
Larkhill, RAF Balloon Section, 84
Lavoisier, 17
Leningrad, 152
Lewis, Flight-Sergeant W.S., 68
Lewisham, 143
Lincoln, President, 31
Liverpool, 93, 102, 115, 123

Livesey, Roger, 142
Lockheed-Martin, 214
London, 88, 94, 97, 115, 121-123, 143, 146-148, 157
Longstreet, General, 36
Louis XVI, 12
Lowe, David, 142
Lowe, Thaddeus Sobieski Constantine, 29-39, 54, 153
Luftwaffe, 85, 87, 94, 109, 118, 120, 122-123, 126, 135, 136, 143
Luke, Frank, 76
Lynch, Maureen, 74
LZ 'Low Zone' balloon, 88

'M' Balloon Unit, 126-128
Macworth, Colonel J.D., 87
Madagascar, 51
Mafeking, 55-56
Mahmoud, Bachirudden, 216
Maidstone, 143
Mainwaring, Captain, 118
Malta, 132
Manchester, 93, 101, 106, 115, 117, 132
Mangin, Gabriel, 43
Manhattan Project, 166
Mannheim, siege of, 24
Maratanza, USS, 37
Marcel, Major Jesse, 168-170
Margat, Jean, 28
Martin Marietta, 206
Mantell, Captain Thomas F., 178
Mars, 131
Martial, 23
Martin, James and Martin-Baker Aircraft Company, 113
Maubeuge, 18, 20
Maudsley, Lieutenant S.G., 132
Mayence, siege of, 24
May Flower, 33
Maxfield, Colonel Joseph E., 52
McClellan, Major General George B., 33, 35, 37, 39
Melford, Dorothy and Joseph, 98, 102, 106-109, 133-135, 147
Melting Pot, 184
Meridor, Dan, 208
Merseyside, 95
Messerschmitt 109, 94
meteorology, 125, 139-140, 178, 181-185, 204-206
Met Office, 204-206
Methuen, Lord, 58
Metz, 45
Mig fighters, 168, 182
Mikesh, Robert, 165
Milan, Siege of, 77
Miles Hawk aeroplane, 90
Ministry of Aircraft Production, 100
Ministry of Defence, 205
Ministry of Information, 94, 103-104, 142
Mitchell, Reverend Archie and Mrs, 157, 164-165
Moby Dick, 181

Mogul, 170-171
Mongoose, 189-191
Montgolfier, Joseph and Etienne, 10-16, 197
Moonshine, 137
Moore, William, 170
La Mountain, John, 29-33
Morgan, Janet, 80
Morlot, General Antoine, 22
Moroccan campaign and rebellion, 51, 132
Morrison, Herbert, 143-144
Moscow, 28, 152
Murmansk, 152
Mustangs, 178

'Nadar' – see Tournachon, Felix
Napoleon, 44
NASA, 174-175, 210
National Security Council, 186
NATO, 204, 213
Naval Meteorological Office, 125
Nelson, Horatio, 26
Le Neptune, 42
Newcastle, 93, 106
New Mexico, 167-175, 211
Newport, Monmouthshire, 95
Niepce, 46
Nile, Battle of, 26
No.23 airship, 85
Norway, Neville Shute, 118

Oberpfaffenhofen, 180
Off-Board Balloon Jammer, 211
Office of Naval Research, 177, 193-196, 199, 212
Open Skies, 179-181
operations – see individual names
Ophelia, HMS, 132
Oppenheimer, Robert, 166
Outward, 123-126

Panama Canal, 155
parachutes, 67-74, 129, 153, 172-174, 178, 200-203
Parachute and Cable, 119-120
Paris, Siege of, 8, 40-50
Parseval, Major von, 61
Patriot, HMS, 132
Pawlett, Somerset, 110-113, 148
Peardrop, 137
Pearl Harbour, 155
Peebles, Curtis, 184
Pepe, General, 116
Perry, Eve, 117
Pershing, General, John J., 73-74
Piccard, Don, 196-197
pigeons, 43-50, 80
Pilot Aerial Survival System, 195-196
Pioneer, 54
Plymouth, 93, 95
poison gas, 80, 158, 184, 216
Poland, 148
Portsmouth, 93, 123
Potomac, 33
Powell and Pressburger, 142

Powers, Gary, 177, 183
Pretoria, 58
Priestley, Joseph, 10
projects – see individual names
propaganda balloons, 77-78, 126-128, 186-192, 204, 213-214
Prospero, 187
Pucklechurch, 106, 148
Pushman, Muriel Gane, 106

Quaker guns, 34

R33 airship, 85
R100 and R101 airships, 92, 106, 118
radar, 137, 171, 178, 182, 206, 208
Radet, Adjutant General, 20
Radio Free Europe, 181, 186-189, 194
radiosondes, 163, 178
RAF Lyneham, 9
Ramey, Brigadier General Roger, 169
Rampont, M., 42
Rastadt, 24
Raven Industries, 195-197, 208-209, 212
Reagan, Ronald, 211
Reitsch, Hannah, 109-110
Renard, Charles and Paul, 51
RFD, 100
Richard Wallace, 48
Rickenbacker, Eddie, 76
Robert, Jean and Nöel, 12-15
Roberts, Lord, 58-59
Rodeghier, Mark, 173-174, 176
Roosevelt, President, 167
Rossia, 131
Roswell, 168-175
Roswell Army Airfield, 168
Röth, Fritz, 75
de Rozier, Jean-François Pilatre, 12-13
Royal Aircraft Establishment – see Farnborough
Royal Air Force, 8, 82-83, 86, 92-93, 99, 100-103, 115, 119-120, 125, 129, 132, 136-137, 200-203, 204-205, 212
Royal Flying Corps (RFC), 60, 65, 73, 77, 81-84, 88
Royal Naval Air Service (RNAS), 132
Royal Navy, 25-26, 118, 124-125, 132, 204, 208
Royal Navy Volunteer Reserves (RNVR), 118, 120
Royal Netherlands Air Force, 212
Royal Observer Corps, 145
Royal Thai Army Special Forces, 203
Russo-Japanese War, 60-61

Santiago, 52
Saratoga, 33
Schiff, Congressman Steven, 170
Schjeldahl Company, 205-206
Second World War, 8-9, 81-129, 132-166, 170, 177, 203, 205, 214
Seek Skyhook, 206
Selle de Beauchamp, 20-22
Sheffield, 93
Shell, 154

Shute, Nevil, 118
'Sierra Sams', 172
Sinclair, Sir Archibald, 147
Sigsfield, Captain von, 61
'silk balloon', US Civil War, 36-37
Skyhook, 175, 177-178, 180
Smiley, Steven, 215-216
Smith, Anthony, 197
Solarc 500, 213
Sopwith Camel, 68, 85
Southampton, 93
South West Research Institute, 211
Spad aeroplane, 76
Spanish-American War, 52-53
Special Operations Executive, 129
Sperrbalone, 149-151
Spitfire, 118, 145
Spuller, Eugene, 45
Stalin, Josef, 166-167, 179
Starkweather, John B, 33
Starstreak, 203
Star Wars, 211
Steenackers, 50
Steiner, John H., 33, 39
Strasbourg, Siege of, 40, 45
Strelzyk, 197-198
Stuart, Sir Campbell, 127
Stuttgart, 24
Sudan, 55, 57
Supreme Truth cult, 217
Surveyor space programme, 174
Swansea, 93
Swialto, Josef, 188

Tait, First Lieutenant, 71-73
Tatsfield, 146
Taylor, Second-Lieutenant L.G., 81
TCOM, 139, 206-208
Teaser, 37
Tempest V, 145
Templer, Captain J.L.B., 53-55, 58
Tissandier, Gaston and Albert, 43-44, 50
Tongking, 51
'torpielle' rocket, 70-71
Tournachon, Felix, 38, 42
Tokyo, 160, 162, 216
Trenchard, Lord, 83
Trewin, J.C., 141
Trichet, J., 45
Trinity, 166, 168
Truman, Harry S., 166, 170
Tudor-Boyd, Air Vice Marshall Owen, 93
Turnbull, Wing Commander Gerry, 121, 195

U2 reconnaissance aircraft, 177, 184
U-boats, 132, 137, 140, 149
Ultra Large Airships, 213, 215
United States, 33
US Air Force, 115, 170-173, 176-181, 183-184, 206, 211-212

US Army Air Force, 150, 170-176
US Army Corps of Engineers, 153
US Army Signal Corps, 208-209
US Coast Guard, 139
US Customs, 206-208
US Civil War, 8, 29-39, 51, 52, 53, 130
US Defence Advanced Research Projects Agency, 214
US Department of Defence, 165, 176, 205, 211, 213
US Missile Defence Agency, 214
US Navy, 132, 158, 164, 170, 177-178, 193-195
US State Department, 191
US War Department, 73, 153

V1, 8, 143-148
V2, 8, 143-144, 147-148
Valenton, 42
Valley Forge, USS, 175
Veligura, 153
Verne, Jules, 197
Very Low Altitude balloons, 135-136, 138, 155
Veto, 187
Vickers, 95
Vietnam, 213
Viking space programme, 174-175
Ville de Florence, 42-43
Ville de Langres, 50
Ville d'Orléans, 48
Vizetelly, Henry, 44
Vittoria, 28
Van Dyk, Herman, 123-124
Venice, 116-117
de Volette, André Giraud, 12
Voyager space programme, 174
Vulcano, 130

Walpole, Horace, 16
Warrington, 115
Washington, 31-32
Washington, 33, 35-36
Watson, Lieutenant, 54
Weaver, Colonel Richard, 176
Weinlings, 55
Wellington bomber, 125
Welles, Orson, 164
Wells, H.G., 86
Westall, Robert, 95
Westinghouse, 206
Wetzel, Günter, 197-198
'White Cloud', 181
Widnes, 115
Williams, David, 200-201
Windows, 137
Winzen, Dr Otto C., 177
Wire Barrage – see Free Balloon Barrage
Wise, John, 29-30, 32
Women's Auxiliary Air Force, 99, 102-108, 140, 147
Women's Royal Naval Service, 124-125, 140
Wöstmann, Second Lieutenant Anton, 70
Wright, brothers, 60
Wright Field, Ohio, 171
Wright-Patterson Air Force base, 165
Würzburg, battle of, 24

Yon, 52
Yorktown, 34
Yost, Ed, 194-196, 199
Yule, Jimmy, 151

Zeppelin, Ferdinand von, 39
Zeppelin airships, 81, 84, 121

If you are interested in purchasing other books published by Tempus,
or in case you have difficulty finding any Tempus books in your local bookshop,
you can also place orders directly through our website

www.tempus-publishing.com